Creole Identity in Postcolonial Indonesia

Integration and Conflict Studies
Max Planck Institute for Social Anthropology, Halle/Saale

Series Editor: Günther Schlee, Director at the Max Planck Institute for Social Anthropology

Editorial Board: Brian Donahoe (Max Planck Institute for Social Anthropology), John Eidson (Max Planck Institute for Social Anthropology), Peter Finke (University of Zurich), Joachim Görlich (Max Planck Institute for Social Anthropology), Jacqueline Knörr (Max Planck Institute for Social Anthropology), Bettina Mann (Max Planck Institute for Social Anthropology), Stephen Reyna (University of Manchester, Max Planck Institute for Social Anthropology)

Assisted by: Cornelia Schnepel and Viktoria Zeng (Max Planck Institute for Social Anthropology)

Volume 1
How Enemies are Made – Towards a Theory of Ethnic and Religious Conflicts
Günther Schlee

Volume 2
Changing Identifications and Alliances in North-East Africa
Vol.I: Ethiopia and Kenya
Edited by Günther Schlee and Elizabeth E. Watson

Volume 3
Changing Identifications and Alliances in North-East Africa
Vol.II: Sudan, Uganda and the Ethiopia-Sudan Borderlands
Edited by Günther Schlee and Elizabeth E. Watson

Volume 4
Playing Different Games: The Paradox of Anywaa and Nuer Identification Strategies in the Gambella Region, Ethiopia
Dereje Feyissa

Volume 5
Who Owns the Stock? Collective and Multiple Forms of Property in Animals
Edited by Anatoly M. Khazanov and Günther Schlee

Volume 6
Irish/ness is All Around Us: Language Revivalism and the Culture of Ethnic Identity in Northern Ireland
Olaf Zenker

Volume 7
Variations on Uzbek Identity: Strategic Choices, Cognitive Schemas and Political Constraints in Identification Processes
Peter Finke

Volume 8
Domesticating Youth: The Youth Bulge and its Socio-Political Implications in Tajikistan
Sophie Roche

Volume 9
Creole Identity in Postcolonial Indonesia
Jacqueline Knörr

Volume 10
Friendship, Descent and Alliance in Africa: Anthropological Perspectives
Edited by Martine Guichard, Tilo Grätz and Youssouf Diallo

Creole Identity in Postcolonial Indonesia

Jacqueline Knörr

berghahn
NEW YORK · OXFORD
www.berghahnbooks.com

Published in 2014 by
Berghahn Books
www.berghahnbooks.com

© 2014 Jacqueline Knörr

All rights reserved. Except for the quotation of short passages for the purposes of criticism and review, no part of this book may be reproduced in any form or by any means, electronic or mechanical, including photocopying, recording, or any information storage and retrieval system now known or to be invented, without written permission of the publisher.

Library of Congress Cataloging-in-Publication Data
Knörr, Jacqueline, 1960-
  Creole identity in postcolonial Indonesia / Jacqueline Knörr.
  pages cm. — (Integration and conflict studies volume 9)
  Includes bibliographical references and index.
  ISBN 978-1-78238-268-3 (hardback) — ISBN 978-1-78238-269-0 (institutional ebook)
  1. Ethnicity—Indonesia—Jakarta. 2. Creoles—Indonesia—Jakarta—Ethnic identity. 3. Creoles—Indonesia—Jakarta—Social conditions. 4. Postcolonialism—Indonesia—Jakarta. 5. Ethnic conflict—Indonesia—Jakarta. 6. Jakarta (Indonesia)—Ethnic relations. 7. Jakarta (Indonesia)—Social conditions. 8. Jakarta (Indonesia)—Politics and government. I. Title.
  GN635.I65K56 2014
  305.8009598'22—dc23
                                                                 2013023315

British Library Cataloguing in Publication Data
A catalogue record for this book is available from the British Library

Printed on acid-free paper

ISBN: 978-1-78238-268-3 hardback
ISBN: 978-1-78238-269-0 institutional ebook

Contents

List of Illustrations — viii

Acknowledgements — x

Introduction — 1
    Creole Identity and Postcolonial Diversity — 1
    Ethnic versus Transethnic Identity — 2
    National Identity in the Context of Ethnic and Transethnic
        References — 5
    The City as Locus and Focus — 6
    Categories of Identification and Social Discourses as Objects
        of Observation and Analysis — 10
    Notes on Field Research — 13

Chapter 1. Creole Identity in Postcolonial Context — 19
    Creole Terminology at the Conceptual Crossroads of History
        and Ideology — 19
    Creolization and Creole Identity beyond the Caribbean — 21
    Towards a Comparative Concept of Creole Identity — 23
    Indigenization and Ethnogenesis as Criteria of Creolization — 25
    Creoleness versus (Post-)creole Continuum — 27
    The CvP Model: Creolization versus Pidginization — 30
    The Pidgin Potential of Creole Identity for Postcolonial
        Nation-building — 32
    Creole Ambivalences — 36

Chapter 2. Jakarta, Batavia, Betawi — 41
    Cityscape and City Dwellers — 41
    Historical Beginnings: Sunda Kelapa, Jayakarta, Batavia — 45
    Social Organization and Interethnic Relationships in Batavia — 46
    Creolization and the Emergence of the Betawi — 52
    Social Marginalization of the Betawi — 60
    The (Re-)discovery of the Betawi: Objectives and Context of State
        Sponsorship — 68

Chapter 3. Orang Betawi versus Orang Jakarta — 74
    Discourses, Definitions, Dichotomies — 74
    Betawi (Asli) versus *Pendatang* — 78

Betawi versus Betawi Asli: Ethnic References With and Without
	'Asli' 82
Betawi as Jakarta Asli   87
The Pidgin Potential of Betawi Culture and Identity   88
Orang Jakarta as a Category of Urban Identification   90
Creolization of Jakartan Identity?   93
Tradition and Modernity in the Relationship between
	Orang Betawi and Orang Jakarta ... and a Miss and
	Mister Jakarta Pageant 94

Chapter 4. Suku bangsa Betawi: Integration and Differentiation
of Ethnic Identity   98
	The Inner and Outer Circle of the Betawi 98
	Betawi Kota: The (Political) Spearhead of the Betawi 99
	Betawi Pinggir: The Guardians of 'True Islam' 103
	Betawi Udik: The Guardians of 'True Tradition' 104
	Betawi Kota, Pinggir and Udik: Integration through
		Differentiation and Diversification from Within 108
	The Arabic Dimension of Betawi-ness 109
	Tugu: Exotics or Enclave? 114
	Kampung Sawah: The (Christian) Betawi in the Paddy Field 121
	Bangsawan Betawi: About the Invention of a Betawi
		Aristocracy 124
	Batak Going Betawi: Or, What Is a Batak Betawi? 129

Chapter 5. Betawi versus Peranakan   135
	Conceptual Disentanglement 135
	Cina Benteng: The First Peranakan 137
	Between Privilege and Expulsion: The Chinese in Batavia and
		Early Postcolonial Jakarta 137
	The Repression of the Chinese during the Suharto Era 141
	Recent Developments: 'Free the Dragon' versus 'Be(com)ing
		Betawi' 143
	The Betawi's Appetite for Incorporation 153

Chapter 6. Orang Betawi versus Orang Indonesia: The Connection
between Ethnic Diversity and National Unity   158
	Pancasila and *Bhinneka Tunggal Ika* as Core Principles of
		National Identity 158
	The Betawi as a Representation of *Bhinneka Tunggal Ika:* On the
		Meaning of 'Diversity of Origin' for 'Unity in Diversity' 163
	National Meanings of Betawi Indigeneity 166
	Betawi-ization versus Javanization of the National Centre 169

Betawi Contra *Orang Kompeni:* Postcolonial Constructions of
    Anti-colonial Heroism   170
  Orang Betawi and Orang Indonesia as Interconnected Categories
    of Identification   180

Chapter 7. Betawi Politics of Identity and Difference   183
  Betawi Goes Politics: The First 'Betawi untuk Gubernur'
    Campaign   183
  Indigeneity in the Production of Authenticity and
    Commitment   185
  Creole Identity in the Production of Commonalities   187
  Islam In and Out of Politics   189
  Jakarta between National and Local Representation   191
  Social Margins Going Ethno-politics   193
  Betawi as a Social Class and as Urban Identification   195

Conclusion. Towards an Open End   198

Bibliography   201

Index   218

Illustrations

Maps

Map 0.1. Central Jakarta/Tanah Abang, Kebon Sirih.   16

Map 2.1. General map of Indonesia   41

Map 2.2. Administrative structure of Jakarta   42

Map 2.3. Jabo(de)tabek metropolitan area   43

Figures

Figure 2.1. Batavia [*Jacatra*] 1619, from Haan (1922) *Oud Batavia*, G. Kolff and Co.   47

Figure 2.2. Roemah blanda – A Dutch house in Batavia, circa 1870 (Antique Maps & Prints of Indonesia, Bartele Gallery, Jakarta)   52

Figure 2.3. Batavia 1895 (from *Brockhaus Konversations-Lexikon*, 16th edition. Wiesbaden, 1952)   57

Figure 4.1. Betawi wedding outfit (cover from *Jakarta Kini*, edition June 2001)   101

Figure 5.1. Glodok, Chinese quarter – end of the nineteenth century (Picture No 10113239/JAVA/DJAKARTA 1881/Djakarta: the Chinese quarter/Mary Evans Picture Library)   139

Figure 5.2. 'Free the Dragon' (cover from *Jakarta Kini*, edition November 2000)   145

Figure 5.3. Programme of Peranakan Festival, Jakarta 2001   147

Figure 6.1. *Garuda Pancasila*, Gunkarta (photographer) via Wikipedia Commons, picture taken at the National Monument (Monas), Jakarta (n.d.)   160

Figure 6.2. Betawi warriors in founding year of the Forum Betawi Rempug (FBR), (this picture appeared in *The Jakarta Post*, 16 February 2001)   168

Figure 6.3. A *jago* in action, cover of Ali's *Cerita Rakyat Betawi I* (1993) (illustrator unknown)   171

All efforts have been made to contact the rights holders for these illustrations.

Acknowledgements

I am grateful to my colleagues for many valuable scientific discussions as well as gatherings devoted to convivial rather than academic exchange. Terima kasih to my friends and informants in Jakarta for their great trust and candour throughout my time with them. Thanks to all those who have in one way or another contributed to the publication of this book.

This book is dedicated to my family and friends at home and abroad.

Introduction

Creole Identity and Postcolonial Diversity

This book is a contribution to the study of the social construction of collective identities in postcolonial societies.[1] More generally, this study focuses on the interaction of ethnic, local and national identifications in Jakarta and on the role that creole identity plays in this regard. While examining contemporary such processes, focussing on the years following Suharto's fall, this study also contextualizes the phenomena under study historically, tracing their origins and development in light of the social conditions prevailing in a given historical period of time.

With an extremely heterogeneous population of around twelve million people, Jakarta is one of the largest cities worldwide, the largest metropolis in Southeast Asia and in many ways an example par excellence of contemporary postcolonial society. It is in such postcolonial settings, which are shaped by a high degree of ethnic, cultural and social heterogeneity – and in which the majority of the world's population lives today – that creole groups and identities often play an important role in processes of interaction and exchange and, hence, identity formation. This is above all due to the fact that, because of their heterogeneous origins, they can be conceptualized and identified with in ethnic and transethnic terms. It is, therefore, particularly in postcolonial societies in which ethnic identities constitute an important dimension of social organization and individual and group identity that creoleness can develop its potential in terms of transethnic integration and – following from this – for the promotion of a specifically postcolonial national consciousness. It is not primarily as an identity-related and ideational 'interstice' in and between minds that creole identity unfolds its particular social and political efficacy but rather in social relationships – on the terrain of the societal reality of contemporary postcolonial societies. However, as a late effect of colonialism and its overcoming, creole culture and identity are often linked with a considerable degree of ambivalence as well.

Processes of societal integration and differentiation are closely connected to (re-)configurations, (re-)constructions and transformations of social meanings, values and actions at a particular time and place. In seeking to understand these processes in terms of actual human experience the current study investigates and analyses them both in their respective historical as well as contemporary social contexts.

Ethnic versus Transethnic Identity

The crucial role frequently played by creole culture and identity in processes of social integration and differentiation, particularly within postcolonial, ethnically heterogeneous societies, stems above all from the fact that, because of their heterogeneous origins, they encompass both ethnic and transethnic dimensions. Before moving on it is therefore important to consider the relationship between ethnic and transethnic identity.

Ethnic identities are collective identities. Both collective and personal identities are socially constructed and have a reciprocally constitutive relationship with one another. The decisive difference between collective identity – one related to a *we* category – and personal identity – one related to an *I* – consists in the fact that the former has only a symbolic form, whereas the latter constitutes a physical and mental entity – a specific *I* or person – and thus has a *natural* boundary. By contrast, a *we* is not physically limited; its boundaries are constituted through the persons making it up. 'Collective identity is a question of identification on the part of the individuals involved. It does not exist "in itself" but rather only to the degree that certain individuals embrace it. It is as strong or as weak as its expression in the consciousness of the group's members and the degree to which it is able to motivate their thought and action' (Assmann 2002: 132).

The boundaries of a group are not only determined by the individuals making up that group, i.e., internally, but are also influenced by outsiders – by other individuals and groups. Just as the individual and the group constitute one another, so too do groups constitute themselves in relation to and in distinction from one another. Assessing who is a member of a certain group can produce different results on both intra-group and inter-group levels depending on the criteria of membership that are applied. Since the publication of Fredrik Barth's *Ethnic Groups and Boundaries* in 1969, it has been widely accepted that in terms of their expression and intensity ethnic identities are dependent on the prevailing historical, social and political contexts and situations that form the framework in which they are constructed. Ethnic identities are thus flexible and dynamic. They are not fixed entities with clear boundaries and invariant cultural features. Barth understands ethnic identity as a form of social organization whose (flexible) boundaries determine the membership of a group. For anthropological research this means that 'the critical focus for investigation becomes the ethnic boundary that defines the group rather than the cultural stuff it encloses' (Barth 1969: 15).

The influence of Barth's work has resulted in self-designation and self-ascription being accorded a central role in most subsequent definitions of what an ethnic group is.[2] In this context, ethnic identity is also regarded as an ascription that is negotiated, defined and redefined in connection with interests, situations and needs.[3] Barth's chief contribution to anthropological theory and research can be seen in the turn from the consideration of ethnic groups as static units with particular historical and cultural characteristics to the consideration of ethnic groups as forms of social organization that are not primarily tied to particular cultural and historical characteristics but rather to boundaries of membership developed in the context of social interaction.

This view functions as a corrective to the formerly dominant conceptualization of ethnic groups as fixed units, but it has also led to a neglect of the investigation of the relationship between ethnic identity and culture – and thus of the question as to the extent to which ethnic identity differs from other social identities (Premdas 2002: 177).[4] This question can only be answered via an exposition of the relationship between ethnic identity and culture because ethnic identity, ethnic classifications, ascriptions and self-designations are reasoned in terms of common culture, origin and history by means of which the existence of one's own (or another) group is substantiated and distinguished from other groups (De Vos and Romanucci-Ross 1982). Ethnic identity is thus both an element of social organization and a cultural element of the respective group of people laying claim to its validity (Vermeulen and Govers 2000). Ethnic identity encompasses a sociopsychological dimension, and it follows that the investigation of ethnic identity needs to include a consideration of the ideologies relating to culture and origin by means of which the respective ethnic identity is constructed and substantiated – despite the fact that these criteria are not in themselves adequate to determining the boundaries of ethnic groups (Vermeulen and Boissevain 1984). Ethnic boundaries can be more or less flexible depending on situation and context and in relation to the subjects constructing them. They are not dependent on the respective features via which they are substantiated but rather on the cognitions and emotions of those who claim these features as their 'own' or as 'ethnic' (Nagata 1974).

Based on these considerations, ethnic identity can be comprehended as the self-attributed and externally attributed membership of a group understood (and understanding itself) as ethnic, which is substantiated by way of a corpus of common historical and cultural characteristics (Premdas 2002). The belief in a common culture as well as in a common origin and history are features of ethnic identity (Eriksen 1993). However, it is possible for self-attribution and external attribution to diverge.

In connection to the theme of this book it is important to emphasize that ethnic identity can be substantiated with reference to the criterion of common origin in both homogeneous and heterogeneous terms. Moreover, ethnic identity may not only be 'inherited' via descent but also acquired and internalized through social convergence and incorporation (marriage, endowment with relevant social and cultural characteristics). This is particularly significant in the case of creole group identities. Furthermore, the expression of ethnic identity is not dependent on whether the history postulated as common and the cultural characteristics deemed to be shared actually correspond to reality or are merely imagined. What is crucial is that they are cogently communicated within the framework of ethnic self-assertion both internally and to the outside world.[5] It is therefore important that the claim of shared history and culture can be conveyed as plausible. This is facilitated, on the one hand, by establishing an extensive congruence between claimed history and culture and, on the other, by pointing to obvious and visible evidence. However, the factual reconstructivity of common history does not determine the intensity of ethnic identity. History – both individual and collective – is always the result of processes of selective reconstructions of memory and the invention of what puts the latter in (situational) perspective.[6]

The level of consciousness of ethnic difference and the degree of intensity of ethnic identification vary and are dependent on the respective social context. In particular, (re-)ethnicization processes – in the sense of the (re-)emergence and (re-)intensification of group identity – are often the result of certain collective interests (Cohen 1974). By the same token, there are variations on an individual and a group level with regard to the perception, communication and staging of ethnic identity (Cohen 2000). In short: 'There is no such thing as one kind of ethnicity' (Leman 1998: 150). This also means that a person can assign himself or herself to different ethnic groups according to the situation and context, given that the respective group boundaries allow for the requisite flexibility (Nagata 1974). Moreover, ethnic identities always exist in relation to other collective – for example, social, political, religious and gender-specific – identities. The meaning that accrues to ethnic identity is related to the meaning that accrues to other identities.

Despite – or because of – their contextual and situational character, ethnic identities are particularly significant for individuals and groups because they simultaneously comprise social and cultural orientations and connect these with a particular origin and history and with a particular place or territory. The connection of social, cultural and origin-oriented affiliations often lends ethnic identity a particular integrative power compared to other identities (Gardels 1991).

The existence of transethnic identifications presupposes the existence of a heterogeneously ethnic society in which ethnic ascriptions matter. Differences in ethnic identity may be transcended by means of different categories of identification – like urban, religious and national ones – according to situation and context. Likewise, categories of identification may on their part – and again dependent on situation and context – assume ethnic and transethnic relevance for an individual or a group. For example, Jakarta can have a primarily ethnic reference for someone who relates to Jakarta in ethnic terms – which, in Jakarta, is the case mostly among the Betawi. Local (Jakartan) identity in this case is connected with ethnic (Betawi) identity; it is a feature of ethnic identity for those who refer to it. Jakarta can also have transethnic reference if referred to as a category of identification irrespective of ethnic identity, if, simply put, a person identifies as Orang Jakarta without being Orang Betawi. I will come back to this later.

National Identity in the Context of Ethnic and Transethnic References

The following remarks focus on the connection between national and ethnic identity in ethnically heterogeneous societies.

First things first: national identity is not the opposite of ethnic identity. The two are linked by extensive structural commonalties and connections. For example, ethnic affiliation is frequently associated with a specific territory and in this context often forms the basis of national identity. 'Ethnic affiliation and territorial location have long been acknowledged as sources of national identification. … Many ethnic communities feel a strong association with a particular relatively clearly defined segment of territory' (Coakley 2003: 2). Ethnic and national identifications presuppose the existence of other ethnic groups or nations, as do their strategies of delimitation. In contrast to ethnic identity, national identity within an ethnically heterogeneous nation(-state) refers to the nation as a whole, which is often represented by a state or aspires to statehood (Eriksen 1993).

Ethnic and national identities are above all emotional in nature and the communities they refer to primarily imagined ones. As Benedict Anderson argues, 'It [the nation] is imagined because the members of even the smallest nation will never know most of their fellow members, meet them, or even hear of them, yet in the mind of each lives the image of their communion' (1991: 6). In his critical analysis of concepts that interpret nationalism as 'imagined' and therefore 'false' in contrast to other communities, Anderson argues that '[i]n fact, all communities larger than primordial villages of face-to-face contact (and perhaps even these) are imagined' (1991: 6).[7]

Specificities relating to ethnic groups are often regarded as constitutive of the national. Which group(s) and characteristics are perceived as representing a specific nation may vary according to situation and context. Internal hierarchies and relationships between and within ethnic groups also depend on their proximity to the national (Heinrich 1984). National communities often exhibit interethnic differences with regard to the intensity and meaning of national identity. Ethnic identities can thus exhibit differing degrees of national reference – some ethnic identities correspond more, others less with the prevailing national identity. In Indonesia, for example, the national identity of the Javanese is generally more marked than that of the Ambonese.

In contrast to the definition of national identity by Peoples and Bailey (2001) – which focuses on the Western model of the nation – ethnic identity is not understood per se as subnational identity here. It is possible for ethnic identity to (also) have a subnational character, but this need not necessarily be the case. Ethnic identities can position themselves in opposition to the nation or accrue meaning largely independently of national references, for example within a framework of transnational networks and alliances.

Ethnic identities are often understood as a breeding ground for national identity or propagated as such by the state, particularly within the framework of postcolonial conceptualizations of the ethnically heterogeneous nation. (State) ideologies of nationalism often avail themselves of a particular selection of what are mostly historical and cultural resources (Elwert and Waldmann 1989; Anderson 1991; Gellner 1999; Hobsbawm and Ranger 1999). In this context, state-prescribed ideologies of national consciousness can be more or less congruent with the actual national feelings of the citizens concerned.

National identity presupposes ethnic identity particularly where the latter constitutes an important factor of societal organization on the level of society as a whole (Knörr 1995, 2007a, b). In this context ethnic groups within a nation are seen as the roots from which the national tree is nourished.[8] Ethnic identities are construed as part of the nation just as the nation is construed as being closely tied to 'its' ethnic identities. Ethnic identity thus has national dimensions just as national identity has ethnic dimensions.

Just as *particular* ethnic affiliations can separate people, so too can the fact of the significance of ethnic identity *in itself* be interpreted as a form of commonality – for instance, as typical of a particular nation, as typically African, etc. As a Ghanaian once told me, 'It's typical for us to belong to tribes, it's typical for us Ghanaians and it's typical for us Africans in general.' According to this conceptualization membership of a particular 'tribe' may separate a person from members of other 'tribes', however, all Ghanaians and all Africans are united by their affiliation with the 'tribe' as a societal and identity-related organizational form.

It is particularly in the capital cities of (postcolonial) nation(-states) characterized by ethnic heterogeneity that the relationship between ethnic and national identity finds specific expressions due to the proximity of the national in the form of state institutions, media, national symbols, etc. In this context, proximity to the national can also generate transethnic ties, which does not imply that the significance of ethnic identities is necessarily diminished, especially if the latter are seen as the roots of the national. Indeed, it is often the case in the capitals of postcolonial nations that the ethnic and cultural diversity of their inhabitants is staged as a national cornucopia rather than as antithetical to the national.

The City as Locus and Focus

This study is based on anthropological research carried out above all *in* the city. This approach is based in part on the assumption that cultural phenomena in the city do not necessarily have to differ from cultural phenomena outside the city – even though this is often the case due to specifically urban circumstances. It follows that cultural change in the city cannot automatically be equated with modernization. In fact, the example of the Betawi shows that the construction and transformation of identity in the urban context can also consist in the development and defence of tradition. Phenomena encountered in the urban milieu thus need not necessarily be 'typically' urban phenomena.

However, this study is also based on anthropology of the city *in itself*, where the reference to the city is central to identity-related processes. We are concerned here with phenomena that exist *in* Jakarta and pertain *to* Jakarta. The 'locus' of this study is thus also understood as its 'focus' (Bommer 1991).

Urban anthropology has often looked at postcolonial cities (cities that developed as the result of colonialism) as somewhat non-native – in much the same way postcolonial nationhood and postcolonial nation-state boundaries were construed as mere outcomes of colonial interference. The maintenance of ethnic and origin-related relationships and the establishment of corresponding networks have been regarded as evidence that identities emphasizing (real) origin and (ethnic) tradition retain their primacy in the (colonially constructed, modern) urban context. This anthropological emphasis on the preservation of people's own and native identity and culture in the urban environment has its justification in that it is often overlooked in research focusing on degrees of modernization in the sense of a purported process of Westernization. However, the downside of such a perspective lies in the fact that the bonds that have developed between urban dwellers and what they perceive as their city as well as the establishment of transethnic identities and interethnic networks have often been underestimated or interpreted as indicative of social disintegration and alienation from the presumed original ethnic culture and identity.[9] The significance of specific urban circumstances for processes of identification has likewise been largely neglected. By avoiding the ethnic lens (without neglecting the importance of ethnic identities) and by focusing on social relationships and identity-related processes in a wider frame of reference it becomes apparent that irrespective of their (partly) colonial origins, both cities and nation-state boundaries have been incorporated by the postcolonial subjects to a significantly higher degree than suspected by the (researching and observing) descendants of their former colonial masters.

In the examination and assessment of the relationship between native and foreign culture, between tradition and modernity in the postcolonial world, there is a persistent tendency to classify tradition as native culture and primarily associate it with the rural space. Conversely, change and modernity tend to be associated with foreign (Western) culture and assigned above all to the urban space. As a consequence, it has been assumed that urban culture worldwide largely conforms to Western lifestyles, values and attitudes. However, more recently, it has been demonstrated that modernity can be configured in a variety of ways that are distinct from the Western variant (Eisenstadt 2005; Knörr 2002a, 2002b).

A further reason for the neglect of urban-oriented (transethnic) identity lies in the fact that city dwellers are often primarily understood and studied as migrants, and the bonds between them and their suspected places of origin are emphasized. To be sure, it is often the case that a large proportion of urban populations can be classified as migrants in as far as they have originally come from areas outside the city. However, this characteristic cannot necessarily be seen as constituting the decisive factor in the identity formation of city dwellers. On the contrary, one finds an increasing tendency among such migrants to identify themselves primarily with the city in which they live rather than with the area from which they originate. An ever increasing number of people are born in cities, grow up there and share the experience of urban life. Jakarta is thus not only a spatial reality for the people living there but also serves them, independently of specific regional origins and ethnic affiliations, as an object of identification, engagement and discourse. In this sense, Jakarta is both a representation and a constituent of urban culture(s).[10]

Although we cannot speak of a universal city or urban culture exhibiting characteristics that are independent of the specific social and cultural backgrounds of its respective inhabitants, the spatial, social and cultural aspects of the city as phenomenon do exhibit certain important structural commonalities. For instance, social and ethnic heterogeneity and high population density lead to city-specific forms of social organization and interaction. It is not the absence of tradition that is characteristic of the city but rather the extensive encounters that occur (1) between different traditional ways of life, (2) between traditional and de-traditionalized or alternative ways of life and (3) between the different de-traditionalized or alternative ways of life (Nassehi 1999).

Cities provide a wealth of material for research into processes of social and cultural change. Groups with different ethnic, cultural and regional origins co-exist in (comparatively) dense spatial conditions. Interethnic relationships and intercultural interaction – preconditions for such processes – are usually particularly marked in cities. Within a city – especially one as large and featuring such a high degree of heterogeneity as Jakarta – the construction and transformation of community and identity always take place in the context of an engagement with what is more one's own and more someone else's culture. Indeed, Bruner (1974: 220) argues that 'As the capital and prime city of a country with over three hundred ethnic groups, Jakarta is the multi-ethnic city "par excellence".'[11] In Jakarta the simultaneous operation of different configurations of sociality and culture has been part of everyday interaction for centuries. It is thus particularly the urban environment that provides an illustration of how, in the course of intensive confrontation and engagement between 'one's own' and the respective 'other', both are socially and culturally implemented, transformed and perpetuated. This also applies in cases where the bond to a place of origin or an ethnic group becomes less significant or undergoes a change of meaning.[12] In a city like Jakarta it becomes particularly clear that external cultural influences are not comprehended and absorbed in their original form. Rather, they are selected, interpreted, transformed and reconfigured in accordance with the respective local background. And just as differences in the adaptation of external culture emerge on the basis of city dwellers' diversity, so too do new identities and communities emerge (Knörr 2002a, 2002b, 2007a).

When it comes to the relationship between ethnic and national identity in the postcolonial context of ethnic diversity, Jakarta, as the national capital of Indonesia, offers a rich source of material. It is particularly here, in a framework of ethnic and cultural diversity in close proximity to the nation(-state), that one can observe how the national ideology of 'unity in diversity' (*Bhinneka Tunggal Ika*) is conceptualized, communicated and staged as the root of (Indonesian) nationhood. I will be returning to this aspect later.

The investigation of the emergence of urban variants of identity also provides general insights into the emergence of shared, transethnic identity against a background of ethnic and cultural heterogeneity and difference. This may enable us to discern how and under what conditions transethnic identity emerges or is hindered or (re)fragmented. Moreover, one can identify the dimensions of culture that are most suited to the endowment of shared identity as well as those in which differences are maintained and defended. Culture, as a process of interaction and negotiation, can be seen as comprising mutually referential and corresponding phenomenal or material expressions, on the one hand, and relational or cognitive-emotional expressions on the other. Phenomenal expressions are understood here as the perceptible manifestations and materializations of culture, relational expressions as people's social actions, perceptions and emotions in relation to them. The phenomenal and relational dimensions of culture interact and influence each other and in order to identify and understand continuities, discontinuities and transformations related to them require investigation and analysis in terms of this very interaction and mutual influence.

Such an investigation and analysis calls for the understanding of the emic meanings of cultural representations and conceptions, hence, the meanings that the insiders associate with the latter.[13] That this is necessary becomes particularly evident where specific social and cultural forms and habits are automatically and naively regarded as evidence of the Westernization of individuals and societies. Such assessments are commonly based on the concept of a contextually and culturally independent equivalence of meanings, on the assumption that the adoption of characteristics of external origin implies the adoption of their original meanings and valencies. In simple terms, there are – for example – McDonald's branches in Jakarta and in Düsseldorf in which (almost) the same hamburgers are sold. However, the social meaning of a visit to McDonald's in Jakarta and the consumption of a burger there differs from the social meaning of a visit to McDonald's in Düsseldorf and the consumption of a burger there.[14] Social meanings and valorizations are thus contextual and are related to the respective societal, cultural and historical situation.

In the process of social and cultural interaction external influences are invested with meaning and deployed in relation to local specificities. A cultural trait of external provenance can thus be adopted without this entailing the adoption of its external meaning and valency, i.e., the meaning and valency it has in its original context as seen from the point of view of the incorporating society. An external cultural trait is invested with new meanings that make sense within the incorporating, local society. The social meaning of any specific cultural feature depends on the respective cognitive-emotional relationship a given society or social group develops towards it. Therefore, its meanings can only be deciphered via an investigation of this very relationship. The emic perspectives and conceptions concerning a given (appropriated) phenomenon are thus part of the phenomenon to be investigated. It is only by deciphering these conceptions that we are able to recognize, for example, that the meaning of purportedly European characteristics found in an African society may be very different from their meaning in the European society from which they originate. Vice versa, the incorporation of African cultural traits into urban European culture does not imply the incorporation of their original African meanings. New and external social and cultural forms are always perceived, selected, interpreted, and (re)configured against the background of the respective locality, and in a context defined by what is familiar, established, one's own. This process is characterized by creativity, activity and exchange and not by one-sided and passive acceptance and adoption. The configuration potential that, given the plethora of foreign social and cultural influences is particularly pronounced in urban environments, is thus limited by the preexisting social and cultural context and the conceptions inherent to it. The incorporation and integration of new, external forms and features as a consequence of exchange and interaction does not entail estrangement from one's own culture but rather a '*de*-strangement' (*Ent*-fremdung) of the external culture via its (meaningful) incorporation into what is familiar. Accordingly, what emerges is not a variant of the external foreign(er's) culture but a variant of one's own, local culture.

Categories of Identification and Social Discourses as Objects of Observation and Analysis

The construction of ethnic, local and national identity in Jakarta operates first and foremost via the categories of '(Orang) Betawi (*Asli*)', 'Orang Jakarta' and 'Orang Indonesia', with the category of '(Orang) Betawi' assuming a key role.

Orang means 'human being' or 'category of human being' – an Orang Jakarta is thus a Jakartan, and an (Orang) Betawi is a member of the group of the Betawi. Because Jakarta is (also) the name of the city, the prefix Orang is required in Indonesian to distinguish the category 'Jakarta human being' from the category

'Jakarta city'.[15] By contrast, although *Betawi* is also the Indonesian term for Batavia, the (Dutch) name used for the city of Jakarta during the colonial period, it is today almost exclusively used to denote the Betawi group of people and thus does not require the prefix Orang. *Asli*[16] means 'original', 'indigenous', 'genuine' and is commonly attached as a suffix to Betawi when the intention is to emphasize the (ethnic) authenticity of a Betawi or a group of Betawi. Terms used to denote this group and its language once varied widely, but the terms Betawi, Orang Betawi and Betawi Asli have now become the established appellations. The term Orang Jakarta is also used on occasion to refer to the Betawi, usually with the attached suffix *Asli*.

The categories Orang Betawi and Orang Jakarta have a reciprocal relationship with the category Orang Indonesia, which refers to the national, Indonesian context of identity, which has particular significance for the capital Jakarta.

The Betawi are regarded as the original inhabitants of Jakarta – as *orang asli*, who emerged at the end of the seventeenth and beginning of the eighteenth centuries via processes of cultural creolization of different groups that had immigrated to Batavia from Indonesia and regions in South and Southeast Asia. The Betawi see themselves as a people or ethnic group (*suku bangsa, kelompok etnik*)[17] and are classified as such by others. They are ascribed particular social, cultural and historical characteristics as ethnic features.[18] Today, the Betawi live for the most part in centrally located parts of Jakarta, in a number of peripheral areas and in the neighbouring cities of Bekasi and Tangerang.

There are several intra-ethnic differentiations among Betawi groups that are significant within the framework of this study and that are recognized both by the Betawi themselves and by others. In the context of the construction and transformation of ethnic and transethnic identities in Jakarta, these differentiations often play an important role.

Orang Jakarta (without the suffix *Asli*) denotes a primarily transethnic category of people whose overriding social and cultural orientation is the Jakarta of the present.[19] A person is Orang Jakarta on the basis of his or her individual cognitive-emotional relatedness to Jakarta, which is expressed in certain views, behaviours and parlance. 'Orang Jakarta as a transethnic label refers to a category of people rather than to a group. No conceptual distinction is made between Orang Jakarta who, besides identifying as such, also ascribe themselves to specific other ethnic groups and those who do not. However, distinctions are gradually emerging with regard to the intensity and authenticity of Jakartan identity that do not necessarily correlate with the absence or presence of other ethnic affiliations but primarily with the expression of social and cultural characteristics that are regarded as typically Jakartan.[20] The orientation to Jakarta is thus not an expression of a collective or ethnic consciousness; rather, it is expressed primarily – and extensively – at the level of the individual and the respective social group. The transethnic category Orang Jakarta is in manifold ways related to the ethnic category (Orang) Betawi – a relationship that finds expression in both the effort to delimit one category from the other as well as in the construction of commonalities.

(Orang) Betawi and Orang Jakarta denote, on the one hand, groups and categories of people who are ascribed Jakartan culture and identity by themselves and others by means of historical, social and cultural ascriptions and delimitations. On the other hand, the concepts of (Orang) Betawi and Orang Jakarta also comprehend meanings that, although they are connected with certain groups and categories of people, are not necessarily identical with them. This applies particularly to the category Betawi, which comprehends a corpus of ascriptions and meanings only some of which are directly connected with the Betawi as an ethnic group, whereas others are increasingly being constructed independently of or only in a loose association with them.

Orang Indonesia denotes all Indonesians as members of the Indonesian nation. The particular significance of national identity in Jakarta as the national capital is constructed, mediated and staged by means of multifarious connections of the national category Orang Indonesia with the Jakarta-related categories of Orang Betawi and Orang Jakarta.

Although Orang Betawi contains a primarily ethnic, Orang Jakarta a primarily local and Orang Indonesia a primarily national reference, the conceptions and social performances connected with these categories constantly relate to, condition and influence one another. They closely interact with one another and with other identity-related categories in processes of inclusion and exclusion in Jakarta. Therefore, their social meanings can only be understood by investigating and analysing the manifold ways in which processes of identification related to (trans-)ethnic, local, and national categories are communicated and socially interrelated.

It is important to bear in mind that identity-related processes do not always become evident in terms of features and actions observable from the outside, but often at the level of conceptualizations and ideologies. This applies, among other things, to the construction of origin in connection to ethnic, local and national identifications. Ascriptions and differentiations in relation to origin can often not be grounded in historical fact and their significance (which is not therefore reduced) cannot be evaluated solely via the investigation of actual, historical processes. This applies all the more to groups – such as the Betawi – whose origins are heterogeneous and who have emerged via creolization processes, in the course of which a new common identity was forged on the background of ethnic diversity (Knörr 2007a, 2008a, 2008b, 2009c, 2010a, 2012). Nevertheless, it is often the more visible, so-called phenomenal level of identification processes that proves more accessible for the initial steps in a research process and provides a platform from which the level of conceptualizations and ideologies can subsequently be accessed.

Identification processes concerning categories of collective identification and groups of people are likely to become evident in central social discourses at the individual and group level. Such discourses are represented, performed, negotiated and related to one another in manifold ways.[21] Discourses are understood here as social praxis that has both linguistic and nonlinguistic dimensions. Discourses do not emerge arbitrarily but rather in connection with particular social developments and at a particular time. They have historical roots, the identification of which facilitates the understanding of their contemporary significance. Their contextual meaning is dependent on ideologies, power structures and aims. Correspondingly, statements and stagings need to be comprehended and interpreted as elements of a particular discourse or discursive strand, of a particular social praxis at a particular historical time. Discourses are processes in which the conceptualizations, values and constraints are formed by means of which reality is comprehended and differentiated. Social reality is constituted by discursive praxis and thus subject to constant change. Discourses are a consequence of historical developments and influence the formation of social reality. They exercise a guiding effect on action. Conversely, social praxis and the institutional frameworks determine what can be said when and how.

The investigation of central discourses is particularly suited to tracing identity-related processes that entail strategies of inclusion and exclusion, integration and differentiation, because they constitute the loci at which identity and its social meanings are negotiated, are rendered visible and audible.[22] These discourses occur parallel and in constant interchange with one another, and their meanings can only be evaluated when their reciprocal dynamic is made part of the analysis. For this reason the central discourses relating to the processes being investigated here also constitute the analytic units around which research questions are organized and according to which the results of research are evaluated and presented.

Notes on Field Research

I refrain from a detailed analysis of the role of the researcher in the field and his or her influence on the research environment and thereby on research results. Instead, I will focus on a number of particularities relevant to the theme of this book. I regard my role in the field as having only a very limited effect on the lives of those I have researched and thus assume that neither the constructions of identities in Indonesia nor Indonesians' conceptualizations of them have been significantly influenced by my person. Good research – including anthropological research – focuses on the research topic and not on the researcher conducting it (except where he or she is the object of study). It is common knowledge that establishing a balanced relationship between proximity and distance is central to the acquisition of knowledge particularly where knowledge of what (other) people think, do and feel is concerned. The degree of proximity/distance needed to conduct good research may vary from researcher to researcher – one needs more proximity, the other more distance. At the latest, it is when the work is done that it becomes evident whether one has been too close or too distant from those studied – in both cases acuity and analytical thickness suffer. It is up to the reader to decide whether either alternative applies to this work.

This study is based above all on so-called classical anthropological research methods.[23] I was a participatory observer in many settings that exhibited or potentially offered a connection to the theme of the study. I conducted interviews, both highly and loosely structured, and had many conversations in which aspects of the research topic were (also) addressed. The interviews were for the most part conducted in an informal atmosphere. They were organized around questions central to the study, which served as a guideline and which, in the course of research and with the accumulation of knowledge were supplemented, varied and changed. I aimed at an open conversational atmosphere that allowed informants as much scope as possible to develop and express their own standpoints. Conversations with representatives of state and non-state institutions occasionally assumed a more formal character. However, even in the course of more formal interviews I endeavoured to create an atmosphere that allowed interviewer and interviewee to develop the theme together and offered informants the opportunity to interrogate the questions I was asking, to raise new and sometimes (seemingly) other issues than those related to my research questions, issues, that in many cases then proved highly relevant for the understanding of the theme of this study. To create a setting that was as informal and relaxed as possible I refrained (with a few exceptions) from recording interviews because this seemed to inhibit informants when it came to freely expressing their opinions and created the impression of a test in which there were correct and incorrect answers. Instead, I took notes during or immediately after conversations.

Particularly when themes are linked with personal emotions, ideas and conceptions it is often expedient to present research questions in the context of personal experience rather than in direct relation to the object of study. We often learn more about – for example – ethnic identity when someone tells us about an experience or an event in which ethnic identity played (or did not play) a role than when someone expresses his or her opinion about ethnic identity as such, hence, without placing it in the context of personal experience. The meanings of identifications unfold above all in specific personal and social contexts. For this reason it makes sense to investigate identity-related ascriptions and processes within the contexts in which meaning accrues to them. The meanings of identifications and delimitations become clear in the context of both discussions and actions. They must therefore be investigated in the context of conversations as well as by means of (participatory) observation of the activities via which they are negotiated, staged and substantiated.

Personal biographies also played an important role in interviews and interactions; they encouraged informants to describe personal attitudes and behaviours and to link them to the questions under discussion. (cf. Lehmann 1983; Knörr 1990, 1995, 2007a).

Apart from the conversations and interviews that explicitly contributed information to the research project, I also had many conversations and discussions in many different places – in *warung*,[24] taxis, buses, bars, government offices, shops, at markets, etc. – discussions that were not initially related to my research but then often led to discussions of particular aspects of it. As a conspicuous foreigner in Jakarta I was constantly asked who I am and what I was doing in the city. My answers often sufficed to initiate a conversation that addressed thematic aspects of my study. Moreover, such random settings make for a more relaxed atmosphere than an interview setting and thus for greater openness. Finding the 'right' person or situation to achieve 'theoretical saturation'[25] is less important than having the appropriate questions at hand (or discovering them) when the 'right' person or situation for the clarification (or discovery) of these questions is encountered.

In view of the theme and scope of my enquiry it did not seem appropriate to restrict my research to one or more city districts or *kampung*.[26] Limiting my work to a particular locality would certainly have been more pleasant in terms of travel requirements, but it would not have allowed me to gain the insight I needed into the complexity and interdependence of the different identity-related processes whose local point of reference is Jakarta as a whole rather than specific *kampung*.

Jakarta's diversity does not only function as a symbol of Jakarta in itself but also represents the diversity of all Indonesia in specific ways. Many public events that stage and celebrate the connection between Jakarta and Indonesia take place at locations that symbolically refer to this special link. The *Abang dan None Jakarta* (Mister and Miss Jakarta) pageant, for instance, is held in the *Taman Mini Indonesia Indah* (TMII)[27] – an extensive area in southern Jakarta where the Indonesian archipelago has been replicated in miniature form and where the cultural variety of Indonesia is represented in the form of typical houses, ethnic artefacts and events. The many public Betawi events organized to commemorate Jakarta's birthday take place for the most part in the inner city at central locations rather than in the *kampung* and areas where the Betawi live. The big meetings of the Betawi organizations are held at locations in Jakarta where the organizations' presence is most noticeable rather than in the areas where their members live.

This is not to say that the processes studied do not exhibit differences relating to particular districts/*kampung* nor that there are no location-based forms of identification. However, these did not constitute a central focus of this study and were not considered as central to the investigation of the complexity and

16 *Creole Identity in Postcolonial Indonesia*

interdependence of identifications and delimitations constructed in relation to the categories of identifications at stake here. This study constitutes what might be termed a selective 'multi-local ethnography' (Marcus 1995), which aims to achieve as 'thick' a description as possible of the interconnections characterizing

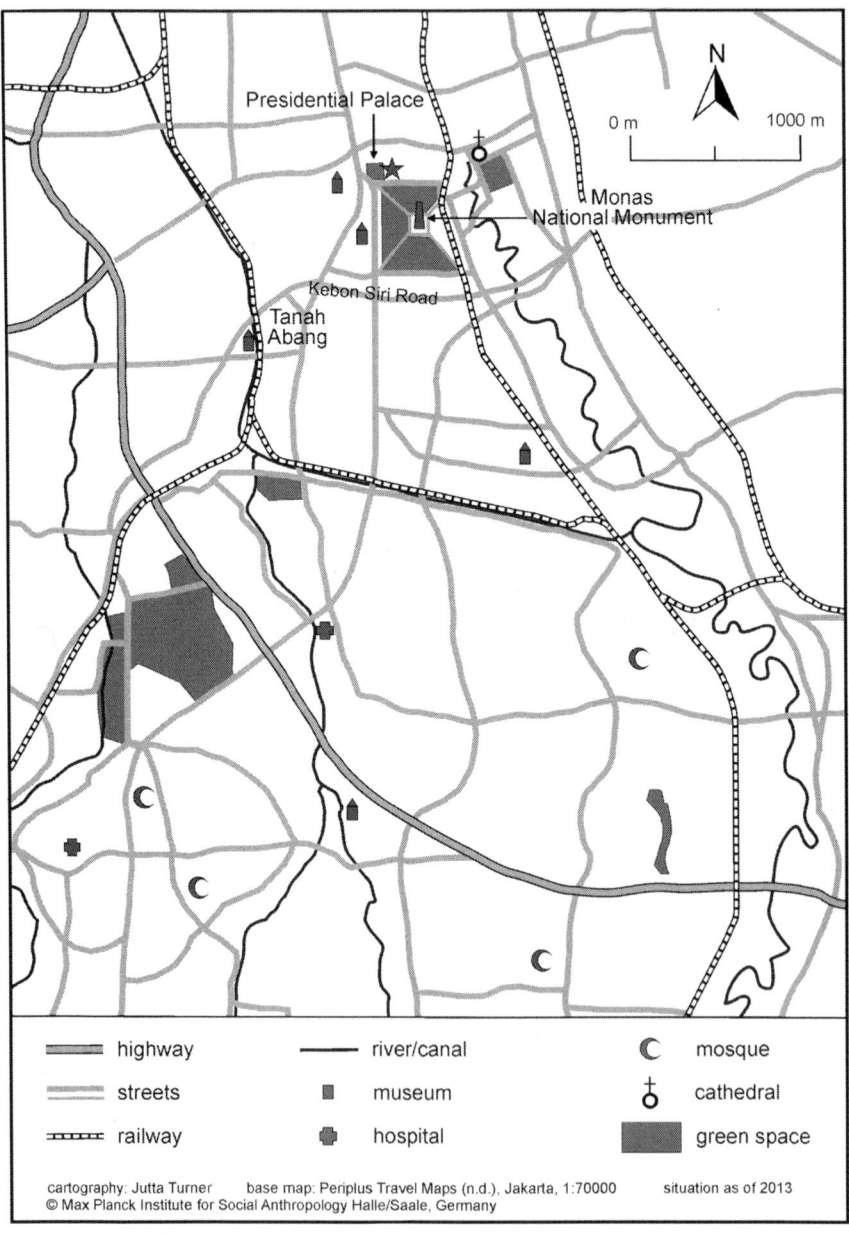

Map 0.1. Central Jakarta/Tanah Abang, Kebon Sirih.

the investigated processes (Geertz 1999). Future research may well identify district and *kampung*-specific differences relating to the interconnections that my own research has identified.

Nevertheless, the central questions guiding my research lent themselves to a certain degree of spatial concentration. Processes of integration and differentiation are best observed and investigated where they unfold in interaction with one another. This is particularly the case in the more central areas of the city, which are very heterogeneous in ethnic terms and where the role of Jakarta as the national capital is particularly marked and a subject of identity-related engagement. I chose to live in the centre of Jakarta on the border between Kebon Sirih and Tanah Abang, which are both commercial districts and residential areas in which inner-city (and old-established) Betawi live and work along with many people who classify themselves in terms of different ethnic and transethnic identities (such as Orang Jakarta and Orang Indonesia).

Notes

1. The term *postcolonial* is used here to denote societies that up until the recent past were colonial territories and that are still shaped – hence *post*colonial – in many respects by the historical experience of colonialism. The erstwhile colonial powers can also be regarded as postcolonial societies in so far as they were part of the colonial system. However, the societies described and treated as postcolonial here are restricted to those that were colonized.
2. E.g., van den Berghe (1975); Parsons (1975); Elwert and Waldmann (1989).
3. E.g., Roosens (1989); Young (1993); Anderson (1991).
4. See also Roosens (1995); Eriksen (2002).
5. See Waters (1990); Hobsbawm and Ranger (1999).
6. See Assmann (2002: 40), who refers here to the philosopher Hans Blumenberg when he writes: 'There are … "no pure facts of memory".'
7. He refers specifically to Ernest Gellner and argues that 'Gellner is so anxious to show that nationalism masquerades under false pretences that he assimilates "invention" to "fabrication" and "falsity", rather than to "imagining" and "creation". In this way he implies that "true" communities exist which can be advantageously juxtaposed to nations' (Anderson 1991: 6).
8. The 'tree with roots' motif as a symbol of the relationship between national entity and ethnic diversity is one I have frequently encountered both in Indonesia and West Africa.
9. Referring to the Chicago school of urban anthropology, Hannerz (1980: 56) writes: 'They conceived disorganization when they described diversity.'
10. The relationship between modernity and tradition in the context of Southeast Asian urbanization is analysed, for example, by Evers and Korff (2000). Among other things they discuss the (own) cultural symbolism and structure of urban space in relation to the 'increased homogenization of the morphology of the cities' (ibid.: 119).
11. See Dhofier (1976: 14) for a discussion of the intensity of interethnic relationships in Jakarta.
12. See Cohen (1974: 271–78) on ethnicity in Bandung (Java) and Medan (Sumatra).
13. 'An emic model is one which explains the ideology or behaviour of members of a culture according to indigenous definitions. An etic model is one which is based on criteria

from outside a particular culture. Etic models are held to be universal; emic models are culture-specific' (Barnard and Spencer 1996: 180). In simple terms, emic models/categories/concepts are those relating to the perspective of the insider, whereas etic models/categories/concepts are those that make sense from the viewpoint of the observer. See also Headland et al. (1990).

14. In Jakarta, visiting McDonald's is an expression of a middle class lifestyle, a modern way of life and certain level of prosperity; see also Gerke (1995), who made a similar observation.
15. This is also the case with 'Indonesia' and 'Orang Indonesia'.
16. *Asli*: derived from the Arabic *asal* = origin.
17. *Suku bangsa*: refers to an indigenous, ethnic group. By contrast, the term *kelompok etnik*, i.e., ethnic group, does not necessarily signify Indonesian indigeneity. The term *suku bangsa* is more common in colloquial usage.
18. Particular features frequently referred to include origin (heterogeneous descent, indigeneity), language (*Jakarta Malay, Omong Betawi*), music (*Rebana, Gambang Keromong, Tanjidor*), street processions of costumed and maked dancers (*Ondel-Ondel*), religion (link between Islamic and ethnic identity), clothing (*kebaya, pasisir*), cuisine (*krak telor, kue-kue*), social manner and characteristics of personality (e.g. directness, humour, gregariousness, conservatism).
19. However, Orang Jakarta is also used to denote a person as Orang Betawi – the given meaning emerges from the context in which the term is used.
20. Characteristics commonly referred to as typical for Jakartans (Orang Jakarta) include modernity, progressiveness, openness, cynicism and quick-wittedness.
21. The concept of discourse used here is based on its use by Foucault (1991, 2002); Fowler (1991, 1996); Wodak (1994); Jäger (2004).
22. On the theory and practice of the dynamics of processes of social inclusion and exclusion, see Schlee and Werner (1996); Schlee and Horstmann (2001); Schlee (2008).
23. Apart from these interactive forms of field research and the utilization of scholarly literature, I also drew on Jakartan television broadcasts, newspaper articles and a range of publications relating to the city produced by state institutions and authorities. A range of websites and publications that were (in part) only available online also provided important information. E-mail contact also allowed for a certain level of continuity in communication with different informants while not in Indonesia.
24. *Warung* = small, roofed eatery or mobile wagon selling simple dishes.
25. Theoretical saturation is achieved when the field under investigation (the studied phenomena) has been elucidated to the point where no new knowledge can be expected from additional data (see Glaser and Strauss 1967; see also Strübing 2004).
26. *Kampung* is the Indonesia term for a village or settlement. In the urban context the term refers to residential areas that, particularly in comparison with the modern environment, tend to exhibit a village character.
27. *Taman Mini Indonesia Indah* = Beautiful Indonesian miniature park; see Pemberton (1994); Errington (1997).

Chapter 1

Creole Identity in Postcolonial Context

Creole Terminology at the Conceptual Crossroads of History and Ideology

The central role that creole identity plays in the processes of identification under study here requires a critical examination of the creole terminology. This is all the more so because the discourses revolving around the etymology and meaning of the term *creole* (in its different variants – *créole, crioullo, Kreo,* etc.) and of the concepts of creoleness and creolization are in many ways influenced by ideological orientations on the part of those conceptualizing.[1] This also applies to discourses relating to the criteria upon which particular creole identities are based. These discourses make use of origin-related, phenotypical (racial) and/or cultural rationales, and they vary according to historical and social contexts and the specific group concerned. Exactly who and what creole denotes remains a matter of dispute. 'Simply put, "creole" and "creolization" have meant lots of different things at different times' (Stewart 2007: 5). Or: 'As such the term [creole] has constantly undergone changes in usage reflecting the changes in culture and society through the ages' (Knight 1997: 273). The ambivalent and conflicting public and scholarly discourses around terms, ethnonyms and etymologies are also an indication of the current relevance of creoleness in many postcolonial, heterogeneous societies and the ambivalence and contestedness frequently linked with it.

Chaudenson has examined a range of different scholarly etymologies of the term creole produced over recent decades and shows how they, in contrast to the old etymology, which traces the term back to the Spanish *criollo,* are in fact untenable in scientific terms: 'Recent lexicographic attempts ... illustrate perfectly how often extreme ideological fantasies can divert serious thinking, even in debates that are reputedly scientific. ... In reality, the facts about the word creole are now well known, even though experts can still discuss some details on its etymology' (Chaudenson 2001: 1; 3). A number of those formulating such new etymologies are apparently primarily concerned with proving who is (or was) the true 'ur-creole' by providing 'evidence' of the origin of the word creole. Thus we find, for example, the construction of a 'white' and a 'black' etymology being used to prove the existence of a 'white' or 'black' ur-creole, respectively.[2]

When was the term creole first used, by whom and for what kind of people? There are good reasons for taking account of the historical context when delineating creole as a conceptual field. Taking into account creolization's – and creole terminology's – historical semantics helps unfold the latter's heuristic potentials as a conceptual field and analytical tool.

The Portuguese *crioulo* is regarded as the oldest variant of the creole terminology. However, the first documented use of the concept is the Spanish *criollo*, which denoted those Spaniards who were not – like the *peninsulares* – born in Europe but in the so-called 'New World' (Stephens 1983, 1999).[3] The origin of *crioulo* (and thus of *criollo*) can be traced back to the verb *crier* (raise, nourish, engender, bring into being) and to the noun *cria* (infant, baby, person without family). Both of these terms can in turn be traced back to the Latin *crear* (create, bring into being).[4] The endings *-oulo* and *-olo* indicate that the term is diminutive, which points to the fact that it was initially used to refer to children born in exile and only later expanded to include adults as well (Arrom 1951).

Subsequently, slaves were also differentiated according to whether they had been born in Africa or in their respective colonies. Slaves born in a colony were referred to as creoles, *criollos, crioulos,* etc., whereas newcomers were termed, for example, New Africans, Saltwater Negroes or Wild Negroes (Morgan 1991: 199–200; Pierce 1998: 222). Individuals of mixed black and white descent were also referred to as creoles. The term came to be applied to all nonindigenous persons born 'here', namely in the respective new home, delimiting them from those born 'back there', namely in their territories of origin, whether Europe or Africa. It was used equally for whites and blacks, although depending on the respective context the term was supplemented (white creole, black creole, etc.) to specify what kind of creole was being referred to. The term creole thus originally had the function of denoting a person in terms of his indigeneity or exogeneity: 'By claiming a "creole identity", people from colonized lands stress their difference from the original colonists and their descendants in the Old Country' (Hoffmann 2003: 5). 'Creolization meant, and means, not only the differentiation from the original settlers, but the amalgamation of all the cultures that different immigrant groups brought in through the years' (ibid.: 11).

Slave exile and early colonial societies in which slaves and other foreign populations of various origins settled offer a classic example of historical creolization processes. Due to their size or relative proximity to their place of origin, some groups were able to maintain their original identities and form diaspora communities even in exile. However, the great distances usually involved meant that the maintenance of social contacts to the group and region of origin was only possible for the few. There were also individuals who became integrated into the ranks of the colonialists or into local populations, often by way of marriage and religious conversion. However, the majority, particularly among the slaves, were forced to reorientate themselves in a new environment and without any contact to their original homelands. Over the course of time, the interaction of groups of different origins led to the development of new and shared cultural features. Different factors determined which and whose social and cultural forms and features were integrated and to what degree and by means of which patterns of exchange colonial and local influences were merged and reconfigured. Such factors included the size of the respective groups, the size of the entire group of slaves or other foreign populations and the (relative) social and physical proximity of the population undergoing creolization to its colonial masters and, where applicable, to local, indigenous groups.[5]

The progressive commingling of different immigrant groups in the colonial settler societies meant that the differentiation of indigenous and exogenous[6] became more and more obsolete. The term creole was increasingly applied above all to groups emerging from unions between (former) slaves and between persons of different origins and skin colour (Stewart 2007). The comparatively homogeneous groups of the first European settlers in the New World, with whom the term creole was initially associated, also commingled among themselves and with persons of indigenous origin, a development that led to an increasing social hierarchization of creoles based on the criterion of skin colour.

Creolization processes occurred among oppressed and dominant groups – among the European settlers of Louisiana and South Africa, among freed slaves in West Africa, and among slaves and servants in colonial Indonesia, for example. It should be noted that creolization does not necessarily require a social context shaped by the marked relations of domination characteristic of slave and colonial societies. Nevertheless, it was in these social contexts that the conditions that (can) lead to creolization were particularly pronounced – such as the distance from place and group of origin, the necessity of interethnic communication and the need for social solidarity and shared identity and language.

Creolization and Creole Identity beyond the Caribbean

The societies commonly associated with creolization in both linguistic and cultural terms are above all those of the Caribbean along with some islands in the Indian Ocean region (particularly Mauritius and Réunion), societies in which creole groups either make up the majority of the population or are one of a comparatively small number of groups that are differentiated along ethnic lines.

The fact that creolization and creole identities have mostly been studied with regard to the Caribbean has given rise to the impression that these phenomena may be regional particularities. For some time, the protagonists of *Créolité* – a discourse originally developed among writers, artists and academics in the Francophone Caribbean and in the Caribbean diaspora in North America and Europe[7] – marketed creolization as a movement countering globalization. The latter was associated with cultural homogenization and standardization from above, with exclusionary discourses of ancestry and the suppression of cultural diversity (Glissant 2000).[8] Creolization, on the other hand, was considered a process by means of which notions of purity, monolingualism and universality were to be repudiated in favour of contact and diversity. The *Créolité* movement's understanding of creolization was developed in conjunction with postcolonial discourses. It assumes that as a result of increased contact and mixture new cultural forms and contents emerge, which are mixed and local instead of ethnic and national. As well, ethnic, racial and national categories of identification are expected to be replaced by identifications with specific localities and their respective cultural representations.

As Khan has pointed out, 'creolization serves as both a model that describes historical processes of cultural change and contact and an analytical tool that interprets them' (2007: 653). The conceptualization of *Créolité* as a postcolonial model of identity, however, seems to result not so much from empirical analysis of social processes and dynamics prevalent in the (postcolonial) Caribbean but rather from wishful thinking – or, as Stewart has put it, 'Their "model of" is thus already a "model for" an idealized Créolité ready to be recommended to the world'[9] (Stewart 2007: 17) – a model, I would like to add, that also tends to neglect the difference between material and relational dimensions of culture – between cultural forms, on the one hand, and a given population's perception of and identification with them (Knörr 2010a).[10]

Anglophone scholars dealing with creolization tend to focus more on the context-specific social meanings and functions of the cultural forms and contents emerging from the process of creolization (cf. Miller 1994).[11] Creolization in their view creates an identity-related, but not heritage-based, reference system within a specific social context by linking cultural forms from a variety of sources. The emphasis lies on creolization's function for social integration rather than on its potential for overcoming exclusionary discourses resulting from colonial suppression (Miller 1994). The normative bent of the *Créolité* movement is averted, yet the historical context of creolization is equally disregarded and creolization no longer understood and analysed as a process of social and cultural interaction embedded in specific social and historical contexts. Instead, the perspective is narrowed down to the (micro-)level of cultural forms and to how individuals and groups relate to them.

As has already been pointed out, creolization is distinct from other forms and processes of cultural interaction because it involves indigenization and ethnicization in specific contexts, whereby old boundaries are dissolved, yet new ones are produced. Thus, not everything creoles do counts (once and for all) as creolization. Even when creole groups mix, this is only creolization if they replace their respective creole identities with a new and common creole identity. Therefore, the Caribbean is a good example of historical, but not of contemporary, creolization. The pan-Caribbean identity propagated by some of the followers of *Créolité* largely obscures the social realities of the Caribbean. Neither the (awareness of) common (African) roots nor the particular Caribbean mix has led Jamaicans, Trinidadians or Haitians to dispose of their ethnic and national identities and to identify themselves instead as Caribbean or Antillean. This fact is ignored by many *Créolité* proponents, including academics.[12] Although parts of the Caribbean population have developed a Caribbean identity that transcends their ethnic and national identities, it by no means replaces the various identifications associated with certain islands, nations and ethnic categories – at most it complements them.[13] Even within specific Caribbean as well as Indian Ocean societies, particular groups are excluded rather than embraced and social hierarchies tend to correlate with ethnic backgrounds and degrees of pigmentation.[14]

Inasmuch as Caribbeanists have contributed to the understanding of what happens when creolization occurs, they have at the same time also sought to assert control over the meaning of creolization, which they tend to regard as a concept native to their region of expertise. This has been a hindrance to developing the term's heuristic potentials concerning the comparative analysis of historical processes of creolization across different societies worldwide as well as of contemporary processes related to them.

Mine is not a Caribbeanist perspective. I, like Hannerz (1987), among others, consider creolization a process not exclusive to any particular region, and it is my aim to explore the social and political meanings of creolization and creoleness *beyond* the Caribbean. I focus on postcolonial societies, which are ethnically heterogeneous and where ethnic identities are important dimensions of social identities of individuals and groups. It is particularly in such settings that creole identities and processes relating to them assume important social and political meanings and functions concerning the construction and conceptualization of ethnic as well as transethnic and national identities. This is due to the fact that in the given societies it is a social and political necessity to acknowledge ethnic identities and cultural specificities inasmuch as there is a demand for identifications across ethnic boundaries and cultural as well as religious differences.

Towards a Comparative Concept of Creole Identity

The criteria applied to the definition of creole identity are an expression of particular social classifications within a society. They provide information about dominant ideologies with regard to origin, race and culture. Today (also) in the classic regions of historical creolization there are still divergent ideas about who is a creole and why. In Louisiana, for example, one finds people who understand creole as applying exclusively to whites of European descent and others who see mixture as the characteristic feature of creole culture and identity. When a white creole in Louisiana says that only white creoles are genuine creoles (or Belles Creoles), then this statement says something about his view of the (not only creole) world but nothing about the existent or nonexistent creoleness on the part of those who are classifying or being classified.[15] The fact is that there are more or less white and more or less coloured creoles and that colour is unsuited to say anything about existent or absent creoleness.

'Being white' is generally (and mistakenly) not associated with mixture; the implicit model of purity versus mixture (in contexts of creolization) suggests that what is dark is mixed and what is white is pure.[16] However, such concepts of purity and mixture in relation to skin colour are social constructions and a person with light skin is not per se less 'mixed' or more 'pure' than a person with dark skin (and vice versa). People and culture alike, irrespective of their appearance, tend to be the outcome of varying degrees of – social, cultural, sexual – interaction and mixture.[17] The insistence of some of the Belles Creoles that the term creole originally meant the opposite of mixture is based on the fact that the white ur-creoles distinguished themselves on the basis that they did not intermingle with blacks. Here again it is assumed – more or less implicitly – that mixing only takes place where it involves people with different skin colours. In fact the Belles Creoles – irrespective of how white and beautiful – are also products of mixing between different immigrant groups who, in the process of increasing indigenization and interaction with one another and their (new) environment, developed a new culture and a new shared identity that progressively became differentiated from their original culture and identity.[18] Furthermore, irrespective of existing hierarchies and boundaries in colonial societies, European and African cultures mutually influenced one another. Many sources describe this mixing of European (colonial) culture with African culture – often criticizing it as a form of creole decadence.[19] The question of who mixes with whom in the course of creolization is thus not decisive for the definition of what creole is.

It is also irrelevant whether an emerging creole group is called by an ethnonym that refers phonetically to its creoleness (for example, Creole, Créole, Krio) or not (for example, Betawi, Martiniquais, American Liberian). It is the given ethno-historical particularities that matter. What is creole from an etic point of view does not have to be so named (or recognized) from an emic point of view: 'In order to pursue such research, one must be prepared to consider situations as involving creolization even when the people concerned do not use the terms "creole" or "creolization"' (Stewart 2007: 13).[20] And, I would add, one must conversely be prepared and able to recognize groups as non-creole even though they may term themselves something creole. Just as (socio-)linguistic criteria are applied to classify a language as a creole, (socio-)cultural criteria must be applied to classify a culture and identity as creole.

Seen against this background, discussions conducted in academic circles as well as in the public sphere concerning appellations for creole groups may be of interest insofar as they provide insight into the ambivalences associated with creole identities particularly in postcolonial societies. However, they offer little to the task of actually identifying creoleness. This is true for example of the long debate over the labelling of the creole population (and language) in Freetown (Sierra Leone) as either Creole or Krio (Knörr 1995, 2007a, 2008b, 2010a; Wyse 1979, 1989; Skinner and Harrel-Bond 1977; cf. Fyle 2000).[21] This debate could be put to rest given that both terms are correct: Creole designates the group (the Krio) as creole in reference to the social and historical context of its ethnogenesis and the ensuing creoleness of its culture and identity, while Krio is the group's ethnonym, which emerged in the process of its ethnogenesis. As regards efforts to determine whether a group is creole or not, its name is irrelevant.

Indigenization and Ethnogenesis as Criteria of Creolization

In the course of a creolization process, new common culture and identity is created (Patterson 1982: 316). The participants in this social process create new cultural representations in the sense of cultural forms and features (ways of life, music, religion, etc.), *and* they are collectively subjected to a process of ethnicization. They develop a new collective identity, which is increasingly based on a shared rootedness in and affiliation with the given cultural, historical and local context. The new, shared identity that emerges in the course of creolization – which, depending on the given social conditions may vary in terms of the degree of ethnicization – is thus the result of a new sense of shared history and belonging. The criterion of specific origin – a central rationale in the case of old, established ethnic identities – is also significant in the case of ethnogenesis via creolization. However, in the latter case origin is neither assumed to be nor constructed as homogeneous but rather as (more or less specifically) heterogeneous.

Creolization is only one of the processes that can evolve as a result of the interaction of people of heterogeneous origins. A precondition for such a process is a need on the part of these groups for a new, shared identity. As a rule, this is only the case when such groups settle in a foreign environment in which their respective identities of origin lose their meaning and function. Moreover, it is probable that the tendency to ethnicize a new shared identity is more marked when ethnic ascription has been a fundamental factor of social organization and identity within the respective societies of origin and when the exile society is characterized by ethnic structuring and classification.

Examining the social and historical context of creolization and tracing the etymology of *creole* and its meanings over time shows that creolization has been distinct in involving indigenization and – to varying degrees – ethnicization[22] of diverse and, in large parts, foreign populations. Irrespective of differentiations relating to what constituted and still constitutes creole, the concept of creolization was thus connected from the outset with indigenization and ethnogenesis against a background of ethnic and cultural diversity.

This process of ethnicization, the emergence of a new ethnicized group, is thus fundamental to the differentiation of creolization from other processes of cultural interaction and exchange.[23] Creolization thus does not mean – as has been proposed by postmodern de-bordering models and, more specifically, by Caribbean creolists and their adherents – the dissolution and overcoming of ethnic, national and other boundaries as a consequence of the continual production of a creatively pervasive farrago. Old boundaries are dissolved in the process of creolization because they cease to make sense in an existentially new social and local context. However, in the process of recontextualizing culture and identity new boundaries are created that do make sense within this new environment. Creolization is thus a process that ultimately subjects identity to (varying degrees of) essentialization.[24] The confusion as to what creole is stems above all from the fact that the social and historical context of the concept's genesis – which involves more than etymology – is ignored when used in an undifferentiated manner to denote everything mixed and somehow intermediate and in-between.

The fact that creolization is often used in a somewhat arbitrary fashion to describe all sorts of contemporary processes of interaction and mixture has resulted in resistance to the utilization of the concept outside the historical context of the slave exile. As Sydney Mintz remarks: 'But the term "creolization" … had been historically and geographically specific. It stood for centuries of culture-building, rather than culture mixing or culture blending, by those who became Caribbean people. They were not becoming transnational; they were creating forms by which to live, even while they were being cruelly tested physically and mentally' (Mintz 1998: 119).

It is clear that equating creolization with transnationalization is a mistake.[25] Nevertheless, the conceptual arbitrariness that is justifiably criticized here is not a (good enough) reason for discarding the heuristic potential that the conceptual field creole has for describing and analysing contemporary processes of social and cultural interaction. Taking into account the social and historical context of the genesis of the concept does not exclude the use and development of the concept's heuristic potential for phenomena of the present. Rather, it may unfold it, given that we look more carefully and more comparatively at the different histories of creolization in different parts of the world, and at the different social contexts within which creole identities and terminologies emerged. Rather than restricting the usage of the term creolization or creole to a specific historical situation and region, we must specify what structurally differentiates creolization and creole identities from other forms of social and cultural interaction and identity formation. This will on the one hand allow us to better distinguish between different historical processes and social contextualizations of creolization and on the other hand may enhance our understanding of contemporary processes of interaction and identity formation in postcolonial societies and beyond. This seems all the more important given that such processes are not only becoming increasingly common in our ever more complexly globalized world, they are also becoming more differentiated. We need to make use of the creole terminology because of its potential for a more systematic and comparative analysis, conceptualization and differentiation of both historical and contemporary varieties of social and cultural interaction and of the processes of identity formation related to them. Or: 'It is not sufficient to point out that mixing does take place; it is necessary to distinguish between different forms of mixing' (Eriksen 2007: 167; cf. Mufwene 2000; cf. Jourdan 2001).[26] Creolization is more than the mixing of people and culture. Creolization is a process that links indigenization with ethnicization against the background of ethnic diversity in a specific social context. What emerges from creolization is not only new shared culture but also new shared identity and belonging. This specificity of creolization is of fundamental significance for the understanding of the social processes described and analysed in the course of this book as well as for the further advancement of conceptual differentiations that these observations and analyses allow us to make.

It should be added that, as a rule, creolization is not an infinite process of integration and incorporation, as suggested, for example, by Balutansky and Sourieau (1998: 1): 'Creolization is thus defined as a syncretic process of transverse dynamism that endlessly reworks and transforms the cultural patterns of varied social and historical experiences and identities.'[27] In most cases, creolization is a finite process that is concluded once a new creole group has constituted itself as the result of mixture, indigenization and ethnicization – social dynamics involving integration inasmuch as closure. In terms of the intensity of ethnic identity and the flexibility of ethnic boundaries, creole groups are just as variable as other, non-creole groups.[28] Due to their heterogeneous origins, creole groups may continue to play an important role within the ethnically heterogeneous society in which they emerged – however, this role is due to the creoleness of their identity, which is the result of a concluded process of creolization, rather than creolization itself.

However, creoleness can become less significant or even completely irrelevant if, for example, diversity of origin is the rule rather than the exception in a given society. Creoleness can also cease to exist if the process of indigenization is so complete that the diversity of origin is forgotten and the once creole group becomes just another ordinary (ethnic) group. Creoleness is often a quality of comparatively young creole groups – which excludes neither the possibility of it enduring nor the possibility of it being awakened to new life if a certain context and situation demand it.

For the moment, it is important to note that it is necessary to distinguish both between creolization and other processes of amalgamation and between creolization as process and creoleness as quality.

Creoleness versus (Post-)creole Continuum

Creole identity, creolization, and creole groups have been taken up as themes and research subjects in a range of disciplines. Current social-science and cultural-studies approaches for the most part have interdisciplinary roots and draw on knowledge and approaches from anthropology, historiography, literary studies and linguistics.

The designation and description of particular creole groups by historians has been taken up by linguists, who have expanded, differentiated and specified the concept in the context of research into creole and pidgin languages. Anthropology has primarily taken up approaches and concepts developed in the linguistic field of creolistics and attempted to apply these to cultural phenomena that emerge in the context of cultural interaction and exchange. The protagonist of the anthropological study of creolization is Ulf Hannerz. He regards creolization as a process that, although characterized by specific societal conditions – a colonial or postcolonial situation and ethno(cultural) heterogeneity – can take place anywhere given that these criteria are met (Hannerz 1987).

For some time the anthropological approach to creolization has been dominated by a focus on cultural forms and features per se, while the cognitive-emotional level, i.e., conceptions and meanings associated with such forms and features, has been largely neglected.[29] Drawing on concepts derived from dependency theory, world-systems theory and linguistic creolistics, proponents of this approach have formulated a centre-periphery model that functions in terms of a continuum (Hannerz 1989; 1998). This model posits a quasi-quantitative and gradual distributive continuum with original native cultural traditional characteristics of the periphery on one side and foreign cultural (Western, modern) characteristics of the centre on the other. In this context Hannerz positions urban culture on the semi-periphery in so far as it is here – in the urban milieu of the periphery – that the culture of the centre is most extensively adopted.

Although this model generally assumes the existence of reciprocal cultural influence, its perspective remains focused on the level of cultural forms and features as such and its interpretations fixed on meanings that correspond to the cultural interpretive model of the interpreter (who as a rule is affiliated with the postulated culture of the centre). Although reference is made to the process of change that these characteristics are subject to, there is insufficient investigation of the local meanings that accrue to these cultural features within the framework of the society incorporating and transforming them. To identify these meanings it is necessary to examine how these features are conceptualized, integrated and classified and which meanings and valencies they are assigned or denied in specific contexts. Hannerz' understanding of cultural creolization reflects a widespread view of the linguistic creolization process as largely determined by the prevailing European standard language. As a result, allegedly modern features are categorized as European and centre culture, while allegedly traditional features are categorized as indigenous and periphery culture. Understood in this way, centre and periphery are utilized as categories that reflect rather than critically scrutinize the perspective of the Western world – the postulated centre (Wallerstein 1974; cf. Knörr 1995, 2002b, 2007a, 2010a).

Hannerz' formulation of the creole continuum has also led to a renewed focus in debates on the anthropological application of the linguistic concept of the post-creole continuum, which emerges as the interim linguistic space between standard language and creole language once the latter has been established. This linguistic concept has informed the anthropological construction of a creole continuum spanning the interim cultural space between creole and standard culture within which creolization processes occur and different variants of creole culture and identity exist: 'The notion of post-creole continuum ... rejects absolute boundaries and instead highlights the existence of variations within a speech community. However, this "post-creole continuum" corresponds quite well simply to the creolization of culture, which does not lead to stable uniformity, but is on the contrary an ongoing process' (Eriksen 1999: 16).

Eriksen (2007) thus understands the fact that in Mauritius it is particularly people of ambiguous origins who are regarded as members of the creole group as indicating the existence of a post-creole continuum in the Mauritian context. In my view, this could have more to do with creoleness as a result of historical creolization than with a post-creole continuum positioned between less ambiguous identities.

Groups emerging through creolization processes are often particularly inclusive. They have emerged in the course of the interaction and integration of different ethnic groups of exogenous and indigenous origins, and this integrative potential often persists after the actual creolization process has been completed. However, this does not mean that the ethnic quality of creole groups is any less marked or robust. Referring to Mauritius, Eriksen observes: 'Creole culture is perceived as stable and fixed ... At the same time, the creole ethnic category is more open to new recruits than other ethnic groups in the island' (2007: 174). This appraisal applies to many creole groups. However, my own observations have shown that while these groups commonly exhibit a particular openness to the inclusion of people of other ethnic identities, they are also particularly persistent in urging the latter to give up their original identity and become fully incorporated into the creole group. Creole identity is thus perpetuated in so far as the historical moment of its emergence – involving the abandonment of old, original identities – is constantly being reproduced. However, this does *not* represent a post-creole continuum in the sense of an intermediate identification. Rather, it represents creole continuity, which is distinguished precisely by the fact that it aims to abrogate the intermediate and otherness and replace it with an unambiguous ascription and with sameness and oneness. This is not to deny that different (sub-)categories can exist or be retrospectively incorporated within creole groups.

The fact that in societies in which ethnic ascription is an important factor of social identity creole groups are often seen as of ambiguous ethnicity and somehow less ethnic due to their heterogeneous origins contributes to the heed paid by the creole group to complete conversion of those included. Where the origin of a creole group is classified as exogenous, it is often the case that so-called real locals regard it as tainted, which in turn can be another reason for ensuring the internal coherence of the group's ethnic identity by means of complete incorporation of people of other ethnic identities. This correlation of open boundaries and complete incorporation also makes clear that we are dealing here with creole continuity in the sense of the conclusive establishment of membership and not with a post-creole continuum in the sense of the continual production of the intermediate.

The CvP Model: Creolization versus Pidginization

This study deals with the meaning of creole identity within postcolonial, ethnically heterogeneous societies. As already discussed, creolization involves both the emergence of new cultural forms and features among people of different origins and the substitution of the latter's different original identities by a new common ethnicized identity developed in the course of indigenization.

This process is rarer in present-day postcolonial societies than a process that, I believe, can best be understood as cultural pidginization. The following elaboration of the CvP model[30] – the differentiation between cultural creolization and cultural pidginization – aims to illuminate the important differences between specific identity-related processes, which are particularly (but not exclusively) characteristic of ethnically heterogeneous postcolonial societies.

The CvP model takes into account the relationship between the phenomenological and the cognitive-emotional levels of culture and can thereby make a contribution to the comparative investigation of variants of identity-related processes and their differentiation in terms of social meaning and significance (Knörr 1995, 2007a, 2009c, 2010a). More specifically, it allows for an investigation of the extent to which identity-related processes are associated with ethnicization. The CvP model is also particularly suited to the investigation and analysis of processes taking place in the interaction between one creole group or identity and a plurality of other ethnic groups or identities, processes that in many postcolonial societies significantly influence the integration and differentiation of ethnic, local and national identities in particular.

The beginnings of the CvP model can be traced back to the work of Gilman (1979), who (like many of his colleagues) focuses on a differentiation of creole and pidgin languages in terms of social and functional rather than linguistic differences. Although linguistic differences can exist, they are not used as the criterion for the differentiation of creole and pidgin languages.[31] For Gilman, the crucial criterion is that of ethnic reference:

> What is clearly true in Cameroon is that Pidgin is the language of reference for no ethnic group ... In view of the confusion between the lan-

guage of ethnic reference and the first-learned language, and of the fact that in multilingual environments there is often no real first language ... [i]t would be better to replace the traditional distinction between creolized and pidginized languages as in one case, the 'native language' of a group of people and in the other case, not. It would be better to recognize that Creoles, such as that of Sierra Leone, are languages of ethnic reference, while Pidgins, such as that of Cameroon, are not (Gilman 1979: 274).[32]

This differentiation allows us to understand linguistic creolization as a process in the course of which the characteristics of different languages develop into a new common language that adopts ethnic reference for its speakers and replaces the original ethnic languages and/or their respective ethnic references.[33] In contrast, linguistic pidginization also leads to a new common language, yet this process is not linked to the replacement of ethnic languages (as languages of ethnic reference).[34]

Accordingly (and in a reasonably simplified manner), cultural creolization can be conceptualized as a process creating new common culture with ethnic reference in specific social (and historic) contexts of ethnic and cultural diversity. On the one hand, new representations of new common culture are produced and old, handed-down ones are recontextualized and transformed. On the other hand, the different identities of origin of those undergoing creolization are increasingly replaced by a new common identity linked to (narratives of) a common territory and new home, to a particular history and heritage and to specific (combinations of) origins and social and cultural particularities. Creolization implies not only the combination of a diversity of cultural forms and features but also the latter's ethnicization, the result being new cultural representations plus a new shared identity associated with them.

Cultural pidginization, on the other hand, can be conceptualized as a process over the course of which common culture and identity are developed in specific contexts of ethnic and cultural diversity as well – yet, in contrast to creolization, this process does not involve ethnicization. No new ethnic group is formed, and original identities based on the heritages of their protagonists remain in existence (Knörr 1995; cf. Hannerz 1987, 1989).

I argue that, unlike in colonial settler and slave societies, it is cultural pidginization rather than creolization that dominates in processes of identity formation in contemporary postcolonial societies (Knörr 1994a, 1994b, 1995, 2002a, 2007a, 2009c, 2010a). This is due largely to today's communication and transportation technologies, which facilitate social contacts and ties over long distances and periods of time. However, we have to keep in mind that what we observe as cultural pidginization in contemporary society today may (partially) result in processes of creolization in the long run. Whether or not creolization has taken place can only be determined, when the process is (largely) completed. Up to this point, creolization may look like pidginization. It generally takes longer for a new ethnic identity to take shape than it does to create new common cultural representations and transethnic identifications.

One possible indication of an ongoing process of creolization consists in certain cultural representations being progressively linked to a specific category of people of different ethnic backgrounds. In (very) simple terms: if small groups of Indians, Ghanaians and French were to find themselves exiled to a small town in the Midwestern United States, they may decide to stick together and while sticking together create a new sort of pie involving Indian, Ghanaian, French and local Midwestern ingredients. This alone, however, would not mean that they were subject to a process of creolization. Only if in the course of cooking – and other forms of interaction such as sticking together as a result of being oppressed and exploited by the Midwestern majority – they were to discard their previous Indian, Ghanaian and French identities and progressively perceive of themselves and being perceived by others as, for instance, the members of the (new) Inghench tribe – as Inghenchians –, would they be undergoing a process of creolization in the course of which they would indigenize (also by including Midwesterners) and feel more and more at home in the part of town, which by then would (likely) have become known as Inghench Town, famous for its Inghench pie.

Should the same groups of immigrants, on the other hand, create Inghench pie while maintaining their Indian, Ghanaian and French identities, they may develop something like an Inghench identity as well, which, however, would not replace their original identities. Their Inghench identity would transcend rather than replace their identities of origins, thereby linking them transethnically amongst themselves and – through the Midwestern ingredients (metaphorically speaking) – to the town, they would probably and increasingly love so well, not least because it enabled them to maintain different identities of origin while developing transethnic connections that allow for a new feeling of belonging and new ways of life and forms of interaction suited to their Midwestern environment. These people would be undergoing cultural pidginization, developing new transethnic culture and new transethnic identifications, yet without undergoing ethnicization, without forging a new ethnic group identity.

The Pidgin Potential of Creole Identity for Postcolonial Nation-building

In many (yet by no means in all) postcolonial societies in which a creole population resides, creole culture and identity – besides being ethnic markers of the respective creole group – have also emerged as a pidgin variant that serves as a transethnic category of self-ascription and, therefore, as a symbol of postcolonial nation-building (Knörr 1995, 2007b, 2009a, 2010a).[35] Some preliminary remarks about why this is so.

Old or established ethnic groups usually emphasize a *single* common historical origin – irrespective of whether this unity of origin can be historically substantiated or has a mythical character. By contrast, creole groups, which are (relatively) 'young' ethnic groups, derive their origin from heterogeneous roots and construct their unity via everything that has become one through the process of mixing of what were once differences – cultural features, ways of life, customs, beliefs, etc. For creole groups, diversity of origin is a constitutive feature of their common identity by means of which they distinguish themselves from other – ordinary – ethnic groups in the society in which they live. Within ethnically heterogeneous postcolonial societies, heterogeneity of origin – or *consciousness* of it – represents one of the fundamental reasons for the particular societal significance of creole groups and creoleness as a culture and identity. In this context, heterogeneity is usually perceived not as an arbitrary mélange but as a specific composite of origins (Haller 2002).

The historical creolization processes that led to the emergence of the creole groups existing today occurred among mostly exogenous groups of heterogeneous origins. However, in the course of these processes indigenous people and local culture were integrated. As a result, cultural features of local groups were subsequently reflected in the emergent creole cultures – all the more where the contact between natives and immigrants within the societies concerned was close.[36]

This combination of (exogenous) heterogeneity of origin on the one hand and the inclusion of indigenous people and culture on the other is rather typical of creole culture and identity and exerts effects on identity-related reference structures both for creole group members themselves and for other (groups of) people in their environment.

For members of a creole group, (their) creole culture has an ethnic reference – as does the other culture regarded by other (creole and non-creole) groups as their own. For members of other ethnic groups, creole culture often has a primarily transethnic reference. Because elements of the respective local, ethnic cultures form integrated elements of the local creole culture, local populations can recognize aspects of their own culture in it and feel connected to it without being affiliated to it in ethnic terms. However, creole culture may also have ethnic references for non-creoles to the extent that it has integrated elements of their respective own (ethnic) culture and thus (partially) represents it. It is thus also such ethnic aspects of creole culture that are conceptualized as 'formerly (also) one's own' that create transethnic connections. In terms of the conceptual differentiation outlined above, this process of (partial) appropriation of creole culture and identity can be understood as cultural pidginization. An additional, transethnic identification is developed that does not, however, replace different ethnic identities but, on the contrary, presupposes them. The pidgin potential of creoleness is grounded in the fact that creoleness is associated with both ethnic and transethnic aspects of culture and identity.

It is not only the *specific* heterogeneity of origin that facilitates a partial identification with creole culture among non-creoles. It is also its heterogeneity *in itself* that is perceived as distinctive in relation to so-called normal, homogenously derived, ethnic identities in a world perceived as increasingly shaped by interaction and exchange – both on the part of members of creole groups and on the part of other protagonists of cultural and identity-related polymorphy.

It is the combination of collective indigenization and identity formation and the diversity of origin that invests creole culture and identity with a particular potential for the integration of ethnically heterogeneous societies of the present that are concerned with both safeguarding ethnic diversity on the one hand and manifesting transethnic connectivity on the other. It is in its pidgin factor that the particular potential of creoleness – in the sense of a quality generated by creolization processes of the past – lies for the societies of the present.

Creole groups, culture and identity have often played a prominent role in independence movements and in processes of postcolonial nation-building. This was the case, for example, in the American independence movements, which confronted European colonial powers with their own national identity, which in turn provided a foundation for aspirations to independence. In this connection, the concept of creoleness – which had previously denoted a purely European origin – was indigenized and thus also rendered transethnic. As a consequence, creoleness was increasingly comprehended as a result of mixing and indigenization. A white creole was now no longer a European born in the colony but an individual of heterogeneous origin born 'at home'. On the eve of independence Simón Bolivar emphasized, 'We are not Europeans, we are not Indians, but a mixed species of aborigines and Spaniards' (cit. in Palmié 2007). Benedict Anderson also underlines the role of such 'creole pioneers' in the emergence of a national identity referring to the new homeland in the 'New World', an identity that progressively replaced that relating to the old homeland in Europe (Anderson 1991: 47–55).[37]

Indigenization also requires the nativization of the imported culture in situ: 'Becoming "Creole" is a process of achieving indigeneity through the migration and recombination of diverse elements that have been loosed from previous attachments and have reattached themselves to a new place of belonging' (Sheller 2003: 276).[38] It is therefore necessary also to draw a distinction between creolization, on the one hand, and diasporization or diasporal culture and identity on the other. Creolization occurs as a process of the dissociation of heterogeneous groups from their different places of origin combined with increasing, collective indigenization, increasing bonding with the new homeland. By contrast, a diaspora involves a group distinguished by a common origin whose members – in exile – have a collective relationship with their original homeland. For a diaspora, the main shared point of reference is the old homeland, whereas for a creole group it is the new homeland.

Why, then, do creole groups and identities often play a central role in postcolonial nation-building? Benedict Anderson has remarked that already at the beginning of the 1960s all his Indonesian acquaintances described themselves as Indonesians even though at the beginning of the century the concept of Indonesia was not even known (Anderson 1996).

In the wake of Anderson's work, much attention has been paid to the question of how such national traditions are generated with a particular focus on the processes of homogenization linked with the emergence of nations (Gellner 1983; Smith 1994). At the same time it has been assumed that the increasing significance of national identity correlates with a decrease in the significance of ethnic identity, that ethnic identities are replaced, as it were, by a common national identity. However, this assumption is not borne out when applied to the processes of postcolonial nation-building. The efforts of what were mostly European-educated political elites in the phase of early postcolonial independence to engineer nation-building in accordance with the European model soon proved unrealistic, including in Indonesia. However, this does not mean that national identities have not emerged in postcolonial societies. On the contrary, national identifications may be quite marked, although they have neither replaced ethnic ascriptions nor rendered them obsolete.

This study delineates an approach that runs counter to the obviously mistaken assumption that ethnic identities must be overcome to allow for the formation of national identities. The commonly posed question as to why ethnicity should persist *in spite of* an increase in national consciousness is based on the assumption that the European path to nationhood represents a universal model. Yet why should the development of a national consciousness in a place like Jakarta and in a heterogeneous country like Indonesia follow the same course as that seen in Europe between the seventeenth and eighteenth centuries? There is no reason for the spread of the nation-state to be accompanied by all its European particularities.

The last two decades have seen a growing awareness within postcolonial societies that national identity can only thrive if preexisting ethnic identities are comprehended as its *foundation* – rather than as its *antipole* – and an increasing expression of this awareness at the political level. This is clearly indicated by political slogans such as 'unity in diversity' and 'rainbow nation'.

It is in this context of postcolonial nation-building that creole groups and creole culture and identity often play a prominent role. They symbolize unity in diversity in a particular way, in their capacity to develop a new, common identity against a background of heterogeneity. This model corresponds to the postcolonial nation, which – as in the case of Indonesia – often has no precolonial roots or forerunner, far better than the European model, which links nationhood to homogeneity rather than heterogeneity. In connection with the development of an independent model of the postcolonial nation, creole groups can function as symbols and pioneers of postcolonial nationhood that has freed itself from the European models of the former colonial masters.

Creole Ambivalences

In regard to processes of integration and differentiation within postcolonial, ethnically heterogeneous societies, creole groups commonly play not only an important but also an ambivalent role. This ambivalence is based in part on the fact that their emergence is tied to the colonial context.

Furthermore, creole identities emerged within a tension between exogeneity and indigenization. The process of indigenization characteristic of the (historical) creolization process usually proceeded (at least for some time) parallel to the effort to preserve old ties and often persists as an ambivalence in that creole groups are often situated somewhere between indigenous and foreign (formerly colonial) populations.[39] Due to their specific background they are often the subject of a societal discourse in the context of which their indigeneity or exogeneity is negotiated and evaluated in relation to a national or even local context. This discourse is most intensively conducted within urban centres in which increasing globalization is particularly noticeable and in which consciousness of the problematic nature of the relationship between local and foreign culture, tradition and modernity, ethnic and national identities is often particularly marked.

Creoleness also facilitates a high degree of manipulability because due to its heterogeneous origins, it can be claimed as one's own also by ethnically marginal and ambiguously defined individuals and groups. Against this background, creole groups develop not only specific strategies of inclusion but also specific strategies of exclusion to safeguard their own identity and to prevent its arbitrary availability.

Whether or not the pidgin potential of creole culture and identity is utilized depends on different factors. If a creole group, for instance, is eager to delimit itself from the natives, it may endeavour – despite or because of existing cultural similarities – to emphasize differences rather than commonalities. If the natives, for their part, want to brand a creole group as nonindigenous or not genuinely indigenous, they may well choose to background transethnic connections and instead emphasize the group's foreign, colonial and sometimes slavery-related background. The explicitly heterogeneous and (partly) exogenous origin of creole groups hence contributes to other ethnic groups denying the former's ethnic quality and indigeneity or classifying them as inferior, ambiguous and impaired. In a society in which ethnic ascriptions and indigeneity are highly regarded, such classifications can lead to social discrimination or be perceived as a disadvantage.

In the ethnically heterogeneous societies of the postcolonial present an often highly controversial discourse is being conducted in connection with the ethnic and transethnic references of creole identity. This discourse particularly revolves around the question of whether it is origin or the presence of creole culture that is crucial in determining whether someone is a (genuine) creole. Whereas in the context of historical creolization in slave and colonial societies the criterion of origin was decisive for the classification of a person as creole, there is an increasing tendency today to include linguistic and cultural criteria. This is connected above all with the fact that creole groups have increasingly integrated indigenous people. Whereas the significance of origin has thus been reduced, the significance of cultural and linguistic features has increased. This is also one of the major reasons why members of creole groups often attribute great importance to even the smallest cultural and linguistic differences between themselves and others claiming (partial) creoleness.

The discourse around the meaning of 'origin' versus 'culture' for the authenticity of creole identity is laden with controversy. Those creole groups and individuals who seek to highlight the inclusive, open boundaries of their group tend to give precedence to cultural features as criteria of creole identity. Proponents of the exclusivity of creole culture and identity tend to emphasize origin and do not accord those whose claim to creole identity is based only on cultural characteristics the same degree of recognition as those claiming creole descent.

Creole culture and identity are often instrumentalized in the service of specific social and political requirements and interests by the respective creole groups and by other societal groupings and state entities. Social and political instrumentalizations of creole identity take place within a range of contexts. They are connected in particular with (1) *national ideologies of unity* as propagated and staged by state entities within the framework of postcolonial nation-building. The focus here is primarily on emphasizing the integrative potential of the respective local creole group – all the more so when this group is localized in a national capital. In the context of postcolonial nation-building, creole groups accrue increasing social and political significance above all because they can be manoeuvred into the political arena as evidence that a common identity can be created against a background of ethnic and cultural diversity. The creole group is presented as a postcolonial symbol of unity in diversity, as a nation en miniature, as it were. Just as the creole group has managed to develop a common identity against a background of heterogeneous origins, so too should the different ethnic groups within the postcolonial nation be able to transcend ethnic differences and embrace a shared – national – identity.

Social and political instrumentalizations also serve (2) the (symbolic) *linkage of foreign and native culture*. In colonial contexts creole cultures developed against a background of heterogeneous origins and as a result of those undergoing creolization engaging with different traditions. Creole groups can thus be seen as socially integrative capacities connecting local culture and external influences. At the same time, the fact that creole populations have also become ethnic groups implies that a connection of the native and the foreign can be achieved in a way that not only permits but even necessitates ethnic identity. This is important in societies in which ethnic identity is regarded as an important feature of the social identity and integrity of individuals and groups. It is particularly in urban environments characterized by marked heterogeneity and progressive modernization that the necessity of safeguarding a certain degree of social cohesion by way of shared – ethnic and transethnic –frameworks is perceived as particularly urgent.

Finally, social and political instrumentalizations of creoleness also serve (3) the *linkage of tradition and modernity*, particularly in urban environments. Due to their transethnic reference for non-creoles, creole groups often provide a bridge between local traditions and modern urbanity. Depending on whether the respective creole group is regarded as traditional or as modern, it provides either a traditional bridge to the modern or a modern bridge to the traditional.

Notes

1. The etymologies of the ethnonyms of many creole groups are likewise often a matter of debate.
2. See Chaudenson (2001) for examples of these ideologically influenced etymological approaches.
3. See Hoffmann (2003). The first documented use of the term is found in a letter written by García de Castro from Peru on 2 April 1567: '[Q]ue esta tierra esté llena de criollos que son estos que acá an nacido, y como nunca an conocido al rey ni esperan concello'/'[T]his land is full of Creoles, which are those who have been born here and […] do not know the king and have no hope of ever knowing him' (quoted in Stein 1982: 162).
4. Houaiss – *Dicionário Houaiss da Lingua Portuguesa* (2001); cf. Spitzer (2003).
5. The involvement of indigenous groups and persons in the creolization process has often been neglected. See, for example, Brathwaite (1971); cf. Knörr (1995).
6. It is more common to state indigenous and foreign and exogenous and endogenous as opposite pairs. Indigenous refers to a whole, independent thing/person that is native to a specific place. Endogenous refers to a part of something else, hence, not an independent thing that is produced or synthesized within a specific system or organism. Examples: One type of rose only grows in Portugal; it is indigenous only to Portugal. Testosterone is an endogenous hormone produced in the testes. Exogenous refers to something that was created/produced somewhere else, beyond the system/organism. However, quite differently from something that is foreign, something that is exogenous may become part of something within a system/organism/society (exogenous inclusion). That is why, in the given context, I prefer to use indigenous versus exogenous rather than indigenous versus foreign or endogenous versus exogenous.
7. Jean Bernabé, Edouard Glissant, and Derek Walcott are some of the major representatives of this movement. See Robin Cohen and Paola Toninato (2009), who deal with the notion of Créolité, creolization and hybridization in literary criticism and cultural studies.
8. Glissant in an interview with *Label France* in January 2000.
9. See also Khan (2007: 653), who claims that 'a kind of optimism undergirds most understandings of the concept' and that '[R]omanticized representations of agency in creoliza-

tion discourse belie the various ways in which agents of creolization can themselves be multidimensional or ambivalent about processes that observers celebrate' (ibid.: 654).
10. Many studies have been carried out on culturally mixed forms, for example food, music, architecture, kinship systems, agriculture, clothing, religion, literature, etc. They tend to focus less on aspects of identity than on material representations of cultural mixing.
11. The established differences between the Anglophone and Francophone creolization discourses do not imply that all Francophone and all Anglophone representatives will argue as described here. On the one hand, these differences are often subtle and graduated, and, on the other hand, there are also representatives on both sides whose position leans toward the other side.
12. Resistance to their model can provoke conflict, as was seen in the Frank Moya Pons affair. Pons enraged members of the Caribbean Studies Association when he asserted that the various creole regions in the Antilles differ more from one another than from the various European countries, whose languages they had inherited (Hoffmann 2003).
13. Jamaican, Haitian and Trinidadian identities, e.g., thus relate to one another in a paradigmatic way – they are normally mutually exclusive in that one can only be one or the other – whereas they relate to Caribbean identity in a syntagmatic way, in that the latter may be shared by Jamaicans, Haitians and Trinidadians alike while existing in different – e.g., Jamaican, Haitian and Trinidadian – variations; see Schlee (2008).
14. There is an abundance of literature concerning exclusionary strategies and the correlation between pigmentation and social classification in Caribbean societies. Concerning some more recent publications, see the contributions in Shepherd and Richards (2002) and in Collier and Fleischmann (2003); see also Miles (1999) concerning the case of Mauritius.
15. See Tregle (1992), who speaks, with reference to Belles Creoles who delimit themselves as pure and white, of a creole mythology that is based on the glorification of cultural and political accomplishments of the past. See also Brasseaux (1990) on the roots of creole culture and identity in Louisiana.
16. Friederici states that creoles are the 'children of pureblooded European parents who were born in America' (1947: 220). Cf. Stephens (1983, 1999).
17. On the relationship between race, origin, birthplace and culture as criteria for creoleness, see Henry and Bankston III (1998); cf. Hoffmann (2003) on the racial connotations of the term creole and on connections between creolization and national identity on Haiti.
18. See Berlin (1998: 105), who refers to the emergence of a new nationality.
19. See, for example, Herskovits (1958); Brathwaite (1971); Mintz and Price (1992).
20. Cf. Eriksen (2007: 173): 'I propose a definition of cultural creolization, thus, which is faithful to its linguistic origins, but which does not restrict itself to societies where "creole" is an emic term or where linguistic creolization has taken place.' Cf. Willis (2000).
21. Put simply, the term Creole is preferred by those Krio who like to emphasize the colonial context, in which their identity emerged, and their perceived closeness to European culture, whereas those Krio, who regard the local context of their ethnogenesis and the resulting indigenization as crucial, prefer the term Krio.
22. I understand both indigenization and ethnicization as relational terms that involve both self-ascription and ascription by others and that may vary depending on who is ascribing identity to whom and in which context and situation.
23. See also Eriksen (1999: 12), who characterizes the creoles on Mauritius as an 'ethnic category' and adds: 'a [Creole] person ... identifies him- or herself as someone ... belonging to a new society founded on the premise of mixing' (ibid.: 13).
24. See Eriksen (2007: 174): '*Creole essentialism* is far from unknown in Mauritius. Occasionally, Creoles will claim that they are the only *vrais Mauriciens*, real Mauritians, since they are the only group who, as it were, emerged from the Mauritian soil.'

25. Transnational refers to processes and identities that transcend the boundaries of the national (while at the same time requiring the national to be able to transcend it). Creolization can also occur in the context of transnational processes but is not identical with them.
26. See also Cohen and Toninato (2009).
27. Cf. Matsuda, who also characterizes creolization as 'open ended' and as 'eclectic, flexible, and mobile' (2001: 6).
28. See, for example, Eriksen (2007) on creole groups on Mauritius, Knörr (1995, 2010a, b) on the creoles of Sierra Leone.
29. This also applies to Chaudenson (2001: 194ff.), who as a linguist concentrates on linguistic creolization yet develops a general theory of creolization that refers to cultural systems, which he understands as domains (cuisine, magic, medicine) within a culture and investigates and analyses in terms of their heterogeneous roots. However, the identity-related aspects of the genesis and development of these cultural systems are hardly considered.
30. I first developed this model in the context of my Ph.D. project and have since elaborated and refined it (Knörr 1991, 1994, 1995, 2007a, 2008b, 2009c, 2010a, 2012).
31. The approaches discussed are limited to those that are of theoretical and methodological interest in relation to the phenomena being investigated here.
32. For Gilman's discussion of this, see Gilman (1979).
33. The languages that serve as the basis for a new creole language may continue to exist, but are usually no longer spoken by the group that is undergoing cultural and linguistic creolization and/or no longer serve as languages of ethnic reference.
34. Ethnic identity does not necessarily rely on ethnic language competence. One can be a Temne, for example, without speaking Temne. However, the perceived authenticity of ethnic identity may suffer as a result (see Knörr 1995).
35. Cultural pidginization does not require a preexisting creole group or creoleness as a culture and identity of ethnic and transethnic reference. However, this study focuses in particular on a case in which a group (the Betawi) formed via processes of creolization and Betawi as a culture and identity of ethnic and transethnic reference are crucial to many pidginization processes.
36. In many cases, immigrants comprised former or freed slaves. As a rule this status led to ambivalences in relation to the free natives, as illustrated by the example of Batavia. One result of this was the reconstruction of ideologies of origin; see also Knörr (1995, 2010b).
37. Cf. Hoffmann (2003), who demonstrates how delimitation in terms of Frenchness by French settlers was continued after independence by new black elites and was deployed by their Haitian compatriots as a means of restricting social advancement. It should be noted that there are other cases where the adoption of the language of the colonial masters as the national language did not (only) contribute to national unity but also manifested social boundaries established in the colonial period between speakers and nonspeakers of that language. This linguistic boundary often correlated with the boundary between town and country, one which in many cases persists today in the form of a social and economic gradient.
38. On nativization as a process see also Brathwaite (1977), according to whom it is not the product (culture) that distinguishes creolization but the parallel process of nativization.
39. Cf. Rath (2000: 99): 'It [creolization] is a way of forming a "native" identity in a situation where there is no natal society.'

Chapter 2
Jakarta, Batavia, Betawi

Cityscape and City Dwellers

Jakarta lies on the northwest coast of Java. It is the capital city of Indonesia, the seat of the national and regional government, the country's most important commercial, financial and education centre and an industrial city. Jakarta is an extremely heterogeneous city in ethnic, cultural and social terms, Indonesia's largest city and one of the world's so-called mega-cities.

According to a census conducted by the *Badan Pusat Statistik* (BPS) – the Central Statistics Office – Jakarta had 9.6 million inhabitants in 2010.[1] It can be assumed from this figure that actually some 12 million people live in Jakarta. This difference is due to the fact that many people live in makeshift housing on the city periphery, in 'residential areas' that are not included in the census. There are also many people living in Jakarta with registered addresses outside the city.

The metropolitan area of Jabo(de)tabek – an acronym covering Jakarta and the neighbouring cities of Bogor, Depok[2], Tangerang and Bekasi – has some 20 million official and around twenty-five million actual inhabitants.

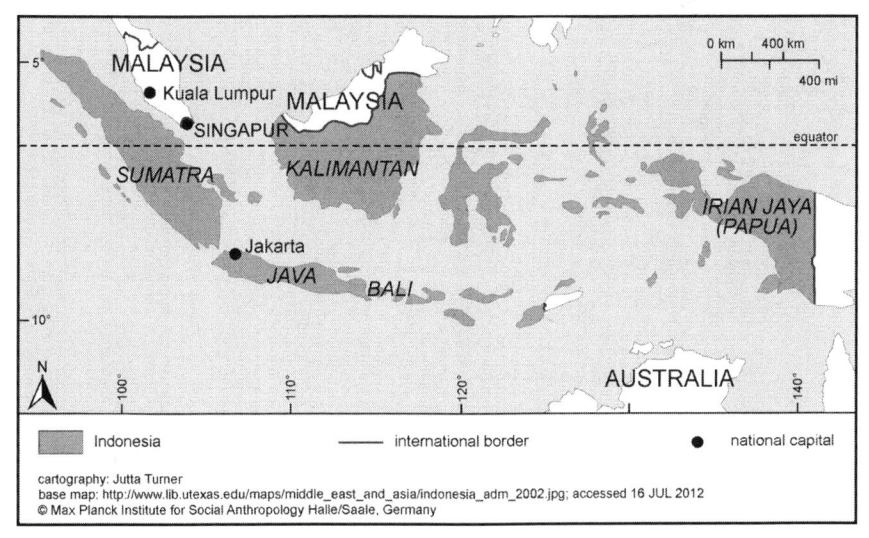

Map 2.1. General map of Indonesia.

42   *Creole Identity in Postcolonial Indonesia*

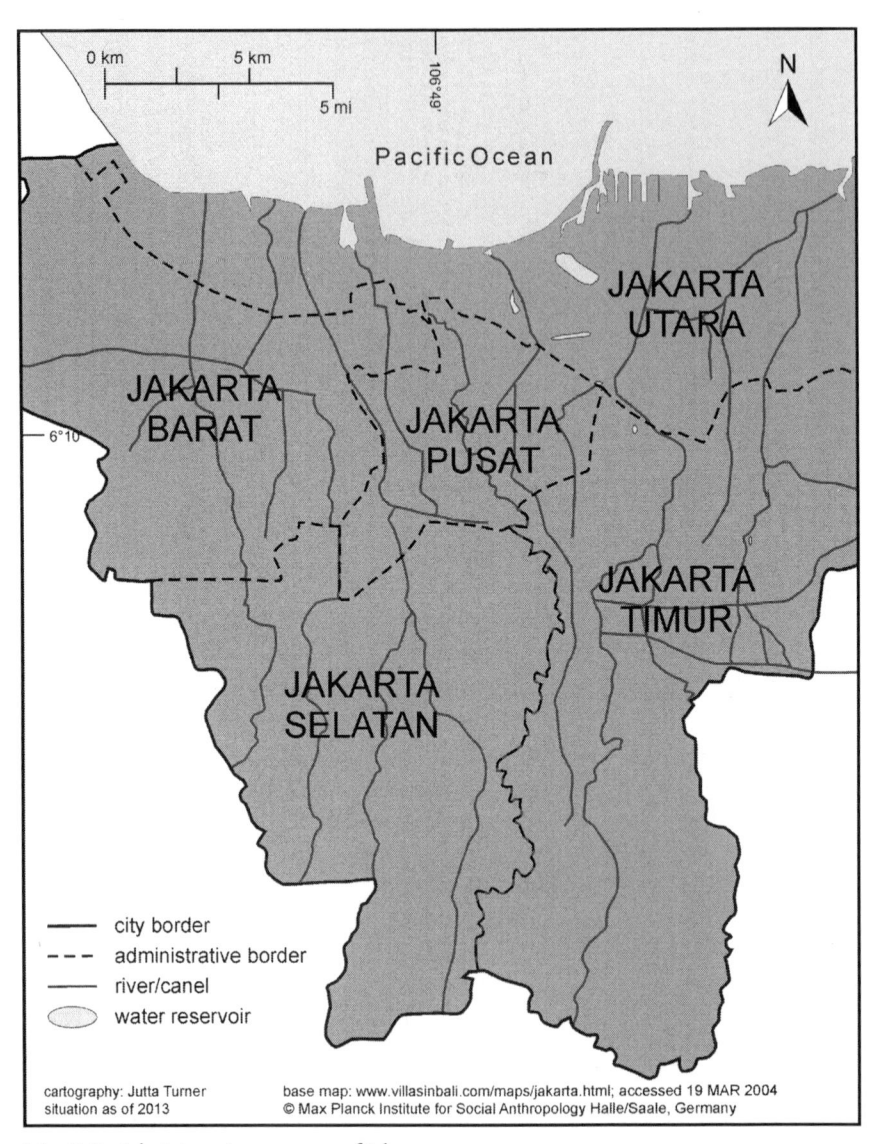

Map 2.2. Administrative structure of Jakarta.

Since 1966, Jakarta has been accorded the status of *Daerah Khusus Ibukota,* or DKI Jakarta (special metropolitan region Jakarta), which corresponds to that of an Indonesian province. In administrative terms, the DKI Jakarta is divided into five districts (*kotamadya*) denoted in terms of their location: Jakarta Selatan (south), Jakarta Timur (east), Jakarta Pusat (centre), Jakarta Barat (west) and Jakarta Utara (north). Jakarta covers an area of some 660 square kilometres.

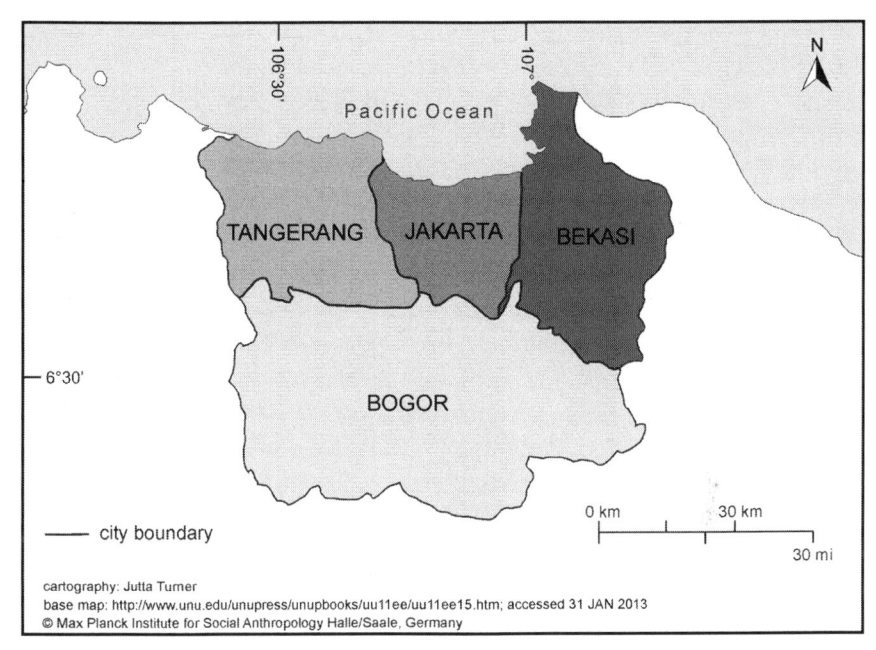

Map 2.3. Jabo(de)tabek metropolitan area.

The majority of the population lives in so-called *kampung*, which are found throughout the city and exhibit marked differences in terms of infrastructure and building quality. One finds, for instance, collections of dwellings that are little more than spaces covered by roofs made of all sorts of materials in areas that are almost devoid of infrastructure and primarily characterized by deprivation and poverty. However, there are also *kampung* that are relatively well equipped in terms of infrastructure and sanitation and have a corresponding level of housing quality. The latter tend to be found in the inner city, whereas the former are located above all in areas on the northern, eastern and western edges of Jakarta (for example, in Jatinegara) and inhabited by the majority of new and temporary migrants to the city (Evers 1982; Nas and Boender 2002). In the districts south of *Medan Merdeka* there are also many so-called *rumah gedongan*, small single-family dwellings often inhabited by government officials. Affluent Indonesians and employees of foreign firms mostly live in the southwestern districts of the city, particularly in the exclusive residential area of Kemang.

According to the 2000 statistics, of the then official 8.4 million inhabitants of Jakarta around 35 per cent (almost three million) were (ethnic) Javanese[3], some 28 per cent (2.3 million) are Betawi and some 16 per cent (1.3 million) Sundanese. The Batak (265 thousand) and Minangkabau (300 thousand) make up just over 3 per cent of the population. The remainder of the population is made up of various Indonesian minorities and foreign inhabitants of the city.[4] Prior to the year 2000, the last official statistics stating the ethnic distribution among Jakartans date back to 1930, and it remains unclear what methods of collecting and evaluating data were used. Between 1930 and 2000, surveys of ethnic affiliation were prohibited on the grounds that ethnic identities were not to be emphasized. Thus, the censuses conducted in 1980 and 1990 only covered inhabitants' place of birth and residence.

Based on the 1930 statistics and a survey conducted during his research, Castles (1967) estimates an ethnic distribution for the year 1961 as follows. In 1930, 54 per cent of the population was Betawi, whereas in 1961 this group made up only 22.9 per cent. The Sundanese made up 34.3 per cent in 1930 and 32.9 per cent in 1961, thus maintaining a relatively constant proportion. By contrast, the proportion of Javanese varied from 9.9 per cent in 1930 to 25.4 per cent in 1961, a change that is connected with their increasing domination of state functions (in particular in the Indonesian capital) following the end of the colonial period. Other ethnic groups formed small minorities.

The data from the 2000 census provide little information about the methodology involved. Suryadinata et al. (2003: 9), referring to the sociodemographic evaluation of the census, ascertain 'that the category of ethnicity used in the 2000 Population Census is self-identity – which is very democratic, but may not always be the "real" ethnic identity of the individual'.

A number of aspects of the data compiled from the census are nevertheless noteworthy in relation to the theme of this book. At 2.3 million or 28 per cent, the Betawi share of Jakarta's population in 2000 seems relatively high, particularly in light of this group's complaints that waves of migration are constantly reducing their relative numbers. Apart from their presence in Jakarta, another 2.6 million Betawi live in the neighbouring towns that belong to the Jabodetabek area. These figures in themselves cannot provide a foundation for Betawi concerns, because they indicate neither a reduction of Betawi nor any danger of their dying out. The impression among many Betawi of their own disappearance is more likely based on the fact that many Betawi are poor and therefore often live in close proximity to the millions of migrants at the fringes of Jakarta and in neighbouring towns.

The percentage of Sundanese in Jakarta has approximately halved both in relation to 1930 and to the projected figures for 1961. This is largely due to the sharp increase in the Javanese population and the general increase in migration to Jakarta. However, it is also related to the conversion of erstwhile Sundanese who now claim Betawi identity. There has been a considerable level of mixing particularly between the Betawi and the Sundanese since the beginning of the colonial period. Whereas there used to be a tendency among those belonging to such mixed families to label themselves as Sundanese, the more recent improvement of the Betawi's reputation has increased the number of those who consider themselves Betawi. As well, more generally, groups and people who have lived in Jakarta for several generations often classify themselves and are classified by others as Betawi. Of all the counted ethnic identities, it is certainly the Betawi who exhibit most ambiguity, because the creole context of their emergence and existence is subject to a particularly high degree of situational and contextual variation.

It cannot be the task of this study to check the validity of statistical information. However, it must be noted that the survey data mentioned here need to be treated with caution. The fact that in the framework of the 2000 census an individual could choose only one ethnic ascription in itself makes the results questionable. A majority of the people in Jakarta have more than one ethnic affiliation, and identities are often situational and context-related. Moreover, the answer to the question of ethnic affiliation in the census was not provided for the most part by each individual within a family but by its (male) head. It is thus not unlikely that family members were often ethnicized to accord with the family head's own ethnic affiliation.

Furthermore, people born in Jakarta or growing up there often regard themselves primarily as Jakartans – as Orang Jakarta – yet, when asked about their ethnic identity, have to refer to one of the ethnic categories designated in the survey – and Orang Jakarta (in contrast to Betawi) is not among them. Therefore they are likely to state the ethnic origin of their parents (or of one of their parents) as their ethnic identity. Thus, those who see themselves primarily as Orang Jakarta but not as Orang Betawi commonly nominate an ethnic identity that actually plays no or no significant role in terms of what they feel their identity to be. Hence, such surveys often reveal more about the implicit theories subscribed to by the statisticians than about those being subject to statistical analysis.

Historical Beginnings: Sunda Kelapa, Jayakarta, Batavia

The first large-scale settlement of the area on which Jakarta now stands took place in the twelfth century B.C. at Sunda Kelapa,[5] a harbour in the north of present-day Jakarta. The area formed part of Pajajaran, the Hindu-Javanese kingdom whose capital – Pakuan Pajajaran – was located farther south in present-day Bogor. Trade brought foreigners and thus new cultural influences to Sunda Kelapa, initially from India, from where Hinduism and Buddhism spread. The first European arrivals, the Portuguese, erected a fort at Sunda Kelapa at the beginning of the sixteenth century. Following the Portuguese conquest of Malacca, Sunda Kelapa profited from a boycott of Malacca by Muslim traders, who relocated their activities to the harbour town.[6] Sunda Kelapa thus became a pawn in the play of Islamic and Christian rivalries instigated by Portuguese and Muslim traders. Faced with a powerful Muslim neighbour to its west in the form of the Sultanate of Banten, the Hindu-Javanese kingdom of Pajajaran endeavoured to hinder the spread of Islam by concluding contractual agreements with the Portuguese. However, these efforts came to nothing when, in 1527, Banten assumed control of Sunda Kelapa. The Portuguese fleet was defeated by the military commander Fatahilla, and Sunda Kelapa was renamed Jayakarta (Abeyasekere 1989).[7]

Although its significance as a trading port declined under the regency of Banten, Jayakarta maintained a good reputation as an anchorage where ships could take on provisions and wait out the rainy season. The port thus continued to be frequented by traders from various regions – from other islands in the Indonesian archipelago, from India, China, England and Holland. The spice trade dominated the commercial interests of Europe's East-India trading companies, whose attempts to monopolize the trade led on the one hand to rivalries between the English and the Dutch and on the other to the decline of centuries-old trade routes within the region.[8]

Jayakarta thus became a bone of contention between the European powers. By means of military force and helped by rivalry between their opponents, the Sultanate of Banten and in the west and the kingdom of Mataram in the east, it was finally the Dutch and their *Vereenigde Oostindische Compagnie* (VOC) that prevailed. In 1619 the old Jayakarta was destroyed by General Coen, the governor-general of the VOC, and rebuilt as Batavia.[9]

The native inhabitants of the city, who were largely Sundanese, were driven from the city and settled nearby. Over the following decades the Dutch extended their authority over large parts of the archipelago, although the enmity of the Javanese kingdom of Mataram and the Sultanate of Banten towards the colonial city of Batavia persisted until well into the eighteenth century.

Social Organization and Interethnic Relationships in Batavia

Due to their fear of rebellion in Batavia, the Dutch opposed settlement within the city by the natives of Java (Javanese, Sundanese etc.). This was one of the reasons for the expansion of the population into the *Ommelanden,* the environs of Batavia, a process that began in the early 1620s, shortly after the city was established.[10] The more Batavia expanded, the more these *Ommelanden* became integrated into the city, while also growing in size themselves. The expansion of Batavia proceeded mainly in a southerly direction, along both sides of the Ciliwung River. This development was driven by the need to ensure a ready food supply for the city from agricultural production and the cultivation of export crops, above all sugar cane. This extended land use and the expansion of agricultural and economic activities to the south was accompanied by increasing immigration into the immediate vicinity of Batavia by those seeking work in agriculture and trading opportunities. Up until the 1650s such immigration was neither monitored nor regulated by the Dutch.

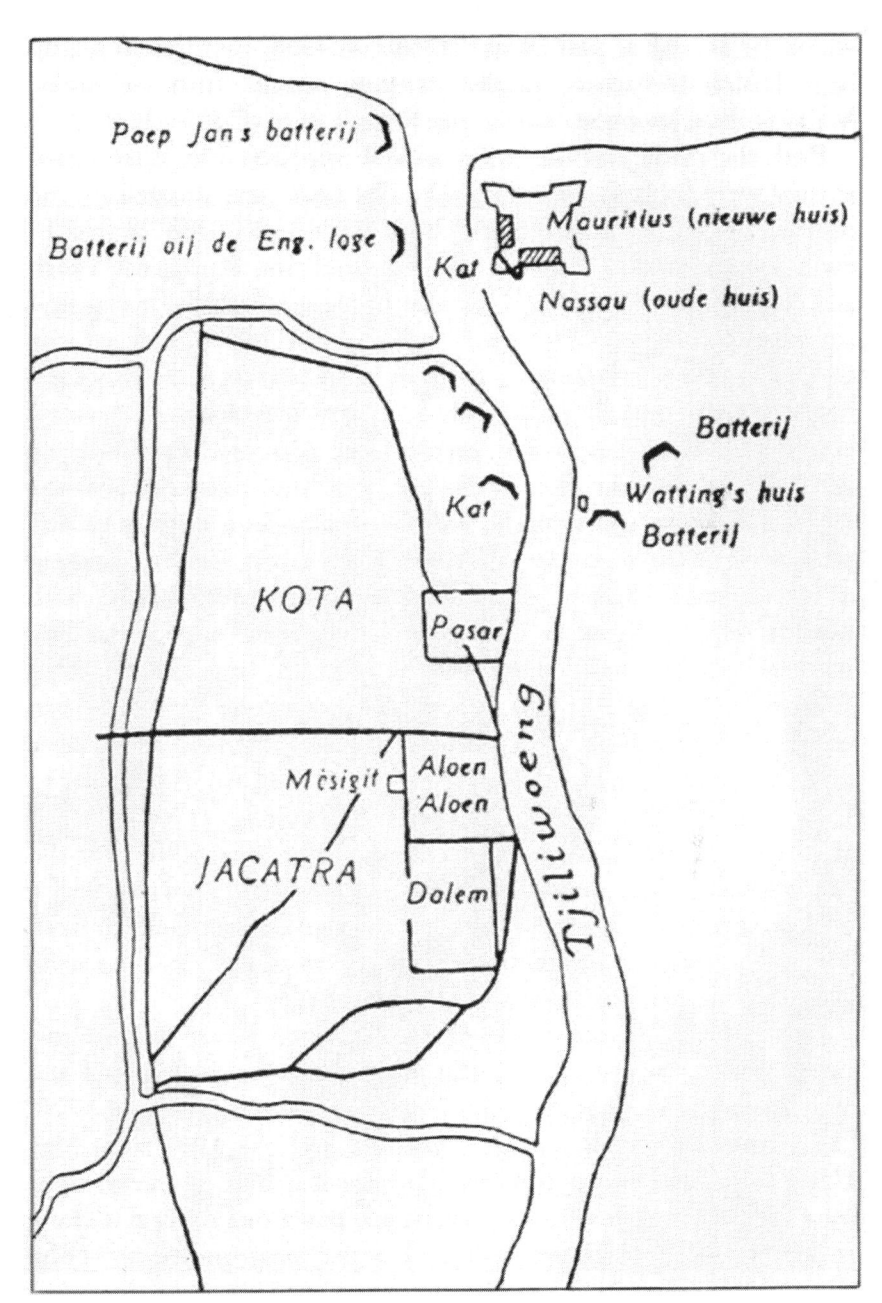

Figure 2.1. Batavia [*Jacatra*] 1619, from Haan (1922) *Oud Batavia*, G. Kolff and Co.

Fearing potential unrest among the native population, the Dutch authorities encouraged Chinese merchants to settle in Batavia, and Japanese and Philippine soldiers were recruited to defend the settlement (Abeyasekere 1989; Haan 1935).

Soldiers, sailors and others in the service of the VOC were often stationed only temporarily in Batavia. Slaves were brought to the city from outside Java to become servants, labourers, mistresses or wives.

During this phase of colonization, the population of Batavia was thus ethnically distinct from the population of the *Ommelanden* and the rest of Java. It was a population that was also largely isolated in social and cultural terms from its surroundings:

> Culturally, Batavia was isolated too. Many of the original Sundanese inhabitants had fled in 1619. All Javanese, the major ethnic group on the island ..., were excluded from the city, and a new population was brought in from many parts of Asia and Europe (Taylor 1983: 20).

The Dutch initially divided the population of Batavia and the *Ommelanden* into three groups: *Europeesche Burghers,* i.e., Europeans (Dutch, German, French, Danes, British, Portuguese), *Vreemde Oosterlingen,* i.e., foreign Asians (Chinese,[11] Arabs, Armenians, Indians, Persians)[12] and *Inlandsche Burghers* or *Inlanders,*[13] i.e., all inhabitants of Indonesian origin (Lohanda 2001). Subcategories also existed. Europeans, Chinese and Arabs were differentiated according to whether they were born in their respective country of origin or in Indonesia. For instance, Europeans born in Holland were regarded as the *eigenlyken Europeaan,* i.e., proper Europeans, whereas those born in Indonesia were commonly termed *liplaps.*[14] Europeans who spent their lives in Indonesia and did not return to Europe were called *blijvers,* i.e., people who stay; Europeans who remained in Indonesia only for a limited period of time before returning to Europe were called *trekkers,* i.e., people who move (on). The natives were classified either as slaves or – as in the case of Europeans, Chinese, Arabs and Moors – *vrijburghers* (free citizens), the latter being subdivided into different classes.[15] To be classified as a *vrijburgher,* a person had to belong to one of the following categories of people:

a) The Portuguese, who were allowed to remain in Batavia because in most cases they had married there. However, they were required to take an oath of loyalty to the Dutch.
b) The progeny of marriages between Portuguese men and native women.
c) The Mardijkers, a group that, from the beginning of the seventeenth century, the Dutch brought to Batavia from (among other places) the former Portuguese colonies they had conquered. In Batavia they worked as soldiers, merchants, VOC watchmen and poultry and vegetable retailers.
d) The Papangers, a group among the Mardijkers whose name derives from Papango, a region (and ethnic group) on Luzon (Philippines) from where they originated (Crawfurd 1971). Like other slaves from the conquered Spanish and Portuguese regions of Southeast Asia, they were brought to Batavia

(among other places) as prisoners of war.[16] They were accorded the status of free citizens after spending many years serving as soldiers of the VOC.
e) Retired employees of the VOC who had married native women and could not return to Holland.
f) Progeny of those in category (e).
g) Colonists from different parts of the world.
h) The *smalle vrijlieden,* the smallest class of free citizens, freed slaves from Makassar, Bali and Ambon.
i) Native inhabitants who had been given a *vrijbrief,* a letter confirming their status as free citizens.[17]

In the 1750s the colonial administration introduced measures to regulate settlement. This was a reaction to the military threat coming from Banten, the increase in the population of the *Ommelanden* and increasing conflict in connection with land ownership. *Heemraden*[18] were deployed to organize land distribution and monitor roads and waterways. Due to the conflicts with Mataram and Banten, the Dutch regarded the Javanese as a particular threat to Batavia. Following the outbreak of war with Banten in 1656, those Javanese still residing inside the city walls were resettled in special areas in the *Ommelanden,* where they were supervised by a *kapitan* who was under the authority of a European state functionary. Other natives suspected of having links to Banten or Mataram were also not permitted to live within the city walls and settled in the *Ommelanden.* A side effect of these measures was that Islam was (temporarily) largely banished from Batavia.

In the course of the seventeenth century soldiers were also settled in the *Ommelanden,* who fought in military campaigns against Ceylon, Sumatra and Sulawesi. The members of this corps were recruited in Ambon, Makassar, Bugis and Bali partly to ensure loyalty among groups that had formerly been opposed to the Dutch regime. These soldiers were allocated land in the *Ommelanden* and were the first people to live in ethnic *kampung.* However, they were soon joined by freed slaves, who rapidly came to constitute the majority of the population of the *Ommelanden.* Javanese *kampung* also expanded due to the effects of immigration. The Dutch in Batavia regarded the rapidly expanding population living in the immediate vicinity of the city as a threat. They feared rebellions and interethnic strife. To them, ethnic segregation seemed the only solution, particularly because they had no interest in engaging with the concerns of the indigenous population and adjudicating in internal disputes. When in 1686 a city watch house was attacked by a group of marauding Balinese, the colonial administration issued comprehensive regulations applying to all settlements in the *Ommelanden,* which remained in force until 1828. The governor and his *Raad van Indië* for the *Ommelanden* decreed that the different ethnic groups had to live in separate *kampung.* Ethnic leaders were appointed who were given the title of *kapitan* and allocated land that they were permitted to cultivate for their own needs and on which they could settle their compatriots.[19] Subject to the authority of their captain, the members of the native population were permitted to provide for their economic needs and dispense justice independently of the Dutch authorities. This system accorded with the principle of indirect rule and involved the colonial government appointing select native individuals – local dignitaries, chiefs, nobles, etc. – who were loyal to the colonial regime and its policies.[20]

The presence of the Chinese in the *Ommelanden* became an issue of increasing concern. The Dutch feared that marriages between Chinese settlers and indigenous women would lead to an increasing indigenization of the former and that these important economic actors might then turn against the colonial authorities. In 1717 the colonial rulers therefore prohibited the Chinese from marrying outside their ethnic group. However, this rule proved impossible to enforce, despite the authorities' attempts to isolate the Chinese in exclusively Chinese *pecinaan* – secluded settlements in the *Ommelanden* (Somers Heidhues 1974).

However, despite these regulations, established interethnic networks continued to exist and interethnic mixture remained common. There was a lot of mixture among slaves of different ethnic origins on the one hand and between slaves and the free citizens of Batavia on the other. Men of nonindigenous origins often married Indonesian women and had children with them. Because very few Dutch women came to Batavia, the majority of male Dutch inhabitants of Batavia lived together with Indonesian women, many of whom were slaves from Bali. In cases of marriage these women were accorded the status of free citizens. According to a decree issued by the colonial government in 1730, children of mixed ethnic unions were to be assigned to the father's ethnic group (van der Chijs 1889). Indonesian women who married European men were attributed their husband's nationality. The goal of the VOC was to create a consistently loyal Eurasian colony that would ensure security and order so that Holland's economic interests could be pursued unchallenged. The social status of children of Indonesian-European unions depended on the status of the father and the extent to which he was prepared to recognize his children by Indonesian women. In addition, skin colour and appearance played an important role. The lighter the skin and the more European the appearance, the greater were the chances that an individual would be accepted within the local European society.[21] Dutch-Indonesian children born in wedlock became part of the growing Indo group, whose members, like the *europeesche burghers,* were accorded the status of *vrijburghers*. However, it was only seldom that such people were fully integrated into the European group. The daughters from mixed families often married Europeans and thus perpetuated the European line.[22] Boys of mixed origin were often trained as soldiers. Others married other Indos, Mardijkers or Christian natives.

Many children of Dutch fathers and Indonesian mothers were raised by their Indonesian mothers and their families. They became members of their mother's ethnic group and often, together with their mothers, were subject to the process of creolization that gave rise to the Betawi within only a few generations:

> Few of these children grew to adulthood counting themselves as part of the European group.... The majority ... were abandoned by the father through either his death, his desertion of the mother, or his escape to the Netherlands. Such children grew up in the mother's ethnic ward of the city ... (Taylor 1983: 8).

Although the Dutch were intent on excluding Islam from the city and promoting Christianity by giving preferential treatment to Christians, Indonesia was not considered an object of evangelization until well into the nineteenth century.[23] However, within Batavia Christian groups and the progeny of European-Indonesian unions were given particular support as part of a programme of Hollandization. This included the establishment of orphanages in which children of Indonesian-European unions were raised.[24] They were often given into the care of women who had proved themselves loyal to the Dutch: 'By the time they left the orphanage, the children were expected to be grateful to society, respectful to their betters, and fluent in Dutch' (Taylor 1983: 27).

However, the number of Indos who were Hollandized as part of their socialization process remained small in comparison to those primarily raised by their mothers in the Indonesian cultural tradition. The practice of Hollandization thus did not result in the emergence of a significant Eurasian population group with a marked Dutch identity, especially since the number of Europeans in Batavia was constantly declining in proportion to the native population (van der Veur 1968).

As a consequence, the VOC framed laws intended to ensure that Dutch settlers remained permanently in Batavia. For example, entry to the colony by Dutch women was significantly limited to encourage Dutch men to establish families with native women. It was also decreed that Dutch widows had to remain in Batavia for many years following the death of their husbands (Taylor 1983). Furthermore, following their retirement Dutch men who had married Indonesian women were not permitted to take their wives back to Holland. They later also lost the right to send their children to Holland. Apart from a number of high officials who managed to circumvent these laws, the latter effectuated that Dutch men with Indonesian families remained in Indonesia for life.[25] However, these measures did not succeed in establishing a permanent Dutch-minded stratum of society either because the more mixing took place and the longer Europeans remained away from their original homeland, the more pronounced Indonesian influences became. 'For most married men, the settlement overseas became home and the only homeland their children knew' (Taylor 1983: 17).

The fact that there was no extensive Hollandization of Eurasian society within Batavia is also witnessed by the failure of the Dutch language to become

52 *Creole Identity in Postcolonial Indonesia*

established: 'Within two decades of settlement the Dutch language was being maintained and spoken only by male immigrants from Holland in the VOC office' (Taylor 1983: 27).

Creolization and the Emergence of the Betawi

Until the end of the eighteenth century, slaves formed the majority of the population of Batavia and the *Ommelanden*. The following figures relating to the population within Batavia's city walls were recorded for the year 1679: Europeans 2,227 (6.93 per cent), Mestizos 760 (2.36 per cent), Chinese 3,220 (10.02 per cent), Mardijkers 5,348 (16.64 per cent), Javanese 1,391 (4.33 per cent), Malayans 1,049 (3.26 per cent), Balinese 1,364 (4.24 per cent), slaves 16,694 (51.97 per cent) (Jayapal 1993).

Figure 2.2. Roemah blanda – A Dutch house in Batavia, circa 1870 (Antique Maps & Prints of Indonesia, Bartele Gallery, Jakarta). The illustration shows one of the plates of the series Gambar-Gambar akan Peladjaran dan Kasoekaan Anak-anak dan Iboe-bapanja (Prints for the education and enjoyment of children and their parents). They were created for Indonesian children to learn Dutch and for Dutch children to learn Indonesian. The plates each illustrate a specific aspect of life in the Dutch East Indies. Source and permission for reprint: Antique Maps & Prints of Indonesia, Bartele Gallery, Jakarta.

Niemeijer (2000) correctly points out that these statistics, particularly in relation to the numbers of Chinese and Mestizos, appear opaque. It also remains unclear in which group children born to Chinese men and (mostly) Balinese women are included. The number of Mestizos, understood as children of European men and Indonesian women, seems very small. Many children born out of wedlock may have been included in their mother's ethnic group or counted as Mardijker.

The most conspicuous aspect of these statistics is the fact that only the *vrije burghers* are differentiated along ethnic lines, whereas the slaves are not. Slaves formed the largest section of the group that in the course of time became the Betawi. They were distributed over the entire area of Batavia and the *Ommelanden*. Most importantly, they ensured that interethnic relationships and mixing continued despite the formal segregation of the population along ethnic lines: 'Slavery as a form of social organization enormously strengthened the multi-ethnic character of daily social life' (Niemeijer 2000: 77).

According to VOC law, it was forbidden to hold Javanese slaves, and in the early days of colonization slaves were shipped to Batavia from the Southeast Asian mainland (Coromandel, Malabar, Bengalen, Burma). After the VOC was compelled to give up its base in Arakan (Burma) in 1665, slaves were imported from the entire Indonesian archipelago. However, the majority came from Bali and South Sulawesi (Abeyasekere 1983; Haan 1935; Lekkerkerker 1918). Many slaves worked as domestic servants, nursemaids and craftsmen in the homes of Europeans and other free inhabitants and later also as agricultural labourers in the *Ommelanden*. Apart from those who gained their freedom – usually as the result of converting to Christianity – the slaves were poor. They often suffered from malnourishment, had substandard housing, were poorly clothed and, in the case of purported misdemeanours, were subject to harsh punishments (Taylor 1983).

The heterogeneous population[26] that lived in Batavia and the *Ommelanden* soon began to create a new, shared culture and identity and their own dialect, *Omong Betawi*.[27]

> They emerged as a cultural category from among the peoples of Batavia: imported slaves; Eurasians deserted as children by white fathers; and peoples from all over the archipelago drawn to the city by the prospect of new opportunities. At the time, this group classified as 'Natives' was by no means homogeneous, for it included Christian and Muslim, and later, people for a while identified separately as Mardijkers. All these groups came together in Batavia and grew from it.... Within the city itself there grew up this special society in isolation from other peoples of Indonesia (Taylor 1983: 19).

Many Chinese born in Indonesia – the so-called Peranakan[28] –, who had mixed with Indonesians over a long period of time already, also became part of the emerging group of the Betawi. As Castles (1967: 162) points out, 'The myth of Chinese unassimilability is thus refuted by Djakarta's own history.' This particular connection between Peranakan and Betawi is dealt with in a later chapter.

Although in formal and official terms a rigid policy of settlement according to ethnic criteria was in force, this policy corresponded neither with the realities of settlement nor social practices. The concentration of specific ethnic groups residing in the *kampung* designated for them quickly dissipated for different reasons. Although a *kapitan* would likely settle on the land granted him, this did not guarantee that all his ethnic compatriots would follow. After some time the *kapitan* were often granted other land or acquired it themselves. This meant that individual settlements were no longer controlled as tightly as before. In some cases a *kampung* lost all its young men because they were active in military campaigns conducted by the VOC. On returning, they would often refuse to settle in the *kampung* designated for them, choosing instead to live elsewhere or move around in search of work (Faes 1893). The larger the ethnic group, the more dispersed was the settlement of its members. The level of mobility was also considerable. Freed slaves – insofar as they were not Christian – were formally obliged to register in the *kampung* responsible for them and to look for work there. However, this formal requirement was not successfully enforced, and freed slaves gravitated to areas that promised them social contacts and economic success. Raben thus concludes: '*Kampung* were anything but closed off, ethnically fixed communities. This supports the proposition that Company categories were arbitrary and in no way reflected ongoing integration' (Raben 2000: 103).

Some ethnic groups were not large enough to establish settlements in their own right and were therefore settled together with one or more other groups.

> Thus the 'Papangers' were united with the Bandanese and the 'Moors' later with the 'Papangers'. In the early nineteenth century, all freed slaves of whatever race were enrolled as 'Papangers'. At the beginning of the twentieth century the guards of the city hall of Batavia were still called 'Papangers', though by that time even the origin of the term had been forgotten (Castles 1967: 159, citing Haan 1917: 220).

Various sources from the period indicate that interethnic contacts, including marriages, were part of everyday life in the seventeenth and eighteenth centuries. By contrast, there are few reports of the kind of interethnic conflicts that the Dutch so feared. Conflicts occurred for the most part on an intraethnic level and were based on social or religious differences (Van der Chijs 1889). The Balinese offer a particular case in point. Balinese who were born in Batavia and were mainly Muslim did not want to settle in the same *kampung* as Balinese immigrants who had arrived in Batavia later on; the former more closely tied to other (Muslim) groups than to their Hindu compatriots (Haan 1922).

The official segregation of the population thus hindered neither interethnic relationships nor the early onset of the process of creolization that gave rise to the Betawi. Although Castles (1967) and van der Aa (1846) assume that the formation of the Betawi only commenced in the eighteenth century and was largely completed by the middle of the nineteenth century, subsequent research has shown that the Betawi in fact emerged earlier. The beginnings of a shared culture and identity were already developing in the early days of colonization:

> The rapid process of amalgamation among Indonesian immigrant groups – in other words, the early emergence of the orang Betawi – undermined official classification. The weakening of ethnic identities and the high degree of intermarriage and mobility made the system of segregation something that existed only on paper (Raben 2000: 107)

The majority of slaves were unable to maintain any relationship with their territories of origin. Within a household there were usually slaves of different ethnic origins; hence, interethnic relationships within one's immediate environment turned out to be more important than the intraethnic ones between slaves living and working in different places.[29] The disappearance of Hinduism among Balinese slaves offers a case in point. Although the Balinese constituted a large ethnic group, slavery meant that they were unable to maintain a Balinese identity or their Hindu faith (Lekkerkerker 1918). Other groups were unable to retain their identities of origin due to their low numbers. In addition, a high mortality rate among slaves due to unhealthy living conditions and the resulting necessity for renewed slave imports meant that, particularly in the eighteenth century, the size of the slave population fluctuated considerably (Haan 1935).

Particularly in the *Ommelanden,* where the majority of slaves and the native population excluded from Batavia lived, Islam played a significant role as a transethnically unifying force that facilitated interethnic relationships as well as the resulting process of creolization. Islam, together with the native population, was largely excluded from Batavia. It thus became a medium of delimitation by means of which its practitioners could distinguish themselves form their (Christian) colonial masters and the latter's (purported) collaborators. Islam forged a bond between those who suffered the greatest level of oppression. The common affiliation with Islam allowed for a boundary to be manifested between believers, on the one hand, and the colonial masters and their allies on the other.

As a transethnic bond, Islam also played a crucial role in the processes of creolization that led to the emergence of Betawi culture and identity. Islam played an influential role in the ethnogenesis of the Betawi because it had a *trans*ethnic effect. For the Betawi today, Islam is attributed an important meaning in the context of ethnic identity due to its function as an ethnogenetic 'catalyst'. Islam is regarded by the Betawi not only as a religious identity but also as an important part of their ethnic identity. For most other groups Islam tends to have a transethnic meaning and, due to its role in the independence struggle, also a national one. However, for the Betawi Islam is claimed and defended as an ethnic particularity, irrespective of the fact that over 90 per cent of other Indonesians are also Muslims. In the words of one Betawi, 'Without Islam we would not exist.'

The perception by Dutch colonialists of Islam as a threat and their exclusion of it from seventeenth-century Batavia increased the social gulf between the Christian colonial masters and their allies on the one hand and the Islamic natives on the other. Christianity thereby became increasingly associated with colonialism and foreign domination, while Islam was linked with anti-colonialism and indigeneity. It also contributed to the establishment of Islam as a unifying force that helped lay the foundations for Islam later playing a nationally unifying role during the struggle for independence.[30] The exclusion of Islam from Batavia thus ultimately contributed to the expulsion of the Dutch from Indonesia.

A further important reason for the *kampung* system not being realized in the manner envisaged by the Dutch authorities lay in the fact that the ethnic categories that were regarded by the European rulers as fundamental did not have much social relevance for the native population at the time of the settlement of Batavia and the *Ommelanden*. Indonesian historical sources reveal that prior to the colonial period the social structure of most Indonesian societies was not decisively influenced by ethnic boundaries. This does not mean that ethnic ascriptions and delimitations did not exist. However, they were permeable and flexible. Moreover, religious and cultural commonalities as well as personal relationships played a more important role than ethnic ascriptions (Anderson 1972; cf. Ricklefs 1993). This meant that foreigners as well as foreign cultural elements could be integrated in a manner that was relatively unproblematic.

It may also have been significant that particularly in the *Ommelanden* – where an ever greater share of people subject to creolization processes came to live – the influence of the Javanese and Javanese traditions was more pronounced than in (early) Batavia, where hardly any Javanese lived. The integration of heterogeneous cultural elements and the incorporation of aspects of foreign cultures are characteristic of Javanese society, culture and religion. It is probable that an environment characterized by Javanese influences facilitated creolization among people of heterogeneous origins. It is also probable that the marked influence of Hinduism and Buddhism on Javanese Islam played a particular role in facilitating the conversion of the (originally Hindu) Balinese to Islam.[31]

The emergence of the Betawi thus involved the interaction of different factors. The enslavement of the bulk of those living in Batavia and the *Ommelanden* distanced and alienated them from their respective ethnic origins and cultural backgrounds. The individual ethnic identities of slaves and free settlers were generally not emphasized and increasingly lost their meaning. The official segregation of the population along ethnic lines had barely any effect on how identity

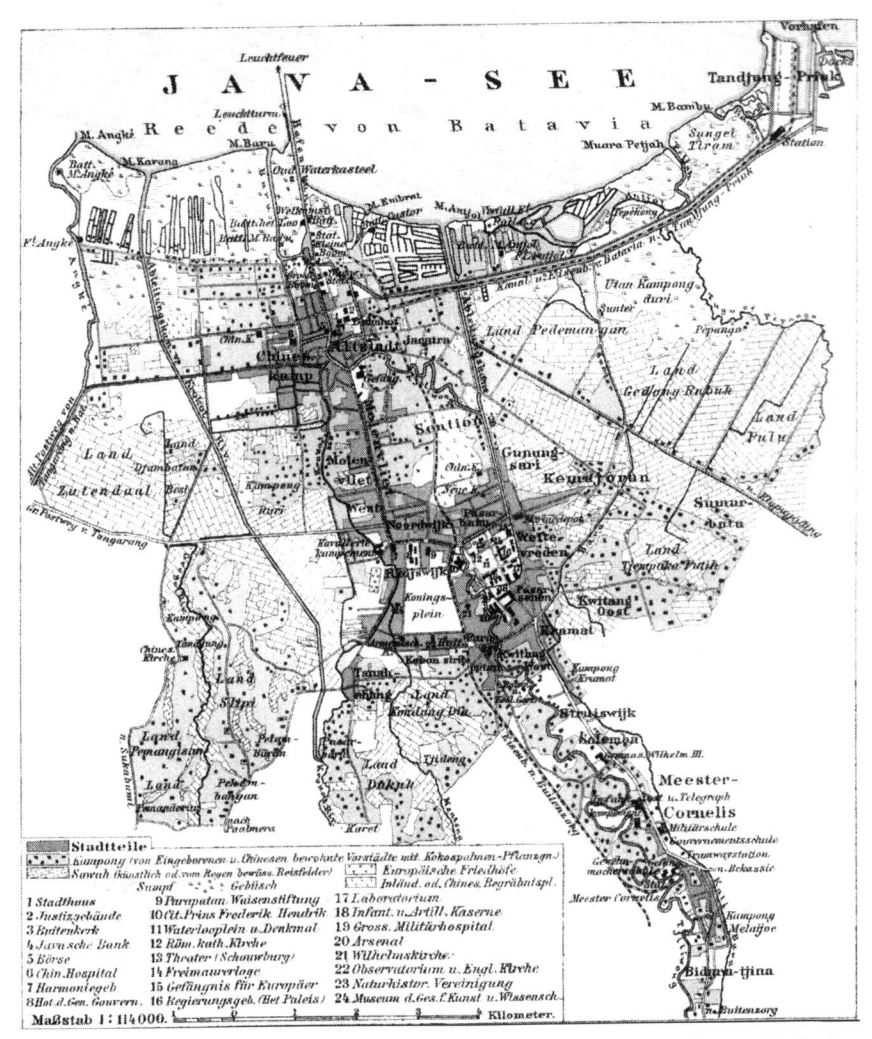

Figure 2.3. Batavia 1895 (from *Brockhaus Konversations-Lexikon*, 16th edition. Wiesbaden, 1952).

was perceived among the population. Against a background of multiethnic coexistence and delimitation from the colonial masters – above all by means of Islam – new cultural representations and a shared identity emerged among the slaves and many free inhabitants of Batavia and the *Ommelanden*, representations and identity which were increasingly attached ethnic – namely Betawi – reference.

Although the individual *kampung* were heterogeneous as regards the ethnic composition of the population undergoing creolization, up until the beginning of the eighteenth century certain settlement patterns can be identified. These patterns are connected with the economic and social functions that different groups assumed. For example, the majority of Javanese settled in what were then the rather remote regions on the western and eastern edges of the *Ommelanden*. Europeans and Indos lived in Batavia or near the city boundaries, where they built houses along the Ciliwung River and the Molenvliet Canal. Mardijkers, Chinese and Arabs often lived in the suburban areas of the *Ommelanden,* where they pursued trade and commerce. In addition, a large part of the Chinese population lived a considerable distance away from the centre, where they ran or worked in sugar mills. In regard to groups coming from other parts of Indonesia, no clear settlement pattern is evident. The significant fluctuations in population numbers evident in censuses conducted by the *wijkmeester* can in part be attributed to the large number of settler deaths caused by repeated malaria epidemics (van der Brug 1994). Extensive military recruitment drives also contributed to these variations.

The pattern of settlement changed at the beginning of the eighteenth century, when diseases decimated large parts of the population. Europeans still living in the marshy *Ommelanden* moved into the southern part of the city, and an increasing number of Chinese immigrated into Batavia's older quarters. However, in 1740 the notorious massacre took place of thousands of Chinese by Europeans and Indonesians.[32] The surviving Chinese fled and old Batavia went into decline. The spice trade dwindled and with it the significance of the VOC. In 1799 the VOC was dissolved and replaced with a colonial government subject to the authority of the government in the Netherlands. The colonial administration and government established itself to the south in Weltevreden,[33] the development of which further disadvantaged Batavia. The governor's residence was moved to Buitenzorg,[34] present-day Bogor. In 1811, as a consequence of Holland's occupation by the French, the French flag was hoisted over Batavia. Soon after, British troops, which had already tried many times in vain to establish a base on Java, exploited the weakness of the Dutch and attacked Batavia, defeated the French and Dutch units and subsequently controlled Batavia for the following five years. In 1816, following the end of the Napoleonic wars, Great Britain returned the colony to the Netherlands. In 1825, the Java War broke out, costing the lives of two hundred thousand Javanese and fifteen thousand colonial-government soldiers and resulting in enormous financial losses.[35] To make up for these losses the obligatory cultivation of coffee, indigo and sugar was introduced throughout Java. Although this measure destroyed the indigenous economy and led to famines, it provided the Dutch with increased yields. Batavia became the centre of the Dutch colonial empire in Southeast Asia (Moosmüller 1989). The new Batavia in and around Weltevreden experienced a boom evident in the construction of parks, churches, large public buildings, colonial clubs and, further to the south, Dutch residences. This new Batavia became the 'Queen City of the East', whereas the old Batavia (Kota) was increasingly settled by Chinese immigrants, who established themselves there as merchants. The increase in its population in the nineteenth century led to Batavia expanding to the south. Ethnic diversity further increased due to the growing number of settlers of different origins. In 1828 settlement as well as military and political administration along ethnic lines were officially ended. In the first quarter of the nineteenth century, the slave trade also progressively decreased and was completely abolished in the middle of the century (Abeyasekere 1985, 1989).

In the late nineteenth century, as communication and transport systems became more efficient and sanitary conditions improved in Batavia, more and more European women accompanied their husbands to the colony, and mixing between Europeans and natives decreased. Whereas interethnic contacts generally intensified, the social, cultural and physical gulf between Europeans and all other groups widened. Although children continued to be born to European fathers and Indonesian mothers, the role of such fathers became reduced to that of biological progenitor, which at best guaranteed mothers and their children a certain level of social protection. Children of such unions grew up with their Indonesian families and married natives. At the end of the colonial period, most of the remaining members of the *tuschenklasse* (intermediate class) of Indos migrated to Holland or established themselves in Jakarta. This latter development led to extensive indigenization through mixing with the native population or, as in the case of the Depok Asli,[36] to a kind of enclaved ethnicization. With the end of the colonial period the so-called *Indisch cultuur*[37] disappeared from Batavia. A successor can still be found among the *Indische Nederlanders* in the Netherlands.[38] In Batavia itself the Dutch thus influenced interethnic relationships and the particular social and cultural features arising from them primarily by creating the administrative structures and social hierarchies within – or beyond – which they were formed and developed.

In the late nineteenth century more Chinese and Arab women came to Batavia. As a consequence, more intraethnic marriages took place among Chinese and Arabs, which in turn facilitated the maintenance and revitalization of identities of origin. These groups, which classified themselves primarily in terms of origin, existed alongside the already established mixed populations. This was particularly evident in the case of the Chinese, where a cleft existed (and to some extent still exists) between the Sino-Indonesian Peranakan and the so-called Totok[39] who arrived in Batavia at the beginning of the twentieth century and barely mixed with Indonesians.

Although during the nineteenth century the population of Jakarta grew from forty-five thousand (1815) to seventy-two thousand (1893) (Castles 1967: 162), this increase was less than the average population growth across Java. It was only in the twentieth century that Jakarta experienced substantial waves of migration. The construction of the port in Tanjung Priok, the expansion of government functions within the framework of 'Ethical Policy'[40] and the abrupt population growth in Java led to a multiplication of the Batavian population. The new migrants, many of them from Java itself but also from other Indonesian islands, established large communities in their new surroundings and founded ethnic associations.

The increasing influx of migrants caused the Betawi to consolidate and organize themselves politically and culturally as *suku bangsa,* as a native ethnic group. In 1923 the first association was founded that explicitly represented the Betawi, a fact it made clearly evident in its name – *Perkumpulan Kaum Betawi*[41], 'Association of the Betawi'. Its goals included improvements to education and health as well as the organization of the economic activity of the Betawi in particular and Indonesians in general (Abeyasekere 1989, Shahab 1994). In 1923 the Betawi thus formally constituted themselves as an ethnic group; the processes, however, that led to the emergence of Betawi culture and identity had already begun in the early colonial period.

The Betawi who had lived in the more central urban districts were increasingly forced into the outskirts of the city. In 1930 more Betawi lived in the outskirts (226,000) than in the centre (192,897) (Castles 1967). Nevertheless, until 1942 the urban life of Batavia was shaped above all by Europeans, Chinese and Betawi. Until the 1950s the latter formed the majority in the central and oldest *kampung* of the city.[42]

It was thus above all *Inlandsche Burghers* – including slaves, freed slaves and free citizens as well as *Vreemde Oosterlingen* – that were subject to creolization processes that led to the emergence of the Betawi. As is typical of creolization processes undergone by groups characterized by significant social hierarchies and cultural differences between them, the processes of creolization in Jakarta gave rise to different Betawi variants, which continue to exist today. This is evident in different sub-ethnonyms such as Cina Betawi, Arab Betawi, Peranakan, etc. These groups have a pronounced Betawi identity but at the same time have preserved an identity-related strand that refers to their specific (ethnic) origin and heritage.

Social Marginalization of the Betawi

During the colonial period most of the Betawi were slaves or descended from slaves, and their social status was correspondingly low. Although the ancestors of the Betawi included individuals of high social status, for example those who had commanded troops and received land for their service, in the course of time this land was for the most part taken over by Europeans or Chinese (Haan 1935).

After independence, the Betawi remained marginalized, and even today their social and economic status is on average relatively low. This applies particularly to the majority of the Betawi who live on the outskirts of Jakarta. This disadvantage has different causes, many of which date back to the early colonial period.

Probably the most important reason for the marginalization of the Betawi was and still is their comparatively low level of formal education. Even in the late colonial period, the Batavia region remained underdeveloped in terms of general education in comparison to other regions. For example, in 1930 Bandung had a literacy rate of 23.6 per cent compared with Batavia's 11.9 per cent (Volkstelling 1930). Most of the people in Batavia who could read and write were not Betawi. The literacy rate in those areas mainly inhabited by Betawi was under 2 per cent and thus one of the lowest in Java. The census of 1961 also reveals a literacy rate below the national average (Castles 1967).

Castles (1967) points to the repercussions of the agricultural system (*cultuurstelsel*) introduced by the VOC as one of the reasons for the conspicuously low level of education among the Betawi. Service to the VOC was in some cases rewarded with land. The owners of this land (*particuliere landerijen*), who were mostly Dutch and Chinese, were also accorded the right to the service and labour of the population living there (van Niel 1992). As a result this population was obliged to work the land and had little opportunity to learn to read and write – '[T]he Betawenese were only servants of the landlords' (Dhofier 1976: 36).

The fact that the Batavia region was far more directly subject to administration and supervision by the colonial rulers than other regions also contributed to the disadvantaged status of the native population. In other regions during the nineteenth century the intermediate levels of administration lay in the hands of members of the local population, who consequently needed to be educated for their tasks. However, in the Batavia region, the Dutch themselves occupied these positions – '[T]he Europeans penetrated to the level of schout or *sheriff*, and there were no indigenous regents' (Castles 1967: 203) – an arrangement based above all on fears of native rebellion.[43] Accordingly there was no perceived need to educate the native population. When in the twentieth century local regents were also installed in the Batavia region as part of the 'Ethical Policy', there were hardly any Betawi who were in possession of the required educational standard, and educated individuals had to be brought from other parts of Java: 'The Batavian sukubangsa accordingly came into existence in an environment in which all the higher elite roles were reserved for other races; whereas elsewhere colonial rule was imposed on pre-existing societies, whose ruling and culture-bearing strata, however modified, remained in existence' (Castles 1967: 203).

Religion also played an important role in the formation of social strata in the Batavia region. It was Christians – whether (converted) natives or immigrants – who occupied the leading roles and positions within colonial society and who were the most privileged by the Dutch also in terms of receiving formal education. In the view of the Dutch, Christians were the most inclined to see their role models in the Dutch and the least likely to undermine, let alone oppose, the colonial system. Privileging Christians was thus not primarily linked to missionary but to economic interests.

The more severe the oppression experienced at the hands of the colonial rulers, the more pronounced became the aversion to their religion and culture and the more Islam took on the function of resistance. The prayer house became the centre of the *kampung,* and Islam became the unifying and empowering link that connected those suffering the greatest oppression.

There was a particularly pronounced aversion towards those who did not number among the colonial masters but – at least from the point of view of the native population – were on their side. This applied particularly to the Chinese, who owned substantial amounts of the land on which the native population provided compulsory labour services.[44] Although the majority of the Chinese were themselves subject to colonial oppression and paternalism, many of them were relatively privileged in comparison to the native population.

Other groups that converted to Christianity or arrived in Batavia as Christians were also privileged by the Dutch and classified by the greater part of the native population as part of the oppressive colonial system. One consequence of this situation was the negative perception of formal education as a first step in the direction of Christianization and thus as undesirable, an attitude that still persists particularly among many older Betawi.

The Muslim population was educated above all in Koranic schools – in *pesantren* and *madrasah*[45] – and in mosques, where Arabic and Malay influences dominated (Lohanda 2001). The Dutch supported the leading role taken particularly by Arabs in the education of the Islamic population, although the authorities restricted such teaching to matters of faith, that is, essentially to the contents of the Koran, Islamic law and the principles of an Islamic lifestyle. The role of Arabs as Islamic scholars and mediators of the Islamic faith thus contributed to the separation of religious instruction and formal education. The importance that was accorded to the *pesantren* and *madrasah* in the education of the native population also led to an increased identification of the Betawi with the 'santri[46] way of life' (Koentjaraningrat 1973: 5–6).[47]

During the colonial period different factors thus combined to push the Betawi to the social periphery and, along with other factors, maintained their marginalization in the postcolonial context:

- the agrarian system of the *particuliere landerijen,* which ensured that the Betawi living in what were then the outskirts of Batavia worked on agricultural estates, where they had no access to formal education;
- the predominance of Dutch officials in the Batavian administration, who saw the provision of education for the native population as unnecessary;
- the 'low' social status of the Betawi, which disadvantaged them from the outset;
- the lack of financial resources to fund schools and education; and

- the combination of religion and social class that privileged Christianity and disadvantaged Islam.

When in 1850, in the course of the implementation of the 'Ethical Policy', the Dutch established the first schools dedicated to providing the local population with Western education, it was only the sons of the indigenous aristocracy, the *priyayi*[48], who were accepted as pupils.[49] Despite the subsequent widespread establishment of state schools, *priyayi* continued to have privileged access to higher education. Other native children were, in part due to the high cost involved, at best provided with basic schooling (cf. Dahm 1971).

This pattern was reflected in the possibilities for social advancement within Batavia; here too the Betawi were largely excluded.

> Even when the colonial system began to open to Indonesians in the early twentieth century, the positions in Batavia went largely to members of extra-regional elites, not to Batavians. Thus the first bupati (regent) of Batavia, appointed in 1924 to bring the region administratively into line with the rest of Java, was a Bantenese, Ahmad Jayadiningrat (Cribb 1991: 13).

Thus, even after independence, the prospects of social advancement were poor for the Betawi. It was others with a better educational background who assumed leadership of the independence movement and subsequently of the new state and its administrative bodies. Furthermore these others had little interest in Betawi participation because for the most part they came from outside Batavia and had little connection to the local population. For them the Betawi were alien.

> The municipality offered a political and administrative training ground for some of the Indonesians who were to run the Republican municipal administration after the declaration of independence in 1945, but these were members of the broader modern Indonesian elite whose involvement in administration, politics or the professions had brought them to Batavia, and few had any direct links with the people of the city (Cribb 1991: 14; cf. van der Veur 1969b).

The Betawi thus continued to be excluded from political power. In 1960 not one government minister or parliamentarian was Betawi, and there were hardly any Betawi employed in the civil service. During the late colonial and early postcolonial periods, access to formal Western-style education remained largely reserved for the members of the traditional elites. It was these elites who gained access to higher positions in the colonial administration and, subsequently, dominated the independent Indonesian state and its administration (van der Niel 1960). Castles characterizes the situation as follows:

> Clearly the Chinese, Sundanese and above all the Batavians form a much smaller proportion of the elite than the mass, while the reverse is the case with the Javanese and the Outer Island people.... The Sundanese and Batavians ... are underrepresented in the elite not only in relation to the population of Djakarta but also to that of the country as a whole (Castles 1967: 200).

This lack of social and economic opportunities for the Betawi meant that subsequent generations were also seldom able to complete a higher education.

The stigma of low origins also continued to exert an effect. Due to their emergence in the colonial context and their link with slavery, the Betawi represented an unpleasant memory of the colonial period. During the first two decades of independence, the desire to create an Indonesian national identity proved a barrier to critical reflection on the colonial period and its problematic legacy, including the Betawi. Instead a precolonial golden age was constructed that drew on concepts of a shared religious and spiritual origin that were supposed to function as a source of shared nationhood (Moosmüller 1999).[50]

The stereotyping of the Betawi as an uneducated group that emerged during the despised colonial period also made them incompatible with (Javanese) constructs of a precolonial cultural community of Indonesians. This negative image also resulted in a tendency among urban Betawi in particular not to identify themselves as Betawi but as belonging to other ethnic groups to avoid social discrimination or to achieve social advancement. Such conversion or situational switch of ethnic identity was relatively easy to do particularly due to the Betawi's heterogeneous origins. The strategy of assuming some other ethnic identity – by means of conversion or according to situation and context – is often applied by members of creole groups, particularly when faced with discrimination.[51] The notion of the Betawi as underprivileged, uneducated and anti-urban is also founded on the fact that Betawi members of the middle class, who often lived in central districts of Jakarta, in many cases did not identify themselves as Betawi in public and were not classified as Betawi by others due to their public appearance as of other ethnic identity and because they did not correspond with the popular cliché.

A further reason for the continuing disadvantage of the Betawi lay in the ongoing effects of the colonial system of *particuliere landerijen*, which was abolished in 1965 (sixteen years after independence) but which continued in the form of the state being allowed to appropriate land when this is deemed to be in the public interest. From the state's point of view the public interest was served above all by the transformation of inner-city *kampung*, where many Betawi continued to live after independence, into locations for prestigious business and residential areas, offices of international firms, embassies, government building, schools, large markets, etc.[52] The state did pay compensation, and residents could apply for a deed of ownership of the land concerned. However, such applications cost more than many Betawi could afford. Moreover, they did not understand why they should apply for ownership of land that from their point of view had long been theirs anyway. Registration as landowners entailed such complex administrative requirements that most Betawi were reluctant even to attempt to negotiate this process. There were also considerable additional costs required to motivate the responsible officials to process such applications. The peripheral social status of the Betawi was thus perpetuated after independence in spatial terms in the sense that they were compelled to move to the outer areas of the city. This meant that the culture of the Betawi also progressively disappeared from the inner city and was confined to the urban periphery: 'In 1930, 143,221 Betawenese lived in the district of Kebayoran; they represented nearly 100 per cent of the whole population. Now [1976] the Betawenese are a minority group compared with non-Betawenese in this district' (Dhofier 1976: 39).[53]

The attitude that developed among the Betawi in the colonial period against a background of discrimination and marginalization whereby they associated formal education with a move towards Western culture and lifestyles and away from their own origins, culture and religion continues to exert a certain effect today. Although the number of Betawi completing secondary schooling and climbing the social ladder is rising, one still encounters the opinion among older people in peripheral areas that Western education is harmful to Islamic morals.[54] In this context it is interesting to note that being forced out of the inner-city districts is associated by the Betawi with the suppression of their traditional values. An old man who still lives in Kebon Sirih, an old Betawi district in Central Jakarta, told me:

> The people from the government wanted the land because they wanted to build office buildings, houses for the rich and foreign embassies. But they also wanted to get rid of the Betawi because our way of life doesn't suit them. We are better Muslims and not as Westernized. That's why they didn't want to see us anymore. But I haven't allowed them to drive me out.

Guinness (1972) argued that the persistently low social status of the Betawi (which, in 1972, when he was reporting on the situation, was more marked than it is today) was also based on the fact that the Betawi cultivated a culture of poverty – in the sense used by Oscar Lewis (1969) and Henry Schapper (1970). According to Schapper, the most important criteria of such a culture of poverty are (1) alienation from state institutions, (2) low levels of income, productivity and security, (3) familial instability and 4) a fatalistic attitude combined with feelings of inferiority in relation to the rest of society, on which one is dependent but from which one also endeavours to delimit oneself.

The models used by Lewis and Schapper refer to subcultures of poverty in the United States and Australia. Nevertheless, several parallels can be drawn with the situation of the Betawi. For example, even today the low social status and the poverty of the Betawi in the peripheral districts of the city is usually classified and evaluated differently from the low social status and the poverty of migrants living in slums in and around Jakarta. Many Betawi see their own poverty – in comparison to that of migrants coming to Jakarta to escape poverty – as an (ethnic) distinction, as God's wish, a condition that positively differentiates them as Betawi and indigenous Jakartans from migrants aspiring to a modern, urban lifestyle and material prosperity. As one young Betawi commented, 'We do not want big cars and we did not want to shop in Sarinah[55] and go to the Hard Rock Café. That's not our culture, that doesn't fit with our religion. We reject it.'

This would seem to suggest that, along with the reasons already discussed, the rejection and disparagement of the Betawi as uneducated, obsolete, uncivilized, etc. have contributed to a Betawi attitude whereby they discredit education, modernity and prosperity of others as foreign evils while classifying and defending Betawi characteristics disparaged by others as indigenous, pure and God-fearing.

A further reason for the low social status of the Betawi that is commonly cited by outsiders but also by many Betawi themselves – and that is congruent with the postulated culture of poverty – is their lack of preparedness to invest in the future, build up savings, etc. An aspect of common parlance that is also supported by the results of Guinness' research is that the Betawi tend to spend money they do not need for their immediate subsistence on consumer goods as quickly as possible or to save it to finance a *hajj*, a pilgrimage to Mecca. There are different reasons for this lack of economic investment in the future. Enduring monetary instability in Indonesia is certainly one reason. Guinness writes of one of his informants: 'Aljar once mentioned that there had been four monies in his lifetime, *uang Wilmina, uang Djepang, uang Bung Karno* and *uang sekarang*.[56] According to him, all of them had failed, but the Dutch money had been the most stable, because it was real silver and could be made into rings' (Guinness 1972: 134).

The Betawi themselves often refer to their religiosity and modesty and to their disdain for the modern way of life as reasons for their neglect of formal education and lack of economic achievement. They often argue that their lack of investment in goods of lasting value is based on the fact that they view material goods as of secondary importance. They argue that their main priority is living according to Islamic virtues, the aforementioned 'santri way of life', which places greater importance on financing a *hajj* than, for example, buying a house or investing in formal education. This attitude is expressed in the following comment by a young Betawi: 'It is more important to go on a *hajj* once than to buy a car. A father who undertakes a *hajj* is more use to his family than a car.'

Today, the contradiction perceived between formal education and Islamic religiosity still appears more pronounced among the Betawi than among other groups. Indeed, there are indications that even today the Betawi undertake pilgrimages to Mecca relatively often. Although most of them are among the less affluent Jakartans, their numbers among the *hajj* pilgrims are particularly high.[57] This suggests that in relative terms they place greater importance on undertaking such a pilgrimage. A *hajj* is an expensive undertaking, and thus there is a tendency to save on children's schooling rather than risk being unable to finance a planned pilgrimage.

However, this leaves the question as to why money that is not required for immediate subsistence needs is often also invested in luxury goods. Although material simplicity is regarded as a virtue, importance is also attached to creating the impression of a secure material existence to guard against the impression of neediness. Should material need become evident, the family would be obliged to support the individual concerned and as necessity to draw on the help of others causes shame (*malu*), it is considered important to demonstrate financial independence as long as this is somehow possible (Guinness 1972). This contributes to a tendency to invest in things that create an immediate impression of material security rather than saving money for the future education of a child or the acquisition of property or other goods of lasting value. To avoid *malu*, impoverished Betawi will often turn to money-lenders rather than members of their family or community. When in the 1960s many Betawi suddenly gained access to money as a result of compensation payments from the government for their plots in the inner-city areas or the sale of these properties, this money was spent primarily on consumer and luxury goods as well as on gambling and wedding ceremonies. Those who had to move often invested only a part of their compensation in new housing: 'When the (opportunity) arose to sell their land most of the Betawi jumped at the opportunity of a quick sale – land was sold, and the money purchased cars, established stalls, or brought luxuries' (Guinness 1972: 131).

A further reason for the social marginalization of the Betawi may lie in their general aversion to state institutions, an attitude shaped by the experience of the colonial period and strengthened by postcolonial marginalization. In recent decades state promotion and professed appreciation of the Betawi have resulted in a higher degree of acceptance of the state's institutions, including its educational system. The Betawi are increasingly emphasizing – both in private and public – the importance of education to improving their living conditions and social status. As one young Betawi man told me in Kebon Sirih:

> It's true that many Betawi living on the outskirts prefer to buy things they don't really need instead of sending their children to school. But if this continues nothing will change. If the Betawi want to advance socially, they have to go to school. That's much more important. We figured this out a long time ago.

However, particularly among Betawi in the peripheral areas of Jakarta, ambivalence persists between an interest in government aid and the endeavour to maintain authenticity and delimitation.

The slave status of many of the Betawi's ancestors is seldom referred to when explaining the Betawi's marginalization. The Betawi generally do not like to be reminded of this detail from their past. Concrete enquires as to whether the ancestors of Betawi were slaves are often answered in the negative. One young Betawi told me: 'I can't imagine that. They were people from all over Indonesia and from other places. But slaves, no, I don't believe that.' Another man said: 'Slaves? No, they were labourers and other poor people, but not slaves.' The delimitation of the Betawi from their colonial masters is also often cited in this context. A young woman told me, 'The Betawi were opposed to the colonial rulers. They didn't let themselves be enslaved by them!' Bringing in Islam to underscore the improbability of a link between the Betawi and former slaves she continues, 'Muslims have only one master, Allah. And since the Betawi are and always have been Muslims they could not have been the slaves of foreign masters.'

Nevertheless, the slave ancestry of the Betawi is referred to, albeit only tentatively and seldom by the Betawi themselves. However, I have never heard this aspect of the history of the Betawi being used against them. A young woman, who was born in Sumatra but had grown up in Jakarta explained to me:

> Earlier on there were slaves in Jakarta who had been enslaved by the Dutch and the Chinese. Later, these people, who came from very different regions, became Betawi. But today the Betawi don't like it when people refer to this. I can understand that. It would be unfair to speak about it, because it's not their fault.

Among the educated Betawi it is no longer possible in the light of historical proof to deny completely the Betawi's former connection with slavery, but even here engagement with this theme is often rejected. Shahab (1994) cites a Betawi commenting on a conference paper given by a non-Betawi that addressed this slave background: 'Okay, we know that the Betawi are the offspring of the slaves in old Jakarta. But we have had enough of it and we do not want to hear it repeated again and again. What is important now, is who the contemporary Betawi are' (Shahab 1994: 333).[58]

The (Re-)discovery of the Betawi: Objectives and Context of State Sponsorship

The late 1960s and early 1970s saw a change in the attitude of the Jakarta government to the Betawi and the introduction of programmes dedicated to the research and promotion of their culture. This (re-)discovery of the Betawi is connected with the discovery of the potential offered by Betawi culture, history and identity as a means of strengthening both transethnic Jakartan and national identity. The pidgin potential of creole identity was discovered.

Within the multiethnic and national context of Jakarta, this identity-related potential has become increasingly significant. The change of heart on the part of the Jakartan government has in turn led to changes in the Betawi's self-perception as well as to a general change in attitudes to them among the population of Jakarta.

Following on from a series of lectures and discussions on the cultural significance of the Betawi for Jakarta and Indonesia, which was organized by the department for culture of the DKI Jakarta, a programme for the promotion of Betawi culture was drawn up and published in 1976 under the title of *Seni-Budaya Betawi* ('The culture of the Betawi', abbreviated as SBB).[59] Then Governor Ali Sadikin in his welcome note (SBB 1976: 9–11) emphasizes that the discussion concerning the necessity to research and promote Betawi culture already began in 1966. The discussions among those who participated in the development of the programme are included in the publication and show that the categories Orang Betawi, Orang Jakarta, and Orang Indonesia were crucial to the interaction of ethnic, local and national identifications in Jakarta already in the late 1960s and early 1970s.

It is argued that research and promotion should be targeted at those aspects of Betawi culture that are understood in the broadest sense as folklore and that are in danger of being lost in the context of modern, multicultural Jakarta. Explicit reference is made to dance, theatre, art, music, literature and language, but mention is also made of traditional medicine, cuisine, architecture and games.[60] The fact that more is at stake than the preservation of the traditional culture and folklore of the Betawi already becomes evident in Sadikin's welcome note (ibid.), in which he emphasizes that the programme for the promotion of the Betawi was created by members of all ethnic groups and not merely the Betawi. Several contributors point out that the promotion of the original inhabitants of Jakarta, the Betawi, must be understood as a means of promoting Jakartan identity more generally, as well of national consciousness, interethnic relationships, and last, but not least, of tourism.[61]

Papers and discussions published in SBB also address identity-related ascriptions and delimitations of Betawi culture and identity in connection with ethnic, local and national references. The invited experts emphasize the significance that folklore can have for the Betawi as Jakarta's original inhabitants, but also for all inhabitants of the city irrespective of their ethnic affiliations. It is stressed that Betawi culture as the indigenous culture of the Indonesian capital can and should promote national identity. The historical significance of the Betawi for present-day Jakarta is underscored, but it is also pointed out that all Jakartans are part of this history. The discussions refer to the question of who is to be classified as

Betawi. The relationship between traditional Betawi culture and modern urban life is debated, it is repeatedly emphasized that the Betawi have heterogeneous origins and that the vibrancy and the integrative dynamics of their culture must be maintained and made accessible to all Jakartans.[62] Furthermore, it is stated that Betawi culture is of significance for all Indonesians also because it represents the indigenous and traditional culture of the Indonesian capital.

Notes

1. *Sensus Penduduk Tahun 2010 Propinsi DKI Jakarta* = Census for the year 2010 / Province DKI Jakarta. The statistics of BPS state a population of 8.4 million for the year 2000. For a sociological evaluation of the 2000 data see Suryadinata et al. (2003).
2. Depok (south of Jakarta, between Jakarta and Bogor) is often not considered in the acronym or on maps of the area. Until 1999 Depok was part of Bogor and the area of Jabodetabek is identical with the one of Jabotabek.
3. In a political-administrative sense all ethnic groups domiciled on Java are Javanese. This usage needs to be distinguished from the term Javanese denoting an ethnic group that makes up the majority of the population of Java. In the present study, discussion of the Javanese refers to the ethnic group, unless mentioned otherwise.
4. I refer here to the figures cited in Suryadinata et al. (2003), a sociological evaluation of the official census taken in 2000. The 2010 statistics of BPS do not give figures concerning ethnic identities.
5. Sunda: region and ethnic group in western Java, *kelapa* = coconut. The name refers to the harbour's function as an outlet for the export of coconuts.
6. The Muslim traders rejected the Portuguese both as commercial competitors and as Christian fanatics.
7. Jayakarta (from Arabic) = glorious victory.
8. Both the English and the Dutch founded trading companies at the beginning of the seventeenth century with the goal of establishing a state monopoly of trade in Asia. The British founded the *East India Company,* and the Dutch the *Vereenigte Oostindische Compagnie.*
9. The name Batavia was chosen by Coen in memory of the Germanic Batavi, the ancestors of the Dutch. In 1942 the Japanese occupiers of Indonesia renamed the city Jakarta, a derivation of its former name. When the Dutch once again took control of Indonesia in 1945 the city was again called Batavia but has been called Jakarta since independence in 1949 (see Jayapal 1993).
10. Today the areas directly abutting the old Batavia are part of the city of Jakarta.
11. The category 'Chinese' in Indonesia is a colonial construct. Those described as such (as well as the native inhabitants) at the beginning of the colonial period saw themselves as members of the Hokkien, Hakka or Teochiu (Anderson 1998).
12. During the rule of the VOC, people from the eastern (Dutch: *oost*) areas of Indonesia were also regarded as *Vreemde Oosterlingen,* although in this case the classification was of a merely regional character and did not alter these people's social status as natives (see Lohanda 2001; cf. van Mastenbroek 1934).
13. Such people were later also termed *pribumi* (natives), a designation that today primarily serves to distinguish between Indonesians of indigenous descent and those of foreign, particularly Chinese, descent (*non-pribumi*). The term is regarded as politically incorrect and is avoided in official discourse, although it is still used in everyday speech (Simbolon 1991).

14. The term *liplap* derives from *berlapsis-lapsis* = arranged in layers (referring to the Indonesian way of dressing). In the colonial Indonesian context *liplap* was a derogatory term for Dutch born in Indonesia who took Indonesian female partners and above all for the children of such unions (*anak liplap*) (Lohanda 2001; cf. Stockdale 1995); see also Multatuli (1992).
15. The distinctions between these groups are explained by Lohanda (2001); cf. Stockdale (1995).
16. According to Haan (1935) the first Papangers came to Batavia in 1633.
17. *Encyclopaedie van Nederlandsch-Indië* (1919).
18. *Heemraden* (Dutch) were people in Holland who guarded dikes and polders (*heem* = home, *raad* = council).
19. In 1773 there were seventeen native *kapitan*, each of whom had responsibility for one *kampung*.
20. The principle of indirect rule is regarded as characteristic of British colonial policy, whereas direct rule is associated with French colonial policy. However, these patterns were not restricted to British and French colonialism (see Furnivall 1944, 1948).
21. Haan (1922) mentions that the widows of Dutch officials had to provide information about their skin colour when applying for widow's pensions. The lighter their skin, the greater was the pension that was granted.
22. A description of the relationship between Indo women and European men in the twentieth century is provided by van der Veur (1969a) as the publisher and translator of the biography of an Indo woman in Holland.
23. A more detailed discussion of this and of the history of the relationship between Dutch colonialism (and Christianity) and Indonesian Islam can be found in Steenbrink (1993).
24. This form of adoption was typical of societies in which creole groups played an intermediate role between the colonial class and the native population. For example, it was common practice among the Krio of Freetown in Sierra Leone to adopt native children and raise them as Christians (Knörr 1995).
25. A description from the European point of view of the relationship between European men and Indonesian women as well as of Java and colonial society in general can be found in Stockdale (1995).
26. On the composition of this group see also Koentjaraningrat (1973).
27. Lekkerkerker (1918) identified a strong Balinese element in this dialect. It is notable that the terminology used to denote it today in both scholarly and everyday contexts varies far more than the terminology applied to the group speaking it. Grijns (1991) identified the following terms: *Bahasa Jakarta, Bahasa Betawi, Asli Jakarta, Bahasa Melayu, Melayu Busèt, Melayu Ora, Melayu Daèrah, Melayu Desa, Melayu Kasar, Bahasa Asli*; cf. Grijns (1979) on the origins of the Betawi dialect. Today, the Betawi dialect functions as a low variety in a diglossic situation, but has covert prestige when used by the upper class in Jakarta.
28. *Peranakan*: derived from the root *anak* (Indonesian for 'child') and thus means 'child of the land'. In Indonesia *Peranakan* mostly refers to Indonesians of Chinese descent unless followed by a subsequent qualifying noun (such as for example *Belanda* (Dutch) or *Jepang* (Japanese). *Peranakan* has the implied connotation of referring to the ancestry of great-grandparents or more distant ancestors.
29. The fact that households included slaves of different ethnic backgrounds is evident from notary documents, inventory lists (of slaves) and court documents, some of which can be found in the *Arsip National* (ANRI) in Jakarta. A number of examples are provided by Raben (2000).

30. On the relationship between Islam and nationalism see Effendy (2003). On the historical background of this relationship see Laffan (2003).
31. On the relationship between the religious variants of Javanese culture and their societal implementation see Geertz (1960); cf. Koentjaraningrat (1975).
32. See also Chapter 5.
33. Weltevreden (from Dutch) = well content.
34. Buitenzorg (from Dutch) = without worries.
35. On the Java War see Adas (1979); Carey (1980).
36. The Depok Asli are descendants of slaves who were settled in Depok by their Dutch owners. They converted to Protestantism and were freed from slavery in 1714. They still maintain a distinct identity and are often deprecatingly termed *Belanda Depok* (Depok-Dutch) by other Indonesians, a term that they themselves reject (see Shahab 1994).
37. The cultural and historical dimensions of this term are explored by Taylor (1983); cf. Milone (1967).
38. See Kortendick (1996), who describes the background to the emergence of this group and analyses the contemporary (re)construction of its identity with reference to the example of the 'Late Late Lien Show' broadcast on Dutch television (1979–1988).
39. *Totok* (derived from Javanese) = new, pure, unmixed. The term is not unproblematic. Many regard it as politically incorrect, while others use it without reservation. Important to note here is that, unlike categories such as *Peranakan* or Betawi, it is not a generally accepted term.
40. 'Ethical Policy' referred to the introduction of a new political style by the Dutch colonial authorities in Indonesia. It was motivated by a mixture of humanitarian concerns and economic interests: 'The practical thrust of the policy everywhere was the same: increased government intervention to improve health, education, and productivity, and to open up the political scene for more local initiative. More schools, more health centres, more political freedom and representative assemblies were among the most obvious signs of the Ethical Policy in Indonesian towns like Batavia' (Abeyasekere 1989: 94ff); cf. Vlekke (1959).
41. Short form: *Kaum Betawi* or PKB.
42. This does not mean that the majority of the Betawi lived in the centre of the city, but only that the Betawi formed a large part of the population there.
43. See Hollander (1895); see van der Aa (1846) for a more detailed discussion of the administration of the Batavia region in the mid-nineteenth century.
44. In 1935, 40 per cent of such land was Chinese-owned; see Sutter (1959).
45. *Madrasah* (Arabic) = religious school in the Islamic world; *pesantren* = Indonesian variant of the *madrasah*. The education offered here to day-students and boarders is supervised by a *kyai*, an expert in Islam. It involves students reading the classical texts of Islam (including the Koran) and related commentaries and interpretations, the so-called *kitab kuning* – yellow books – so-called because the first editions brought to Indonesia from the Middle East were printed on yellow paper.
46. *Santri*: abbreviation of *pesantren*.
47. Cf. Wahid (1974); see Geertz (1960) on the distinction between *abangan*, *priyayi* and *santri* and the social, political and religious groupings (and functions) linked with them.
48. *Priyayi* (Javanese): the term originally referred only to members of the Javanese aristocracy and today is used to refer to the Javanese elite in general (Koentjaraningrat 1975). The cultural forms linked to the Javanese court are also termed *priyayi*: 'The priyayi culture takes form in the cultivation of a highly refined court etiquette, a very complex art of

dance, drama, music, and poetry, and the multi-faceted system of Javanese philosophical mysticism' (Darmaputera 1988: 78).
49. See Sutherland (1979) on the transformation of the Javanese *priyayi* as a consequence of colonization.
50. All citations from Moosmüller have been translated from German to English.
51. The Krio of Sierra Leone have also utilized this strategy of conversion when faced with discrimination – whether from the native population or their British colonial masters – to gain advantages or decrease their level of disadvantage; see Knörr (1995); Spitzer (1974).
52. On property speculation in Jakarta see Dorléans (2002).
53. Dhofier cites the figures for 1930 from Castles (1967).
54. My observations in this regard accord with the work of others who have done research in this area. Shahab (1994) used a sample of 100 people to compare the educational levels of Betawi Kota and Betawi Pinggir (living mostly on the outskirts of Jakarta). She concludes that the educational level of the Betawi Kota is significantly higher due to the fact that in comparison to the Betawi Pinggir the former place a higher value on formal education and are more affluent.
55. *Sarinah:* modern department store in the centre of Jakarta.
56. *Uang* (Indonesian) = money. *Uang Wilmina* (from Wilhelmina, the Dutch Queen, i.e., Dutch money), *uang Djepang* (*Djepang* = Japan), i.e., Japanese money, *uang Bung Karno* (money in the Sukarno era), *uang sekarang* = present-day money.
57. Writing in the 1970s, Dhofier (1976) reported that 13 per cent of Indonesian pilgrims came from Jakarta although Jakarta's population made up only 4 per cent of the entire Indonesian population. It might be argued that the concentration of wealth in Jakarta was a contributing factor here. However, the majority of the pilgrims in fact came from parts of Jakarta mainly inhabited by Betawi. Although I do not have more recent data, it is obvious that today as well a large number of Betawi journey to Mecca and save for many years to do so.
58. My translation of Shahab's original text in Indonesian.
59. Compiled by Wijaya (1976).
60. In the following years a range of works on these aspects of Betawi culture were published, e.g., Lohanda (1989); Probonegoro (1977, 1987); Sispardjo (1978/79); Muhadjir (1986). In addition, numerous conferences were held on *Wayang Betawi, Keroncong, Lenong* etc.
61. See in particular the contribution by Danandjaja (1976: 36–46) and Budhinsantoso's comment concerning the latter (1976: 47–53).
62. See particularly 32ff.

Chapter 3

Orang Betawi versus Orang Jakarta

Discourses, Definitions, Dichotomies

The Betawi are classified as an indigenous and ethnic group (*suku bangsa, kelompok etnik*) and as such are ascribed certain features as so-called typical Betawi. At the same time Betawi-(ness) has transethnic dimensions that (also) non-Betawi can relate to and identify with in manifold ways.

As categories of people, both Orang Betawi and Orang Jakarta convey ambivalent and contested meanings. These make way for a complex of possible ascriptions that people select from according to situation and context that are also informed by specific power relations and ideological constructs. This polyvalency of ascriptions is reflected in a discourse on the meanings of the categories Orang Betawi and Orang Jakarta and on how they are related to one another and to other categories of belonging.

Orang Betawi and Orang Jakarta can be used synonymously as well as to refer to different categories of people: 'The evidence suggests that "Jakartan" and "Betawi" people are used as interchangeable terms. The Betawi claim to be Jakartan and the other way around' (Shahab 1994: 47). However, this does not mean that the categories Orang Betawi and Orang Jakarta are not differentiated. One may say Orang Jakarta and mean Orang Betawi and vice versa, without this terminological arbitrariness implying an arbitrariness of the phenomena described. The ambivalent terminological connotations do not dissolve the boundaries between the categories of people they refer to. Orang Betawi and Orang Jakarta are perceived of as different categories of people despite the existing overlaps and ascriptive ambivalences.[1] In most cases it is clear from the discursive and social context which category is being referred to. However, misunderstandings are predetermined and often people identified as Jakartan (Orang Jakarta) will point out they are, however, not Betawi, and Betawi will feel the need to clarify they are not just Jakartan, but Jakarta Asli/Betawi.

The ambivalence connected with the designations Orang Betawi and Orang Jakarta is largely based on the fact that both have various ethnic and transethnic connotations that may supplement, but also challenge and contradict one another and cause boundaries between them to be challenged and contested.

In 1984 a Betawi pavilion (*Anjungan Betawi*) was constructed in the *Taman Mini Indonesia Indah* (TMII). There had only been an *Anjungan Jakarta* before, a Jakartan pavilion, which the Betawi felt did not adequately represent them. A committee representing a range of Betawi organizations was established to organize the construction of a typical Betawi house. As this example shows, Betawi is not perceived of as (more or less) identical with (Orang) Jakarta. Rather, differentiation and separate representation is aimed at, as exemplified in the TMII in form of a specific house and territory as symbols of Betawi uniqueness.

Seni-Budaya Betawi (SBB; Wijaya 1976), the publication outlining a programme of state support for the Betawi (see above), shows that the discourse Orang Betawi versus Orang Jakarta has long been crucial for the assessment of the relationship between ethnic, local and national identifications in Jakarta (and beyond). In the (published) individual papers and the follow-up discussions, the question as to whether it might not be sensible to replace the designation Orang Betawi with that of Orang Jakarta is raised repeatedly, claiming that Orang Betawi has a negative connotation associated with backwardness and a lack of education and modernity (SBB: 55ff.). The preference of the official side (moderator) quickly becomes clear.

> Since there are two conceptions regarding the use of the terms Jakarta and Betawi, this question will have to be discussed separately.... As far as the terminology Jakarta and Betawi is concerned, there are positions both pro and contra. This matter has to be decided. Obviously a number of those participating here think that the term Betawi can continue to be used (which is also the opinion of the Governor of the DKI) (SBB: 57).[2]

From the contributions made by the official moderators – who can be presumed to be supportive of the governor – it becomes obvious what the governor considers the correct decision and that those who (continue to) oppose the use of the term Betawi will also be opposing his will. Why is the term Betawi preferred by representatives of the state and major state actors? Several explanations can be found in or concluded from the individual papers and the question-answer sessions following them.

In different articles of the programme it is argued that the term Betawi should be used not primarily as the designation of an ethnic but rather of a geographic group of people (SBB: 73) on account of the heterogeneous origins of the Betawi and Jakarta(ns) (SBB: 72). Jakartans and Betawi are not differentiated and all Jakartans are in effect (also) classified as Betawi. The fact that the Betawi consider themselves and are considered by others to be an ethnic variant of Jakartans is ignored.

The special promotion of the Betawi is justified by state institutions as a means of promoting the indigenous and traditional culture of Jakarta and preventing it from dying out. Thus, the state classifies the Betawi as a traditional variant of Jakartan culture and identity rather than as an ethnic group, thereby trying to avoid the impression of one ethnic group being preferred over others and to create the impression that the promotion of the Betawi is a means of enabling all Jakartans to preserve the traditions of their city. As a DKI Jakarta official told me: 'The culture of the Betawi is the traditional culture of Jakarta. It belongs to all people in Jakarta. What is at stake here is preserving or reviving the traditional image of Jakarta, for all Jakartans, for all Indonesians.' Whereas the term Betawi is retained, its meaning is de-ethnicized in that the (promoted) traditions classified as Betawi are presented as belonging to all Jakartans irrespective of ethnic identities. Whereas Betawi is associated with history and tradition, Jakarta is associated with the present and modern life. Because the aim of cultural promotion in the sense outlined above is to imbue Jakarta with a sense of autochthonous history and tradition it would make little sense to replace the traditional term Betawi with the modern term Orang Jakarta.

The promotion of tourism also plays an important role for investing Jakarta with tradition via Betawi culture and for the preference for the term Betawi over that of Orang Jakarta. This becomes evident in the following extract from a conversation I had with a DKI Jakarta official.[3]

IN: We want more tourists to come to Jakarta rather than just changing flights here. And tourists are interested in traditions, not just shopping. This is why it is important that we show them the traditions of Jakarta. This includes the people who embody these traditions. In Jakarta these people are the Betawi. Who else should it be?

JK: Is that why you say Betawi and not Orang Jakarta?

IN: No, I say Betawi because that is the name of Jakarta's indigenous inhabitants [*Jakarta asli*]. What tourist wants to see Orang Jakarta? (laughs). That's nothing special. Tourists want to see something of the traditions of a country or a city. And the only people here who still have traditions are the Betawi. (Pause) Well, perhaps other people too, but those are traditions from other places, not from Jakarta.

JK: You just referred to the Jakarta Asli. Why don't the Betawi simply call themselves Jakarta Asli? You said that the culture of the Betawi is the culture of all inhabitants of Jakarta and that everyone gains from the promotion of the Betawi. If the term Jakarta Asli was used, perhaps everyone would feel they were being included.

IN: One could also say Jakarta Asli but the traditional term is Betawi, and that's why I think one should say Betawi. Furthermore, one could also refer to people as Jakarta Asli who have been in Jakarta for many generations but are nevertheless not Betawi. Therefore, Betawi is clearer. And, as I've said, it is important that there are traditions and people who embody these traditions. When one hears Betawi one thinks of tradition; when one hears Jakarta one thinks of modern life and a large city and pollution.

The following extract from a conversation I had with a young DKI Jakarta official who was an uncompromising supporter of the synonymization of Orang Jakarta and Betawi reveals some of the underlying assumptions concerning different subcategories of Jakarta.

JK: What is the difference between Orang Jakarta and Orang Betawi then?
IN: We are all Orang Jakarta, including the Orang Betawi. My parents come from Lampung [Sumatra], but I am Orang Jakarta.
JK: And you are also Orang Lampung?
IN: My parents are from Lampung. So my roots are in Sumatra. But I grew up here, so I am Orang Jakarta.
JK: Are you also Orang Betawi?
IN: We are all Orang Betawi.
JK: All those living in Jakarta are Orang Betawi?
IN: Yes, all those who have been born and grown up here. And those now arriving will also become Orang Jakarta in the course of time.
JK: Will they also become Orang Betawi?
IN: That's the same thing.
JK: But many people think there are differences. They say that the Betawi are those descended from people who already lived here when Jakarta was still called Batavia.
IN: They are the Betawi Asli.

Ethnic connotations with Betawi are being pushed into the background to promote a transethnic Jakartan identity and avoid the impression that a particular ethnic group – namely the Betawi – is being favoured by the state. By classifying all Betawi as Orang Jakarta and all Orang Jakarta as Betawi, the impression is created that in fact all people in Jakarta are being promoted. In this view, the Asli variant of the (Orang) Betawi is also the Asli variant of all Orang Jakarta.

Official statements include ethnic and transethnic notions of Betawi identity that are voiced in relation to the given political context. Sometimes, the indigeneity of the Betawi is foregrounded, their historical importance for the city and their role as the bearers of traditional Jakartan culture. Other times, the transethnic quality of Betawi-ness is emphasized in that Betawi culture is defined as the culture of all those living in Jakarta. Due to its heterogeneity of origin, Betawi culture allows for both ethnic and transethnic references.

The discourse around the designations Orang Betawi and Orang Jakarta also takes place in informal social settings and in society at large. However, although arguments and definitions are taken up that have been disseminated by the government, the media and different Betawi experts and activists, the dogmatic attitude of some of the latter is usually not carried over. Rather, attitudes and arguments depend on and relate to concrete social relationships, and specific historical and personal experiences.

Betawi (Asli) versus *Pendatang*

The distinction between the Betawi and other groups living in Jakarta is based primarily on – the more or less rigid – classification of the Betawi as the indigenous population of Jakarta on the one hand and all others living in Jakarta as *pendatang*, or migrants, on the other.[4]

The differentiation between *pendatang* and Betawi has its antecedents in colonial society. Those classified as natives in Batavia (and later also in the *Ommelanden*) were neither Europeans nor Asians of foreign origin (*Vreemden Oosterlingen*). They often had Indonesian origins but did not belong to the group of Batavia's precolonial natives, namely the Sundanese and the (ethnic) Javanese who had been banned from the city by the Dutch and replaced by only relative natives from islands beyond Java, who then became the Betawi and the new natives – the new *orang asli* – of Batavia, a status they have maintained ever since and that, until recently, has rarely been contested by common folks and experts alike. Some voices:

> The Betawenese are the natives of Jakarta (Dhofier 1976: 20).
>
> Historically, the Betawi people were the indigenous people of Jakarta or the descendants of the indigenous people of Jakarta in contrast to the Jakartan people which refers to all Jakartan dwellers (Shahab 1994: 47).
>
> Betawi is the name of the indigenous ethnic group [*suku bangsa*] living in the DKI Jakarta and environs ... The name Betawi derives from the word Batavia (Lexicon: 337).[5]
>
> The Orang Betawi are one of the ethnic groups of Indonesia. It is the ethnic group whose home is Jakarta (civil servant, *Dinas Kebudayaan* DKI Jakarta).[6]
>
> The dominant view is that the Betawi are the descendants either of slaves or of predominantly lower class free Asians in Batavia (Nas and Grijns 2000: 12).

The Betawi are usually considered to be the only real original inhabitants of Jakarta despite the fact that the Sundanese in particular had already settled the area prior to the Betawi. Their area of ethnic origin, however, is commonly regarded to be West Java, not Jakarta. A Betawi explained this situation to me as follows:

> The Betawi own Jakarta; it is their land. Like the Sundanese – West Java belongs to them. And the people from Sulawesi – Sulawesi belongs to them. Each ethnic group has its own land, the land the group comes from. And the Betawi only have Jakarta and the surroundings of Jakarta. So we are the real natives here [*suku bangsa asli*].

Another explanation that links ethnic identity and indigeneity with the belonging to and the possession of a particular territory was provided by a man who classified himself both as Sundanese and Orang Jakarta:

> The Sundanese were already here earlier, but our own land is West Java. Therefore it's okay when the Betawi say that Jakarta is their land. After all they come from here. They came into being here. Without Jakarta there wouldn't be any Betawi. And Jakarta without the Betawi? That would be a land without a people.

Hence, just as all groups defined in ethnic terms are assigned a certain territory, so are the Betawi assigned Jakarta. Without territory the Betawi would not be a real ethnic group, and without an ethnic population Jakarta would not be a real (social) place.

Although most Betawi tend to regard all non-Betawi as *pendatang*, the Sundanese are accorded a special status. Apart from having settled the area extensively for so long, there have also been close social ties between the Betawi and the Sundanese since colonial times, particularly in what used to be the *Ommelanden*. A Betawi man married to a Sundanese woman explained the close connection between the Betawi and the Sundanese as follows:

> The Sundanese and the Betawi are rather close because they are culturally similar, they have both lived here for a long time. We often marry Sundanese and we live together in the same *kampung*. Although the Sundanese are not as closely linked with Jakarta as the Betawi, because they are from West Java and have their origins there, they are more closely tied to Jakarta than the Javanese or people from Sumatra or the other islands.

There are also groups in North and West Jakarta, in Tangerang and in small pockets on the southern outskirts of Jakarta that classify themselves as Betawi Sunda. Referring to a village in the south of Jakarta, Koentjaraningrat writes:

> The villagers believe that their ancestors were recruited as workers by the first landlord, Tuan Amen [a Dutchman], from the area to the north as well as from the Bogor area to the south. Therefore, they believe that they are of mixed Jakartan and Sundanese descent (Koentjaraningrat 1973: 14).

Even where no Sunda-specific subgroup of Betawi has developed, the boundaries between the Sundanese and the Betawi are often fluid. A young man living in Kebun Kacang, an inner-city *kampung*, explained to me:

> I should probably say I'm Sundanese because my great-grandparents came from Bandung to Jakarta. But my grandfather married a genuine Betawi woman [*perempuan Betawi Asli*], my grandmother. My father is half Betawi, half Sunda, my mother half Sunda, half Javanese. But we've always lived among Betawi. The people in the area I grew up in often call themselves Betawi Sunda because they're mixed. My mother often says, 'Actually I am Javanese.' But we are more like the Betawi because we have adopted their culture, since they are the genuine Betawi and have always lived here. Only my mother still has strong contacts with her family and is not really a Betawi. But I see myself more as a Betawi, as a modern Betawi.

The classification of the Betawi as the indigenous population of Jakarta, as *orang asli Jakarta*, is confirmed by state institutions (and publications). In official brochures and tourist-information material, which is also disseminated via the Internet, the Orang Betawi are presented as the original inhabitants of Jakarta: 'The city's indigenous people, Orang Betawi, emerged from the melting pot of races, ethnic groups and cultures of Indonesia.'[7]

However, despite the fact that up to date *pendatang* are mostly considered to include all those not belonging to the group of the Betawi, more subtle differentiations are increasingly being made both by the Betawi and by those designated as *pendatang*. It seems that *pendatang* increasingly refers only to those who have migrated to Jakarta relatively recently, whereas people who have been living in Jakarta for a long time are regarded and referred to as residents of Jakarta (*penduduk Jakarta*) or as Orang Jakarta. A Betawi who lived close by to both new immigrants and long-term Jakarta residents commented on this distinction as follows:

> I don't like the term *pendatang*. You can use it to refer to people who are very new here but not those who have always been here. They belong to Jakarta; they are not *pendatang* anymore. If you have lived here a long time you are no longer *pendatang* but a resident of Jakarta [*penduduk Jakarta*]. It doesn't matter where you came from originally.

Pendatang status thus recedes into the background the longer a person has lived in Jakarta. As well, a person's lifestyle and attitudes matter in determining his or her position as *penduduk* and *pendatang*. Anyone can undergo a process of Jakartanization (*Jakartanisasi*). Jakartanization, however, is often associated with the loss of one's identity of origin, as a young woman pointed out to me: 'Many *pendatang* become Orang Jakarta when they live here for a long time and lose contact with their origins. Thus, although they are *pendatang* because they come from somewhere else, they actually become Orang Jakarta.'

Betawi-ization of *pendatang* may also take place. From the viewpoint of the Betawi, it is above all contact between *pendatang* and themselves that is a basis for Betawi-ization. An older man noted: 'When someone new comes to Jakarta and lives in an area where there are many Betawi, he will often become like a Betawi.' However, the differentiation between Betawi Asli and Betawi is upheld, particularly in areas that experience increasing levels of immigration. Aversion against newcomers has long been quite pronounced, especially where immigrants achieved a certain degree of prosperity in a relatively short time:

> The relationship between the Betawenese and newcomers in the fringe areas of Jakarta have been coloured with tensions and conflicts. The Betawenese are said to be under-privileged and deprived, and to feel that they are being 'pushed out' by wealthy newcomers (Dhofier 1976: 34).[8]

A Betawi man (48) in Condet told me:[9]

> For the *pendatang* we are poor, backward natives [*orang asli*]. They would prefer it if we weren't here at all. But we were here first. They have to adapt. If they don't, then we avoid all contact with them. We do not want to become like them and we do not want our children to become like them.

Conversely, such a newcomer complained about the situation as follows: 'They always keep to themselves. It doesn't matter what you do. If you want to become friendly with them you first have to become like them. But who wants to do that?'

The relationships that develop between Betawi and *pendatang* are thus also dependent on the social and economic conditions characterizing their coexistence. The fact that the two groups have long lived together in the inner-city *kampung* has resulted in relations being relatively relaxed. It has also led to many Betawi preferring to designate themselves as Jakarta Asli rather than as Betawi to avoid conspicuously differentiating themselves from their neighbours by referring to the ethnic quality of their Jakartan identity. Adding Asli to Betawi underscores the authenticity of the Betawi in question. As one young man told me:

> Betawi are those whose ancestors were already Betawi when the Dutch were governing in Batavia. They lived in Batavia and the surroundings of Batavia. They originated from different groups, which mixed and be-

came Betawi. Only those who are descendants of Betawi are genuine Betawi [*Betawi Asli*].

According to this definition those who are not descendants of Batavia Betawi cannot be classified as Betawi (*asli*), a view held by many Betawi but also by others, including people who have always lived in Jakarta. A thirty-four-year-old man, whose parents originate from Sumatra and who classified himself as 'Orang Jakarta from Sumatra' [*Orang Jakarta dari Sumatra*], told me:

> Even if I would like to say I am Betawi, I cannot. Although Jakarta is my place of birth and the city I grew up in and now live and work, I know that I am not a Betawi, that is, not a member of the indigenous ethnic group. I know that and the Betawi know it too. In their view, I am and remain a *pendatang*.

Although the boundaries between the Betawi (whether *asli* or not) and other groups are considered more open by many, Betawi with roots dating back to Batavia are regarded as particularly genuine particularly among the more urban Betawi. The more peripheral Betawi tend to prioritize the practice of cultural traditions and religious devoutness as major criteria for Betawi authenticity.[10] Such internal differentiations among the Betawi will be dealt with in more depth in the following chapter. For now, it is enough to point out that the authenticity of Betawi identity is associated with both origin-oriented and sociocultural features, which in turn are associated with particular territories.

Betawi versus Betawi Asli: Ethnic References With and Without 'Asli'

As mentioned earlier on, the term *Asli* is sometimes suffixed to the term Betawi to emphasize the latter's authenticity. Thus, a Betawi Asli is considered a particularly genuine Betawi. All Betawi Asli also understand themselves as Jakarta Asli, as genuine Jakartans. From this point of view, Betawi Asli and Jakarta Asli are identical.

The criteria used as a benchmark of Betawi authenticity are descent and specific social and cultural features. Betawi satisfying both criteria are regarded as particularly authentic. A woman whose father is Betawi and whose mother is Sundanese classified herself as 'somewhere in-between' and explained to me:

> A Betawi Asli is someone who is descended from the Betawi who have always been in Jakarta. My father is a Betawi Asli. I'm not, because I'm mixed. A Betawi Asli is also very familiar with Betawi traditions, he knows the real traditions. He speaks Betawi and prays five times a day. Religion is more important to him than schooling and more important

than money. The Betawi Asli are fairly conservative and always want everything to remain as it is, even in Jakarta.

Betawi Asli is a designation commonly reserved for people who are indigenous in the sense that their Betawi-ness dates back to Batavia. However, it is also common for people to be described as Betawi (without the addition of *Asli*) whose great-great-great-grandparents were not Betawi but whose families have lived in Jakarta for several generations, have mixed with Betawi and have adopted the latter's lifestyle. They are assumed to have lost their original ethnic identity at some point, a loss that is associated with removal and estrangement from a primary origin. Social and cultural characteristics are also significant, particularly where they also function as a kind of compensation for the absence of genuine descent. In this context, less importance is placed on a knowledge of old Betawi traditions than, for instance, use of the Betawi dialect, membership of the working class and the devout practice of Islam. Hence, it is a long-term social and cultural association with Jakarta and the Betawi rather than the criterion of descent that is pivotal to this understanding of Betawi-ness.

The following extract from a conversation I had with a young man illustrates that an often implicit distinction is made between Betawi and Betawi Asli.

JK: And what would you describe yourself as?
IN: As Betawi, because my family has already lived in Jakarta for four generations. At some point one of my ancestors came to Jakarta from Sumatra. He married a Sundanese woman. But when you have lived in Jakarta for four generations, then you are Betawi.
JK: So your forefathers were not Betawi?
IN: No, they came from Sumatra and West Java. But they became Betawi in Jakarta.
JK: But at some stage all Betawi were something other than Betawi and then became Betawi.
IN: No, the Betawi Asli were always Betawi. Earlier, in Batavia.
JK: How do you mean earlier?
IN: Earlier, when the Dutch were there.
JK: But if your ancestors were here four generations ago, then that means the Dutch were also still here and Jakarta was still called Batavia.
IN: Yes, but there were already Betawi here then and my ancestors only turned into Betawi after coming to Jakarta.
JK: I don't really understand. Is there a difference between Betawi and Betawi?
IN: Yes, the Betawi Asli are those descended from Betawi. But there are also people who only later became Betawi: they are also Betawi, but they are not Betawi Asli. They are Betawi, they are Jakarta Asli, because they have been

here so long and do not belong to any other indigenous ethnic group [*suku bangsa*].
JK: So is Jakarta Asli something different from Betawi?
IN: Sometimes. But the Betawi are of course also Jakarta Asli. But not all Jakarta Asli are Betawi Asli [laughs]. It's rather complicated, isn't it?
JK: Yes, but I think I understand. You are a Jakarta Asli and you are a Betawi, but you are not a Betawi Asli. So are you a kind of Betawi Baru?[11]
IN: Precisely. A Betawi Baru [laughs]. That's me.

This dialog shows (initially only implicitly, but anthropologists can be an insistent lot) that a distinction is drawn between those who became the first (and therefore) original and genuine Betawi (Asli) and those who only later became Betawi. The Betawi Asli are conceptualized as those who gave up their original ethnic identities and became Betawi in the initial phase of creolization that began in the early days of Batavia. Although few people are actually familiar with the details of these historical processes, they are reflected in ideas pertaining to identity-related differences that correlate with the different phases of creolization, which in turn are linked with ideas relating to who is which sort of Betawi today. According to this relatively traditional conceptualization of Betawi identity, the latter's *Asli* dimension is primarily based on genealogical descent from the first Betawi, hence, from those who made ethnogenesis happen through creolization. However, Betawi identity may also be based on social and cultural rootedness in Jakarta and on the multigenerational association and mixture with the Betawi (Asli). This conceptualization of Betawi identity is not uncontested both among the older and younger generations of Jakartans. While some of the former deny the authenticity of Betawi identity in cases where it is not based on genealogical descent, some of the latter refer to the original heterogeneity of Betawi identity and consider ethnic mixture and identity-related complexity and variability as evidence of genuine Betawi-ness. A young woman who described herself as Betawi and Orang Jakarta addressed this issue as follows:

> The Betawi Asli emerged from different ethnic groups. So when I say today that I am Betawi even though I am not descended from the very first Betawi, from the people who have always lived here, then that's actually typically Betawi, isn't it? It is typically Betawi to be mixed in origin. That is what Betawi identity was all about in the first place.

Heterogeneity of origin thus in itself contributes to facilitating an ethnic ascription as Betawi where the person concerned is not descended from the Betawi Asli. Such people may claim to be continuing the process of creolization that historically gave rise to the Betawi. What emerged in the process of creole ethnogenesis in – and as the result of – a very specific historical situation is today being claimed as typical Betawi particularly by those who regard themselves as mixed in origin and ambiguous in ethnic ascription and who would (therefore) not be considered genuine Betawi by many of those Betawi Asli who insist on genealogical reasoning and thereby on ethnic closure and on the end of creolization. The difference between these two categorical conceptualizations of Betawi authenticity is based in different emphases being put on the two major inherent dimensions of processes of creolization in general – one being initial mixture and inclusion, one being progressive closure and exclusion. Whereas the Asli-faction insists on genuine Betawi-ness being (genealogically) based on a distinct ethnic identity that resulted from an historical and concluded process of creolization, the non-Asli-faction insists on continued creolization, hence, on an ongoing tradition of mixture and inclusion as a contemporary continuation of genuine Betawi-ness. This understanding of Betawi-ness is rejected most by older Betawi who fear that the mixing of Betawi with non-Betawi will result in the loss of what they consider Betawi authenticity, a fear reflected in the following extract from a conversation with an older Betawi man.

IN: It's best if we marry Betawi so that our traditions are kept alive. Today, more and more *pendatang* are coming to Jakarta and moving into our area. This is not good for the Betawi because we will forget our own traditions.
JK: But surely the Betawi are descended from the mixture of different groups.
IN: Yes, but that was a long time ago. But today we are in the minority, so we have to be careful that mixing does not lead to us completely disappearing.
JK: There are people who say they are Betawi even though they are not Betawi Asli. They say that mixing is typical of the Betawi.
IN: Those people are not Betawi Asli. They have become Betawi, because they have been living among us. But they are not Betawi Asli. They don't know what to say they are, because they have lost their roots. So they say they are Betawi. But they have no idea what that is. They have no idea about our traditions.

In this context it is important to bear in mind that the social significance attached to ethnic identity by the large majority of Indonesians means that the absence of ethnic identity – the 'loss of (ethnic) roots' – cannot simply be remedied by adopting another, non-ethnic identity (cf. Bruner 1974; Skinner 1959). This has ramifications for most people who have lived in Jakarta all their lives, who do not speak their ethnic language, know little about their ethnic traditions and have no socially relevant kin ties beyond Jakarta. One way of re-asserting an ethnic identity is to undergo ethnic conversion by way of marriage to a person who is clearly defined in ethnic terms. However, for people who identify primarily with Jakarta due to the fact that they have grown up there and have roots in the city extending back over several generations the most attractive and authentic option lies in ethnicizing their Jakartan identity. However, an ethnicization of Jakartan identity is only possible by adopting a Betawi identity, because Jakartan identity represents an identity of ethnic reference only in its Betawi variant. People or groups who classify themselves primarily as Jakartan and who have no additional identity of ethnic reference can thus lend their Jakartan identity an ethnic or quasi-ethnic quality by including themselves in the Betawi category. Although Betawi-ness may still be associated with unfavourable stereotypes, it remains a better option to be a Betawi than to have no ethnic identity at all. It is in this context of ambiguous self-ascriptions that Betawi-ness is being corrected, renewed and shifted in the direction of modernity, as exemplified in the following conversation with a young man.

JK: You sometimes refer to Betawi Asli, sometimes to Betawi. Is there a difference?

IN: The Betawi Asli are Betawi who still live in a traditional way. The other Betawi are people who no longer really belong to the group from which they are originally descended. They become Betawi in the same way as the first Betawi became Betawi because like them they have lost their original roots. But these Betawi are a different type of Betawi, not traditional but modern and progressive. I am one of those Betawi, but I am not a Betawi Asli.

JK: Why do you call these people and yourself Orang Betawi then and not, for instance, Orang Jakarta?

IN: I think you could also say Orang Jakarta. But I also think that in many ways they are like the Betawi. They are also impertinent, don't let themselves get talked into things and they talk like the Betawi. But actually … how should I put this – Orang Jakarta are all those who have lived here for a long time and … how should I put it? But not all the people living here are Jakarta Asli. That's why I think it's better to say Betawi.

JK: Are the people you're referring to a new type of Betawi, some type of Betawi Baru?

IN: Yes, precisely [laughs]. That's what I mean. Precisely. Betawi Baru. And Orang Jakarta are all those who were born here, but they are not all genuine Orang Jakarta to the degree the Betawi are. Betawi Baru … like me. Betawi Baru, that's good.

This young man perceives of Betawi identity primarily in terms of specific features concerning social class and personality – such as straightforwardness, impertinence, self-reliance, down-to-earthness and a proletarian, working-class consciousness. Although he does not classify himself as Betawi Asli he perceives of himself as Betawi due to his own social and cultural rootedness in Jakarta and on the basis of what he considers typical Betawi features. He considers himself a typical Jakartan but at the same time ethnicizes his Jakartan identity by categorizing it as Betawi (as well).

Betawi as Jakarta Asli

Because the Betawi see themselves as the original inhabitants of Jakarta, it is hardly surprising that they also regard themselves as (genuine) Jakartans – as Orang Jakarta (Asli). A middle-aged Betawi commented: 'As Betawi we are Orang Jakarta, Jakarta Asli, established Betawi. The Betawi are the original ethnic group that has always resided here. We are thus Jakarta Asli and our culture is the traditional culture of Jakarta.'

However, there are also Betawi who prefer not to call themselves Betawi but rather Orang Jakarta or Jakarta Asli. There are different reasons for this. One is that Betawi is linked with the period of colonial rule. Betawi is a derivation from Batavia, the name given to the city by the Dutch. Those who want to avoid being linked with Batavia and the colonial period thus often reject the term Betawi and favour the term 'Orang Jakarta (Asli): 'Betawi is considered to be associated with colonialism and can be seen as a rude word so that some Betawi are not prepared to be called Betawi, but pronounce themselves as Jakartans, instead' (Shahab 1994: 47). A Betawi woman I spoke to expressed the following opinion on the subject: 'Betawi is not a good or appropriate term for us. We are not residents of Batavia but of Jakarta. Batavia is the name given to the city by the *orang kompeni*.[12] It is not an Indonesian name. I am a Jakarta Asli.'

At the same time, the colonial period is related to slavery and to the historical link between enslavement and the emergence of the Betawi. Many Betawi deny that (some of) their ancestors were slaves. In some cases this denial of historical facts is accompanied by a denial of the link between the Betawi of the present and the Betawi of the past: 'I am not a Betawi because the Betawi were those who lived in Batavia. There are people who claim the Betawi were slaves. But that means that I can't be Betawi because I am not descended from slaves' (twenty-four-year-old man).

The negative stereotypes still associated with the Betawi provide yet another reason for the designation Orang Jakarta being preferred. In particular many younger, educated Betawi emphasize that they regard themselves as Orang Jakarta rather than as Betawi because they cannot identify social and culturally with what is regarded as typically Betawi. As one young man (twenty-three) explained, 'I am a modern and educated person. I go to UI,[13] I speak English, I seldom go to the mosque and I drink beer. A real Betawi is different from me. I'm not at all familiar with Betawi traditions. This is why I see myself more as an Orang Jakarta. Betawi doesn't apply to me.'

Social and economic points of view also play a role in the preference for designating oneself as Orang Jakarta rather than as Betawi:

> I know that there are an increasing number of Betawi associations in which Betawi traditions are fostered and a lot of value is placed on be-

ing Betawi. I sell *sate*[14] to all kinds of people regardless of whether they are Sunda, Betawi or from Sulawesi. However, I think we poor people should understand ourselves as Orang Jakarta and work together to improve our situation (thirty-six-year-old man).

This man thus emphasizes a proletarian consciousness, which is regarded as typically Betawi. At the same time it is this consciousness that informs his rejection of the ethnonym Betawi.

A further reason for the preference for the designation Orang Jakarta is linked with the fact that Jakarta is a culturally diverse city in which interethnic relationships are a normal aspect of social life. Today, the Betawi living in inner-city *kampung,* and increasingly also those living on the city outskirts, live among people of different ethnic origins. Interethnic marriages as well as social and economic interaction are common features of everyday life.[15] In such an environment, it often seems to make little sense to claim a special status as Betawi, just as it makes little sense to delimit oneself from one's own family in terms of ethnic boundaries. Kin relations, social interaction and economic exigencies are often far more important than ethnic identifications in general. Particularly in areas where the Betawi are a minority – and this applies to most areas of Jakarta today – particularly young Betawi prefer to designate themselves as Orang Jakarta because this stresses commonalities rather than differences. They do not want to be perceived as more original and more genuine Jakartans, but as integrated and recognized members of an ethnically heterogeneous (local) community: 'I'm actually Betawi and my wife is Sunda. But we are both Orang Jakarta and so are our children. I think it's better to say that we are both Orang Jakarta and not members of different groups. The difference really isn't important. We are both Orang Jakarta and our children are too' (thirty-four-year-old man).

The Pidgin Potential of Betawi Culture and Identity

Based on their heterogeneous origins, Betawi culture and identity also allow for transethnic identifications. As a young Sundanese woman explained: 'The Betawi are mixed, they are, so to speak, a melting pot. For example, the Betawi language contains lots of Sunda words. When I hear it, I know that the Betawi and the Sundanese are related, that they have common roots. That's why I'm actually very fond of the Betawi.'

It seems that the more one can identify – or assume – elements of one's own ethnic background in Betawi culture, the easier it is to (partially) identify with it. Thus, the Sundanese, Balinese and Chinese, whose ancestors played a decisive role in the historical formation of the Betawi, generally feel closer to the Betawi than, say, the Javanese and the Batak.[16]

However, it is not merely the recognition of specific ethnic features but also the general knowledge about the Betawi's heterogeneity of origin as such that facilitates transethnic identification – as well as the political propagation of Betawi culture and identity as a transethnically connecting link. A functionary in the cultural department of the DKI Jakarta, assessed this situation as follows:

> It is important for people to understand that the Betawi are a 'melting pot' and not merely a *suku bangsa,* to understand that everyone has a share in their culture. Irrespective of the fact that, as *suku bangsa,* the Betawi have of course their own culture. They are mixed and that is something we have to communicate. Then it is easier to make Betawi culture accessible and comprehensible for everyone. Betawi culture belongs to all people in Jakarta.

More recently, the term creole is being used more frequently when referring to the Betawi:

> Batavia was a meeting point for traders of various origins, many of whom settled and intermarried with the Malay natives and formed a unique Creole culture and identity.... Since cultures evolve over time, and the Betawi are a Creole people to begin with, defining the Betawi identity has never been an easy task (Susetyo 2011).[17]

This attitude is increasingly finding echoes in the wider population. To be sure, there are still many people in Jakarta who associate the Betawi above all with backwardness and a lack of education. However, there are also an increasing number of (young) people who associate the Betawi with heterogeneity, mixture and ambiguity – features that reflect their own experiences of urban life and which are therefore instrumental in generating transethnic connections and identifications. As one young man told me:

> The Betawi are mixed. Their culture is mixed; it has all kinds of features that come from somewhere else. It's typical for Jakarta that everything is mixed, we all experience this every day. So in fact all of us are in some sense Betawi, because we continue to mix. I'm actually from Bandung and I'm proud of that. But the Betawi fit to Jakarta because they are mixed. I mean the Betawi here in the city. Those further out, I think, are not as open. They want to keep to themselves more.

In the contemporary context of urban life, Betawi identity, which is not associated with urban modernity when referring to the Betawi in ethnic – *suku bangsa* –

terms, can thus be recontextualized in such a way that it symbolizes modern diversity and transethnic interaction. Betawi-ness as a transethnic concept is thus associated with meanings other than those associated with the Betawi as an ethnic category of people. In its transethnic contextualization one particular ethnic feature of the Betawi – namely heterogeneity – is extracted from its ethnic context – i.e., de-ethnicized – and invested with new, modern meaning.

One may wonder, why, instead of conceptually transforming and altering Betawi-ness in such a transethnicizing manner, heterogeneity is not simply referred to in terms of Jakartan – or urban, modern, contemporary – identity. This, I believe, has to do with the fact that Indonesian society – as other societies in which ethnic identifications are considered important dimensions of social organization and self-esteem – renders identifications more social and political relevance and power when imbued with some degree of ethnic and territorial rootedness. In the mega-city of Jakarta, it is (only) the people and the culture classified as Betawi that can symbolize and represent (Jakartan) authenticity because it is (only) the Betawi who are considered indigenous and territorially rooted in Jakarta. Hence, it is not least the ethnic dimension of Betawi culture and identity that allows the Betawi's creole background – and the recontextualized notion of heterogeneity attached to it – to function as a powerful transethnic link among Jakartans. The transethnic potential of Betawi identity also depends on its ethnic potential, namely on the Betawi being considered a *suku bangsa*, an indigenous ethnic group.

Orang Jakarta as a Category of Urban Identification

The meaning of Orang Jakarta depends on the situation and context in which it is used. As explained earlier on, Orang Jakarta (Asli) is often used synonymously with Orang Betawi (Asli) when referring to the ethnic category of people. However, Orang Jakarta is also used to refer to all those who are considered Jakartans without being Betawi. Orang Jakarta then refers to those who consider Jakarta their home and who share specific social, cultural, linguistic features and styles. Being Orang Jakarta links people across specific ethnic and local affiliations. Responding to my question concerning her feelings of home and belonging, a young female student explained:

> I am Orang Jakarta because I have grown up here and have never lived anywhere else. This is my home. Nevertheless, I am Minangkabau and I always will be. So will my children. Even though we've never lived there. That's were our roots are, our ethnic roots. I am proud to be Minangkabau. That's something special. Being Orang Jakarta is nothing special.

The meanings of Orang Jakarta as a primarily urban category of identification reveal themselves first and foremost at the level of individuals and social groups.

Being Orang Jakarta then does not involve an ethnic reference (i.e., as Orang Betawi). Rather, a person is considered Orang Jakarta on the basis of his or her social and cultural rootedness in Jakarta and his or her orientation towards urban ways of life, which reveal themselves in certain views, behaviours and styles, that are considered typical of contemporary Jakarta(ns).

The phenomenon Orang Jakarta seems to have predated the explicit category Orang Jakarta. A young woman who introduced herself to me as Orang Jakarta and Orang Lampung (Sumatra) told me: 'I don't think Orang Jakarta have existed for that long, perhaps since independence or later. Because earlier only Orang Betawi were Orang Jakarta. Everyone else was *pendatang*.'

It is the association with the Betawi that is responsible for Jakartan identity finding it difficult to find its name. The transethnic Orang Jakarta does not want to be regarded as (ethnic) Betawi. Therefore people will often explicitly point out that they are a different type of Orang Jakarta. Two examples:

> I am Orang Jakarta but not Betawi. The Betawi often say they are Orang Jakarta. But there are different kinds of Orang Jakarta. I'm not a Betawi, not a Jakarta Asli. Because I'm from Sulawesi … well, my parents are (man, twenty-three).

> In some ways I think the term Orang Jakarta is really good, because that is what I actually am. But I don't like it when someone thinks I'm Betawi. Because I'm not. I'm a Javanese. But of course, I am Orang Jakarta (woman, twenty-four).

The conceptual ambiguity of the designations Orang Betawi and Orang Jakarta is a key reason for many people shying away from referring to themselves as Orang Jakarta. They are afraid that this will lead them to being taken for Betawi. As a young woman explained to me:

> I am actually a typical Orang Jakarta. I am certainly not a Betawi Asli. Never! I am a modern, young woman and not one of these conservative, old-fashioned Betawi who have no interest in modern life. That's why I often avoid saying I am Orang Jakarta, because this might make people think I am Betawi.

This reservation towards referring to oneself as Orang Jakarta can be problematic and often leads people to claim an ethnic identity that has actually lost its meaning for them: 'Aside from the Betawi (native Jakartans), if you were to ask people on a Jakarta street where they came from, you can rest assured that most would give the name of just about anywhere other than the capital, even if they were born in Jakarta.'[18] Thus, although the claim to an ethnic identity may express actual ties with an ethnic group (outside Jakarta), it may also be a strategy to avoid giving the impression of lacking ethnic identity or to avoid being classified as Betawi. The following statement by a young woman may help to illustrate the dilemma:

> In Indonesia one must be the member of an ethnic group because that's the way things are. So I simply say that I come from Sulawesi even though only my grandmother came from there. What else can I say? Orang Jakarta would be correct, but that isn't an ethnic group, except if someone is an Orang Jakarta Asli. But I'm not. I'm not a Betawi.

The fact that people born and raised in Jakarta continue to designate themselves – for example – as Sulawesian is often misunderstood in that it is assumed to indicate a continued importance of a person's original ethnic identity. However, the meaning of such designations often derives from the fact that ethnic affinity is an important element of social identity and that the category Orang Jakarta has not (yet) acquired an ethnic reference of its own, i.e., an ethnic reference not associated with the Betawi.

However, there are also many people who reject ethnic categorizations or see them as irrelevant. They tend to refer to themselves as Orang Jakarta without supplementing this with an ethnic classification. In most cases these people are young and regard ethnic ascription as an unnecessary evil that divides people from one another and creates enmities.

> I am Orang Jakarta because I live and have grown up here, because I'm typically Jakartan. I'm a modern person and I don't really know much about ethnic traditions. I respect them but I can't really relate to them. And anyway it's clear that it's not a good thing when people always emphasize that they belong to this or that ethnic group. That just results in conflict and war (twenty-year-old man).

Many people do not feel (or no longer feel) they belong to a particular ethnic group and reject the idea that they should be able to identify themselves in ethnic terms – as one young man who was obviously irritated by my question concerning his ethnic identity. He replied: '*Suku bangsa, suku bangsa,* I really don't care. My mother was born in Jakarta, my father too. We are not *suku bangsa*. I could say we are Betawi because we were born here, but that also isn't true. We don't have anything to do with them.'

Among those who classify themselves as Orang Jakarta while rejecting ethnic categories, it is common to emphasize national (besides Jakartan) identity. Just as ethnic categories are seen as outdated and anti-modern, national identification is seen as modern and progressive: 'I feel that as Orang Jakarta we are above all Indonesians, modern Indonesians. Whether or not I'm a member of an ethnic group [*suku bangsa*] is really irrelevant. But what is important is that I am an Indonesian, just as you are a German. That is something which is important for you, too' (man, twenty).[19]

Creolization of Jakartan Identity?

There are indications that, beyond the group of the Betawi, the category Orang Jakarta is being subject to varying degrees of creolization – hence, a process of ethnicization and indigenization, in the course of which different ethnic identities of origin (i.e., Sunda, Sulawesi, Chinese, etc.) are being substituted by a new, common identity (i.e., Orang Jakarta) linked to the locality (i.e., Jakarta) within which it emerges. This process seems to be triggered by the desire to acquire an ethnic identity – or something that comes close to it – which is felt to be (more) authentic. The following extract from an interview with a young man (twenty-seven) attests to this observation.

JK: You describe yourself as Orang Jakarta and say you are not Betawi and also not Betawi Baru or a member of some other ethnic group. So you don't belong to any ethnic group?
IN: Not really. But a little bit. The people who have lived here for many generations and do not have any homeland other than Jakarta are somewhat similar. But they are not an indigenous ethnic group [*suku bangsa*]. Maybe later. [He thinks for several seconds] That's a good idea. A really good idea.
JK: What is a good idea?
IN: Well, that Orang Jakarta can also be an ethnic group like other groups. I think we should also be an ethnic group. Not traditional and so on, but modern, Jakartan.
JK: Why is that a good idea?
IN: Then we wouldn't always have to explain which ethnic group we belong to but could simply say Orang Jakarta. That would be simple. Not belonging to an ethnic group is not good in Indonesia.

Another young man, who was born and had grown up in Jakarta to parents from Sumatra, told me:

> It isn't good that we Indonesians always have to belong to an ethnic group. If you are asked in Jakarta where you come from and you answer 'from Jakarta' you are immediately asked if you are Betawi. If you say: 'No, not Betawi but from Jakarta', people immediately ask: 'So where

do you come from?' So coming from Jakarta is only enough if you are Betawi. It would be good if one could say one is from Jakarta and that would be like saying one is Javanese or Sulawesian or whatever.

There seems to be a growing desire for an independent Jakartan identity that is not devoid of ethnic reference while not being equated with being Betawi.

Tradition and Modernity in the Relationship between Orang Betawi and Orang Jakarta ... and a Miss and Mister Jakarta Pageant

The particular role of the Betawi as representatives of local, i.e., Jakartan, and national, i.e., Indonesian identity, is substantiated by state institutions who propagate that, as the indigenous inhabitants of the national capital, the Betawi play a significant role in representing Jakarta both as a city in itself and as the national capital. It is emphasized, on the one hand, that Jakarta is the capital city of all Indonesians, irrespective of specific ethnic affiliations. On the other hand, it is argued that as the indigenous inhabitants of the city the Betawi have preserved its cultural heritage and therefore deserve to be accorded a special role – namely as hosts of all people living in Jakarta.[20]

However, Jakarta is a city that is perceived as being modern rather than traditional. That tradition and modernity should not be conceived of as a dichotomy, but as mutually influencing one another seems self-evident, however, tradition is primarily understood (also in Jakarta) as encompassing representations of society and culture which are associated with historicity, intergenerational transmission and continuity, while modernity is primarily understood as encompassing representations of society and culture which are associated with change, ethnic and cultural diversity and with overcoming or transforming traditions to fit contemporary needs.

The shaping of the relationship between traditional Betawi culture and modern urbaneness is referred to in the programme for the promotion of the Betawi (SBB, see Chapter 2), where it is repeatedly emphasized that the issue at stake is not one of preserving the Betawi and their traditions but one of retaining their vitality and integrative power to benefit all people in Jakarta (SBB 32f.). It is obvious that the promoters of the Betawi are concerned with promoting – via the Betawi – Jakartan identity in general and national consciousness, interethnic relations and tourism in particular.[21] Hence, they aim at mediating and contextualizing Jakartan tradition represented by Betawi culture and identity in ways that fit the social requirements of contemporary Jakartan and Indonesian society.

One of the measures designed to meet this goal was the creation of the *None dan Abang Jakarta* (Mister and Miss Jakarta) pageant. Because Mister Jakarta has only limited significance for the issues at stake here, I will focus on the election process of Miss Jakarta only. The pageant is organized every year by the government of Jakarta and its tourism division. The procedures involved illustrate how tradition and modernity are differentiated from as well as linked with one another by means of ethnic and transethnic ascriptions and by mediating them via the notion of Betawi on the one hand and the notion of Jakarta on the other.

None is a Betawi term for a young woman, thus, the Betawi aspect of the event is already referred to in linguistic terms. However, it is the *None Jakarta* and not the *None Betawi* who is elected, hence, besides referring to the traditional (Betawi) dimension of the contest, the pageant's theme also refers to contemporary Jakarta and is open to all young women irrespective of ethnic affiliation.

I accompanied one candidate as she progressed through the competition for the *None Jakarta* 2001 and another one (less closely) in 2006. One applicant (twenty-one) was born in Jakarta to parents from Sumatra. She described her feelings of belonging as follows:

> I was born in Jakarta and Jakarta is my home. My parents come from Lampung in Sumatra, so I am somehow attached to Lampung and Sumatra, although I have only been there once. I see myself first and foremost as an Orang Jakarta – a little bit Betawi as well, but only because they are the natives of Jakarta and their traditions somehow belong to all of us in Jakarta. Furthermore, I had to familiarize myself with Betawi traditions as part of my preparation for the *None dan Abang Jakarta* competition. That made me realize that some things are regarded as Betawi that I thought of as typical for Jakarta as a whole.

The selection of candidates involves different ballots. Initially, all applicants are judged by a panel made up of representatives of the state institutions involved and a range of experts.[22] Criteria for reaching the next round include good appearance, intelligence, general education, language skills and – very importantly – knowledge of Jakarta and Betawi culture. All candidates must present themselves once in the traditional Betawi outfit and once in modern, Western dress. Depending on situation, the *None Jakarta* is expected to cut a good figure both as a *None* in the local Betawi outfit and as a modern Jakartan lady dressed in the global office look. Some interviews are conducted in English to test the candidates' language skills. Questions put to candidates regarding the culture of the Betawi focus on aspects of everyday culture such as cuisine, dress, ceremonies and dance as well as particularities of the Betawi language. The questions the candidates are asked about Jakarta focus above all on architecture, history and politics. Candidates are also expected to be able to speak competently about the significance of tourism for the development of Jakarta and Indonesia. They are asked about how they envisage the promotion of tourism in Jakarta, what aspects of Jakarta they regard as particularly interesting and how they see their role as a potential *None Jakarta* in promoting their city. Among the prizes awarded to the candidate who is ultimately crowned *None Jakarta* is a contract that obliges (or privileges) her to accompany the Governor of Jakarta over the course of a year to official events designed to promote Jakarta, particularly as a tourist destination.

The *None Jakarta* pageant provides an illustration of the ethnic and transethnic potential of Betawi-ness and publically demonstrates that urban modernity and (Betawi) traditions are both elements of contemporary Jakartan society that complement rather than contradict one another. Ethnic tradition and transethnic modernity are linked, and, in the form of the *None Jakarta*, given a highly visible and attractive appearance (Knörr 2000, 2002).

Notes

1. These boundaries are drawn by those under study and by observers alike.
2. My translation. The original Indonesian is as follows: 'Karena ada dua pendapat tentang pemakaian istilah Jakarta dan Betawi, maka akan diperbincangkan secara khusus. ... Tentang peristilahan Jakarta dan Betawi ada yang pro dan kontra. Hal ini perlu diputuskan. Ternyata sebagian perserta Pralokakarya menganggap kata Betawi tetap bisa dipakai (cokok dengan pendapat Gubernur DKI Jakarta).'
3. JK = Jacqueline Knörr, IN = informant. This applies to the entire text.
4. Lohanda (2001) points out that among the Betawi terms still exist for groups of people whose ancestors lived in Batavia and the *Ommelanden,* but who were neither Dutch nor Betawi. These include the Cina-Benteng, Belanda-Depok, and the Arab-Pekojan.
5. The lexicon in question was in a very poor condition. It was impossible to decipher the title or the year of publication. Only the page number was legible.
6. *Dinas Kebudayaan* DKI Jakarta = Cultural authority of DKI Jakarta.
7. See www.traveljakarta.com
8. Dhofier is reporting here on research conducted in Mampang Tegalparang, a neighbourhood to the southeast of the centre.
9. Condet is located in Eastern Jakarta and is one of the old *Kampung Betawi*. Despite the fact that it has been designated to serve as a preservation area for the Betawi and their culture it is nowadays ethnically heterogeneous with many migrants having moved in; see Budiati (2000).
10. On inner-city migration in Jakarta see Somantri (1995a, b).
11. *Baru* (Indonesian) = new.
12. Term for the Dutch colonial rulers derived from *Vereenigte Oostindische Companie*. Today it tends to be generally used as a derogatory or facetious reference to the Dutch.
13. UI = abbreviation for *Universitas Indonesia,* referring to the university in Depok (south of Jakarta).
14. *Saté:* meat on skewers served with a sauce.
15. Based on her research in 1989 Shahab (1994) concluded that among the inner-city Betawi the quota of interethnic marriages at that time amounted to 73 per cent. The quota of interethnic marriages within the parental generation was 30.8 per cent. By contrast, the quota of interethnic marriages among the Betawi Pinggir in Condet was only 2 per cent. Warnaen (1978) conducted a study of 591 students in Jakarta and found that 24 per cent came from ethnically mixed families. Today this quota is probably higher. Tan (1983) found that the quota of interethnic marriages per Indonesian province was between 2 and 3 per cent.

16. It is interesting to note in this context that while in historical terms the Balinese contribution to the emergence of the Betawi was significant, less reference is made to it today than to the Sundanese influence. One reason for this is that Bali and the Balinese are not associated with Islam – which most Betawi still see as a criterion of genuine Betawi identity – but with Hinduism. It is therefore probably less obvious today that the Balinese played an important role in the creolization processes that took place from the beginning of colonization onwards and in the course of which an Islamic Betawi culture was created. Furthermore, as a consequence of marriages to Dutch colonialists and other settlers, many Balinese converted to Christianity and became part of the European or Eurasian population group. Those who underwent creolization processes soon converted to Islam, became Betawi and were no longer perceived as Balinese.
17. The notion creole has recently become increasingly popular among Betawi intellectuals and in academic writings concerning the Betawi. I daresay (and have been told) this also has to do with some of my publications in which Betawi culture and identity are contextualized in terms of their creoleness.
18. In *The Jakarta Post*, 5 September 2001.
19. I do not know how this young man reached his conclusion concerning the degree of national identification on my part.
20. http://www.indo.com/destinations/betawi.html.
21. See in particular the articles by Budhinsantoso (1976) and Danandjaja (1976).
22. This group includes people from the tourism and fashion industries, teachers, journalists and others whose expertise I was not able to discern.

Chapter 4
Suku bangsa Betawi
Integration and Differentiation of Ethnic Identity

The Inner and Outer Circle of the Betawi

The social and cultural reevaluation of the Betawi due to their promotion by the state and the increased public attention they attract go along with specific strategies of intra-ethnic integration and differentiation among the Betawi.

Pauline Milone (1966) distinguished between three groups of Betawi, namely the Betawi Kota (also called Betawi Tengah), Betawi Pinggir and Betawi Udik, without, however, revealing the criteria she draws her differentiation on.[1] The Betawi Kota, Pinggir and Udik can be classified as the inner circle of the Betawi – within which the different groups are in turn categorized in terms of their proximity to the inner circle's centre. Until recently such differentiations were primarily made by outsiders, and although the Betawi were aware of them, they usually designated themselves merely as Betawi or differentiated groups with reference to certain localities (Shahab 1994). Within the inner circle, social and cultural differences are being accentuated to differentiate between different groups of Betawi. At the same time, emphasis is placed on the community and unity of all Betawi. The processes of integration and differentiation within the inner circle of the Betawi are accompanied by inclusive processes through which parts of what – from the point of view of the inner circle – constitutes the outer circle of the Betawi. This outer circle encompasses small groups that until recently have usually not been perceived or recognized by the (inner-circle) Betawi as so-called real Betawi because they are either Christians or are primarily identified with certain localities or origins that are not or only marginally associated with the Betawi. They consider themselves Betawi to varying degrees. Religion and origin are assigned meanings that operate as socially and culturally differentiating factors. These more marginal groups in terms of Betawi-ness have on their part often delimited themselves from the (inner-circle) Betawi. However, they are now finding themselves drawn into an incorporating process driven by inner-circle Betawi who are motivated not least by political interests and who invest the outer circle with particular functions that are seen as giving the Betawi more social and political weight as a whole. Conversely, the more marginal Betawi are exhibiting greater aspirations to be regarded and recognized as genuine Betawi and shift more into the direction of the centre of Betawi-ness. Furthermore, there are also processes of inclusion involving people of other ethnic identities – processes that are the result of inclusive efforts on the part of the Betawi and of specific Betawi-ization efforts on the part of the state. To some extent this outer circle also includes the Indonesian Chinese. However, their identity is negotiated and situated in a specific complex discourse which is dealt with in a separate chapter.

This talk of inner and outer circles, of central and marginal Betawi, may seem to lean towards a centralistic model that reflects the point of view of those classified as being in the centre (of the inner circle). However, this model (also) corresponds to the perceived spatial and social reality on the part of the different sorts of Betawi. The different circles are linked both with their relative proximity to the centre of Jakarta and their relative proximity to the social centre of the Betawi. As well, the increased level of public discourse regarding the Betawi has led to these originally external categories also gaining increasing currency and becoming the subject of disputes among the Betawi themselves. Despite continuing reservations against them, they are now applied in addition to their own local categories of differentiation.

Betawi Kota: The (Political) Spearhead of the Betawi

The Betawi Kota live (or have until recently lived) in the central and at the same time oldest districts of Jakarta and include descendants of the city's oldest Betawi. These central districts – Kebon Sirih, Petojo, Kramat, Kampung Bali, Tanah Abang, etc. – are all densely populated and ethnically heterogeneous. The Betawi Kota live side by side with people of diverse ethnic origins, most of whom have lived in Jakarta for a long time.

The Betawi Kota see themselves as the (most) modern and urban variant of the Betawi and as such distinguish themselves from the Betawi Pinggir and Betawi Udik, i.e., from the Betawi living on the outskirts of Jakarta (cf. Krausse 1975). The Betawi Kota are often relatively well educated and more often found in professional jobs than the general bias suggests.[2] Religious and traditional education tends to play a less prominent role among the Betawi Kota than among the Betawi living on the outskirts of Jakarta.

That the members of the upper social strata among the Betawi Kota now refer to themselves as Betawi is a relatively new development. Milone, for instance, only refers to socially disadvantaged people when she reports on the Betawi Kota.[3] In fact there have always been Betawi among the middle and upper classes, people who were well educated, well paid and engaged in urban lifestyles. However, the negative stereotype associated with the Betawi meant that well into the 1970s Betawi who were relatively prosperous and well educated were usually not recognized as Betawi and preferred to claim an alternative ethnic identity.

Betawi traditions were seldom observed in public among upper class Betawi Kota and were often rejected as inappropriate in the private sphere as well. Shahab (1994: 115) describes how middle-class Betawi Kota in particular rejected Betawi traditions on the basis that these were 'too humble and not compatible with their position'. Referring to a broadcast of a traditional Betawi wedding ceremony on Indonesian television (in the 1970s) she observed that 'they could not accept its introduction to the public since the paraphernalia looked poor and shabby' (ibid.: 116). An informant told her that although she accepted this was a Betawi tradition, its public presentation was not in the interest of the modern Betawi because 'we are now struggling to change the image of the Betawi, while her show only reaffirms the old image of poor Betawiness' (ibid.: 116).

The promotion and valorization of the Betawi by state institutions has meanwhile led to a decreasing tendency among the Betawi Kota to assign themselves to other ethnic groups. In the initial phase of their being promoted, they were eager to point out that being Betawi should not be equated with a lack of education and modernity. Therefore, public representations of the Betawi as poor, uneducated and tied to tradition were rejected. The Betawi Kota have in any case long tended to differentiate themselves more from the traditional, socially marginal Betawi on the outskirts of Jakarta than from their neighbours of different ethnicities within the inner-city residential areas they lived in. In 1975 Krausse observed:

> The kampungs of Kebon Sirih, Petojo, Kramat, Kampung Bali, and Paseban are inhabited by many families who came to Jakarta during the colonial period. ... These old-time city residents ... refer to themselves as 'Jakarta asli' (natives of Jakarta). ... The extent of urban adaptation among city-born residents is reflected in their tendency to hold more jobs of higher educational status than other groups. ... Through these occupations native Jakartans have increasingly come to see themselves as 'city dwellers' rather than villagers (Krausse 1975: 50).

In the course of the revitalization of Betawi culture, the Betawi Kota have re-adopted traditions that were once regarded as inferior, such as the type of traditional wedding ceremony referred to above. It is now becoming increasing chic to marry in Betawi style, a style that is being embraced not only by the Betawi themselves but also by people who have maintained few links with their own ethnic traditions. The qualitative upgrading of the wedding ceremony and outfit, but even more so the upgrading of the Betawi themselves, have made this Betawi style become socially respectable. One informant interviewed by Shahab (1994: 116) responded to the question as to why one of her daughters who married a non-Betawi in 1989 had a Betawi-style wedding as follows: 'They did it since there is a newly luxurious Betawi wedding tradition.'

On the other hand, there are also many not-so-stylish and not-so-(nouveau-) riche Betawi Kota who classify the new *Abang Betawi* wedding outfit, which was officially introduced as a symbol of Betawi identity by the city of Jakarta in the 1970s, as aristocratic and therefore do not accept it as genuinely Betawi. This gesture is symptomatic of the rejection of social hierarchies and aristocratic gestures by the majority of the Betawi in general and of their critical attitude towards state-prescribed identity (Shahab 2000).

Among inner-city Betawi, a distinction is sometimes made between Betawi Tengah and Betawi Kota, according to which all Betawi living in inner-city districts are Betawi Tengah, whereas only those who have obtained education, relative wealth and/or a certain level of influence are Betawi Kota. A Betawi who drew the distinction explained the difference as follows:

> Betawi Kota I call those who are modern and not as traditional as the other Betawi. Betawi Kota are those who have a say in what happens in this city and who, for example, want to ensure that we get a Betawi governor here in Jakarta. They are the people who tell the other Betawi here what they have to do to ensure we gain more influence.

Figure 4.1. Betawi wedding outfit (cover from *Jakarta Kini*, edition June 2001). The photo appeared with an article on 'Forgotten Tradition' by Veronica W. (the full surname was not supplied).

The Betawi Kota are the most likely (although not the only) Betawi to be positioned at the (political) centre of Betawi-ness. They are often active members of *Bamus*,[4] the umbrella organization of all (official) Betawi associations. While many Betawi associations – often organized along kinship lines – originally concerned themselves primarily with internal Betawi issues and shut themselves off from the outside world, the work of the *Bamus* includes the formulation and publicizing of concrete political aims and interests today.

Contrary to the early postcolonial phase, it is particularly the Betawi who live in central city districts and belong to the middle and upper classes who publicly emphasize their Betawi identity today. They represent and promote Betawi particularities, stress Betawi indigeneity, publically formulate Betawi interests and demand more political influence. Due to their comparatively high levels of formal education, their familiarity with the urban milieu, their membership of different social, professional, religious and cultural organizations and their proximity to the centre (of the city and of power), they manage to assert themselves as the political leaders of the Betawi.[5] As well, interethnic links and exchange have characterized Betawi life for centuries, and the Betawi Kota in particular are acclaimed for their interethnic competence that has won them respect both from the Betawi and others.

Thus, in the context of the Betawi revival it is above all those who on account of their relatively high social status or because they wanted to maintain or achieve such status used to conceal their Betawi identity who nowadays due to their social status are most likely to gain prominent positions both within the Betawi community and the public sphere more generally. Although some of them now claim always having been committed Betawi, others quite openly admit that their attitude has changed as a result of the upward revaluation of the Betawi. This is illustrated by the following statements.

> Previously it didn't matter to me whether I was Betawi or not. In fact, when someone asked me about my ethnic identity I would tend to answer Orang Jakarta, Jakarta Asli or something like that. But now I say that I am Betawi, because today the Betawi have a better reputation than they used to.

> I find it amusing. I know a lot of people who now say they are Betawi, even Betawi Asli, whereas earlier they would have said they were Sunda or something else. Now, with the Betawi gaining prestige and influence, a lot of people are saying they are Betawi who would not have said so before.

However, to achieve more political influence, the Betawi Kota need support beyond their own group. The increased kudos of the Betawi within the Jakartan population is above all the result of an increased general awareness that the Betawi are the only ones who can lend Jakarta a traditional and authentic profile. Although the socioeconomic status of the Betawi Kota is comparatively high and their indigeneity undisputed, they are not a Betawi group renowned for their knowledge of Betawi traditions. In the course of increasing urbanization, the cultivation of traditions has generally declined in Jakarta, but due to the social stigmatization the Betawi experienced and the denial of Betawi identity that followed from it, this is particularly true of the Betawi Kota.

This is a major reason why the Betawi living in the more peripheral areas of Jakarta – the Betawi Pinggir and Betawi Udik – consider the Betawi Kota to be less authentic. Moreover, within the Jakartan population in general it is assumed that the Betawi living on the city outskirts are more genuinely Betawi in terms of their knowledge and practice of Betawi traditions. Because Betawi traditions, conceptualized and promoted as Jakarta's indigenous traditions, provide a major reason for the promotion of the Betawi by state institutions, the politically active Betawi Kota need the Betawi Pinggir and Udik to provide an authentic and convincing representation thereof. As a result, socially marginal Betawi within the inner circle are being increasingly co-opted by the Betawi Kota to guarantee the traditional accoutrements required to conquer political territory. A Betawi official told me:

> We have to make clear that the Betawi have their own culture, a rich and vital Betawi culture. We Betawi in the city have maintained our culture and our traditions less than the Betawi on the outskirts, mostly because we are all mixed here. In order to become familiar with and preserve our cultural roots we have to take care of the Betawi Pinggir.

To make the Betawi as a whole appear bigger and more encompassing, Betawi previously regarded as socially marginal and less visible within the inner circle of the Betawi are thus increasingly drawn into the centre of the Betawi. The legitimacy of the demand for more political influence increases with the number of Betawi.[6] Conversely, the more marginal Betawi (Pinggir) need the Betawi Kota to gain a hearing in the public arena. The following chapter will reveal the different roles and functions they adopt in connection to current processes of integration and differentiation among the Betawi.

Betawi Pinggir: The Guardians of 'True Islam'

The Betawi Pinggir live on the fringes of Jakarta. Whereas the Betawi Kota constitute their status primarily by means of their socioeconomic background, their formal education and degree of modernization, the status of the Betawi Pinggir is based above all on religious piety and erudition. They are regarded as the Betawi who practice the purest form and have the most profound understanding of Islam. There are still many Betawi Pinggir today who consider religious instruction as more important than formal education. Many spend a considerable proportion of their income on sending their children to one of the prestigious *pesantren*, Islamic boarding schools, where they are instructed by *ulama* and *kiyai* (religious leaders/scholars) to acquire knowledge about Islamic philosophy, ethics, literature, laws and rituals. The best-known *pesantren* in Jakarta are run by Betawi Pinggir.[7] Those who can afford it sometimes also send their children to

104   *Creole Identity in Postcolonial Indonesia*

the Middle East to attend prestigious educational institutions there. In residential areas dominated by Betawi Pinggir an Islamic scholar tends to be ascribed more social recognition than, for instance, a university graduate. Great importance is attached to those Betawi Pinggir who as *kiyai* exercise a high degree of influence within their (multiethnic) communities both as advisors and teachers.[8]

In the context of the promotion of the Betawi, the religious weight of the Betawi Pinggir is significant in manifold ways. As leading Islamic scholars and guardians of Islamic tradition, they enjoy a high reputation among and beyond the Betawi, and their religious status increases the kudos attached to the Betawi as a whole. Betawi Pinggir who are recognized *kiyai* are also accorded a high status within the *Bamus,* the central Betawi association. The Betawi Pinggir thus help the Betawi as a whole to present themselves as a group that (largely) accords with the ideals of Islam. This is very important in a city (and a country) in which about 90 per cent of the inhabitants profess to the Islamic faith. The religious status of the Betawi Pinggir thus also serves to increase the religious and thereby social prestige of the Betawi. It is all the more important in light of the fact that the reputation of the Betawi as Muslims has been undermined in Jakarta, above all due to the secularization of the Betawi Kota. When asked whether the latter are more devout Muslims than others, a young Betawi answered, 'No, I don't think so. But that's only true of the Betawi here [Tanah Abang, in the centre of the city]. The Betawi who live further out are stricter.'

The Betawi Pinggir, and particularly their religious leaders, feel obliged to ensure that Islam continues to play a key role for Betawi and Jakartan culture and identity, and many are campaigning for Islam to have more influence in social as well as political life.[9] One *kiyai* explained to me:

> As a Muslim I would like Islam to play a key role in our political and legal system. For this reason it is important that as Betawi we ensure that Islam is not driven out of Jakarta. That is why I am involved in the *Bamus*. I would like the Betawi to reflect more upon their faith and Islam to play a more influential role as we become more involved in politics.

He adds, probably to avoid the impression of religious intolerance, 'That does not mean we want to fight against people of other faiths.'

Betawi Udik: The Guardians of 'True Tradition'

The Betawi Udik live on the far outskirts of Jakarta as well as in Tangerang, Bekasi and Bogor, i.e., in the cities bordering Jakarta. Their ancestors included agricultural labourers in Batavia's *Ommelanden.* Due to their distance from the centre and their relative isolation, they have preserved their traditions more than other Betawi. Seen from the centre – a view reflected also in official statements –

the Betawi Udik are the most marginal of the Betawi both in terms of their distance from central Jakarta and their social status. As a result of the mixing of specific groups at different locations during colonial times and in the course of historical creolization, the Betawi Udik living in North and West Jakarta as well as in Tangerang have been shaped above all by Chinese and the Betawi Udik living in East and South Jakarta as well as in Bekasi and Bogor above all by Sundanese traditions (Shahab 1994; cf. Lohanda 2001).

Until recently most Betawi Udik referred to themselves by means of specific local origins (Orang Pintu Air, Orang Sukasari, Orang Batuceper, etc.). They used 'Betawi' to refer to the city and 'orang kota' to refer to the city's inhabitants. While there was an awareness of an affiliation with the Betawi, it was of subordinate relevance in social life. It was only in the confrontation with cultural features and traditions classified and propagated as Betawi in the course of the revitalization and promotion of the Betawi from the end of the 1960s onwards and because of the desire to delimit oneself as native from the increasing number of *pendatang* that a more pronounced consciousness developed of (also) being Betawi. Moreover, the promotion of Betawi culture made it appear increasingly advantageous to join the collective Betawi camp. Shahab (1994) reports the following about two informants:

> Pak Rasin was born fifty years ago in Poris, a small district of Tangerang. When he left for Jakarta in 1950 the whole population was made up of natives.... Pak Rasin realised that he was a Betawi only in the 1970s, when he found out that those traditions that had been encouraged as Betawi traditions were the same as the traditions in his area of origin, which meant that he was a Betawi himself (Shahab 1994: 122).

> Ibu Noma was born in Tangerang in 1946 ... [and] moved to Jakarta in 1967.... In her new place she was confronted by a variety of ethnic groups. She, therefore, felt she needed to have an ethnic affiliation herself [sic]. By chance, she had been introduced to the concept of Betawi through the mass media in Jakarta and she recognised that their characteristics were similar to those of her traditions. Since then she has identified herself as a Betawi. She says that nowadays many educated people of the younger generation in her area identify themselves as Betawi, although there are people who still call themselves according to their area district level (ibid.: 122).

It was not only among the Betawi Udik themselves that identification as Betawi long remained weak. Other Betawi groups did not recognize the Betawi Udik as genuine Betawi either, although for other reasons. Evidence of this includes the fact that they were also referred to as Betawi Ora,[10] which can be translated as 'not really/genuinely Betawi'. However, the very fact that a group is referred to as 'not' being a 'real' or 'genuine' element of a category of people suggests some kind of relatedness to the latter.

One reason for the dismissive attitude towards the Betawi Udik has to do with their religious practices. The Betawi Udik distinguish between two forms of Islamic practice, which are in turn associated with two different groups – the *orang mualim,* who are regarded as strictly devout and orthodox Muslims, and the so-called *orang biasa,* the majority of the Betawi Udik, who see themselves as avowed but conventional Muslims. They do not practice a strict form of Islam, do not adhere strictly to its prescriptions and syncretize both Islamic and non-Islamic elements in their religious rituals.[11]

Betawi Udik who have been influenced primarily by the Chinese have syncretized religious traditions differently from those who have been influenced mainly by the Sundanese. This is indicated by the fact that until the late 1970s Buaran, an area in Tangerang in which many Betawi Udik live, was also referred to as *Kampung Buda* on account of the fact that the religious rituals practiced there involved sacrifices to different spirits and the use of amulets to ward off misfortune and were therefore regarded as Buddhist. The large majority among the Betawi Pinggir and the Betawi Kota regard these non-Islamic elements of religious practice as anti-Betawi – the former because they see them as being directed against the true Islam and the latter because they consider them to be uncivilized. Addressing this subject, a somewhat older Betawi Pinggir explained: 'The Betawi Udik are not true Betawi because they do not practice true Islam. They practice rituals that we reject because they are not Islamic. That's why I can't say they are true Betawi, because true Betawi are Muslims who practice true Islam.' A young woman, herself a member of the educated middle class, expressed different reservations: 'Well, they may be Betawi in some way, but they are not Betawi that I accept because they practice religious rituals that are uncivilized. In this way they present the Betawi as uncivilized and uneducated and that is detrimental to us as Betawi.'

The promotion of Islam by the state since the 1970s – in part as an antidote to communism[12] – subsequently saw Muslim leaders and teachers arrive in the area who conducted religious courses, built a prayer house and publicly condemned the practice of non-Islamic rituals. Buaran now has three mosques and five prayer houses, and religious courses are offered on a continuous basis. There has been a corresponding decline in the practice of rituals designated as Buddhist. A similar development has taken place among the Betawi Udik in Cibubur (South Jakarta).[13] This is in turn making them more acceptable to other Betawi.

In the case of the Betawi Udik, Islamization went along with (increased) Betawi-ization. Because the Betawi as a whole claim to be so-called good Muslims, a practice of Islam marked by non-Islamic rituals is regarded as inappropriate to the representation of Betawi identity. As long as being Betawi was seen as neither advantageous nor reputable, there was no reason for the Betawi Udik to give up non-Islamic practices in the interest of greater conformity with the majority of the Betawi. The increased turn to Islam on the part of the Betawi Udik thus was not originally motivated by a desire to integrate themselves in the Betawi majority. The fact that non-Islamic elements were weakened was the result of increased proselytization by Islamic scholars. However, the fact that there was a turn away from non-Islamic practices had a secondary effect of strengthening religious conformity, which in turn facilitated a shared identification as Betawi.

Today, the Betawi Udik are still unable to draw on formal education and a proximity to power (as in the case of the Betawi Kota) or on the quality of their Islamic practice (as in the case of the Betawi Pinggir) as the basis for augmenting their social status. However, it is the Betawi Udik who can claim to have best preserved original Betawi traditions. Compared with the Betawi Kota and the Betawi Pinggir, the Betawi Udik are not only more familiar with Betawi traditions; they actually practice these traditions and act as a conduit for them. It is through the dances, music and language of the Betawi Udik that specific cultural particularities of the Betawi become particularly recognizable. The Betawi as a whole therefore also need the Betawi Udik to provide them with a specific profile that legitimates their being promoted as the city's natives and to assert their political interests.

Many Betawi Udik on their part tend to consider the Betawi Kota as lacking authenticity, an assumption that is based on the latter's urban lifestyle and their lack of knowledge about Betawi tradition. A middle-aged Betawi Udik explained to me: 'They are Betawi because they have lived in Jakarta for centuries. But because of their continued contact with migrants and people from Europe and America they have forgotten much of their own culture.' Whereas the socioeconomic status of the Betawi Kota is relatively high, their status in terms of cultural competence is relatively low. On several occasions I have heard Betawi Udik severely criticize public presentations of Betawi culture by the Betawi Kota as unauthentic. This critique was particularly vehement in cases in which such a Betawi performance was sponsored by state institutions. The Betawi Udik are increasingly seeing themselves as experts in matters of Betawi culture. An older woman said to me: 'The Betawi Kota have little idea of Betawi traditions. We [Betawi Udik] are the ones who know these traditions. That's why they need us, because we are able to show them what the true Betawi tradition is.'

Strategies have been developed that allow for a relatively smooth integration of the Betawi Udik into the Betawi category while at the same time avoiding an incorporation of their stigma as being 'not-so-good Muslim' and not so civilized. One of these strategies involves the abandonment of the designation Betawi Udik and the latter's terminological incorporation into the Betawi Pinggir category, thereby combining cultural authenticity with religious purity (rather than with religious practices suspected of dubious origin). Some voices:

> We [Betawi Kota] now call them Betawi Pinggir, because Betawi Udik and particularly Betawi Ora have a negative meaning. That is unfair, because they are precisely the Betawi who know the most about our traditions. Betawi Pinggir is okay, because it refers more to the fact that they live on the outskirts of Jakarta and in Tangerang and so on.
>
> The Betawi who are often referred to as Betawi Udik are actually Betawi just like us [Betawi Pinggir]. There are still some who are not truly Islamic, but their numbers are shrinking all the time.

However, the integration of the Betawi Udik and the Betawi Pinggir goes beyond the terminological level and has been facilitated by the fact that non-Islamic practices among the Betawi Udik have been largely abrogated – not least by Betawi Pinggir who have moved into Betawi Udik areas to propagate a purer Islam.

Betawi Kota, Pinggir and Udik: Integration through Differentiation and Diversification from Within

The public image of the Betawi needs to be both differentiated and integrated enough to underscore their worthiness of promotion and legitimate their social ambitions and political demands. It is through the integration of differences, namely the integration of the Betawi Kota – who are seen as modern, urban and educated – the Betawi Pinggir – whose status is based on religious piety and professionalism – and the Betawi Udik – who are classified as experts of tradition – that one recognizable yet differentiated Betawi profile is being forged. What appeared as 'too different to be one' is reinterpreted as 'diversified enough to be integrative'. Diversification from within serves as a means of integration as it ascribes specific, yet mutually dependent and interconnected meanings to mutually dependent and interconnected categories of Betawi. Different aspects of Betawi culture and identity are represented and given a public face by different Betawi subgroups, thereby promoting a distinguishable public image of the Betawi as both diversified and integrative. This internal complementary differentiation of the Betawi also serves their social, cultural and political mobilization. Because none of the Betawi groups is in itself capable of representing all social, cultural, political and religious aspects of the Betawi as a whole, such representation requires intraethnic differentiation and specialization. By means of ascribing specific particularities to specific Betawi groups, the Betawi appear as internally diversified and unified at the same time. Differences that used to be interpreted as separating and dividing the Betawi are thereby reinterpreted as internal variation unifying and strengthening the Betawi as a whole – an interpretation that also fits the national motto of 'Unity in Diversity' (*Bhinneka Tunggal Ika*) very well. Further down we will see how this also impacts the Betawi's role as symbols of Indonesian nationhood.

In the process of internal diversification and unification, the Betawi Kota function as the social and political spearhead of the Betawi. They also have a certain definitional suzerainty when it comes to determining who is what sort of Betawi and why. However, the Betawi Kota are on their part highly dependent on those who are able to lend the Betawi as a whole a recognizable, indigenous and promotion-worthy face. This has led to an increasing number of Betawi outside the Betawi Kota group obtaining influential positions within Betawi associations. Intraethnic social hierarchies are thus being increasingly relativized and transformed.

The high rate of Betawi migration within Jakarta also plays a significant role in the context of the ongoing (re)constructions and transformations of the Betawi phenomenon. In particular, the fact that many Betawi Kota have been pushed into the outskirts of Jakarta or have preferred to sell their land in the centre and move to the outer districts has meant that now more than before different Betawi groups live together and are coming to recognize their common Betawi identity by way of their collective confrontation with non-Betawi. Because most areas that were previously inhabited primarily by Betawi are becoming increasingly heterogeneous in terms of their ethnic composition, the Betawi there are, as it were, closing ranks. As one woman in Condet explained to me, 'Formerly, people in the inner city did not classify themselves as Betawi. They were all simply "orang kota". But now, with people from the city moving into this area, I've realized that some of them are Betawi. We Betawi have to keep together so that we are not pushed out by the *pendatang*.'

In the face of this intra-Jakartan migration, the (sub)categories Kota, Pinggir and Udik, which refer to the distance from the centre of Jakarta both in sociocultural and spatial terms, are difficult to maintain. It is becoming increasingly obsolete to categorize the Betawi in terms of a continuum that links social and cultural characteristics with spatial proximity to the centre. This means that Betawi centrality is no longer automatically equated with superiority. The centre and periphery of the Betawi are reliant on one another in the endeavour to position the Betawi as a whole in the social and political centre of Jakarta.

The Arabic Dimension of Betawi-ness

The large part of the Indo-Arabic population considers itself and is considered by others as part of the Betawi. However, some still differentiate themselves by referring to the Arabic dimension of their identity. Specific designations – Indo-Arab, Peranakan Arab and 'Betawi Arab – still exist, which refer to the Arabic share of an individual's or group's origins. However, the Arabic element is seldom explicitly referred to, as it is regarded as an integrated, natural aspect of Betawi culture and identity (in its Kota and Pinggir variants). Nevertheless, the Arabic element dimension does play a specific role for Betawi identity.

Reference has already been made to the Arabs who lived in Batavia in the initial phase of colonization and who played an important role in the early processes of creolization that led to the emergence of the Betawi. However, the majority of Arabs arrived in Batavia from the beginning of the nineteenth century onwards and settled predominantly in Pekojan[14] in the so-called Moorish quarter.[15] The quarter was already established at the beginning of the colonial period in the early seventeenth century, when Moors from Gujarat and later Coromandel and Malabar (India) started settling there.[16] In the course of the nineteenth century this quarter increasingly took on an Arabic character. Following the opening of the Suez Canal in 1869, Arabs came to Batavia in increasing numbers. The majority of them were Hadhrami from Hadhramaut in South Arabia. By the beginning of the twentieth century, Arabs constituted the second-largest immigrant group after immigrants from Asia.[17]

Initially Arab men almost exclusively married Indonesian women. As this group grew so too did the number of marriages taking place within the group itself, which at this time consisted mainly of the descendants of Arab-Indonesian unions. The Arabs officially belonged to the *Vreemden Oosterlingen,* as did the Chinese and other Asians of non-Indonesian origins. Many Arabs were successful merchants who earned their living through trade and money-lending.[18] During the period of segregated colonial administration, the majority of the Arab population lived in Pekojan. Following the abolition of segregated administration, many prosperous Arabs moved to the better residential areas – like Tanah Abang, Krukut and Petamburan, areas that were also home to nonindigenous Asians and Europeans.[19]

The status of the Arabs drew heavily on their religious prestige as Islamic scholars. This applied particularly to those who as Orang Arab were distinguished from the Orang Hadhramut or Hadhrami. The former were descendants of Arabs who had come from the Arabian Peninsula, the heartland of Islam, and therefore enjoyed a particularly high religious status among the Islamic population of Batavia. A number of them were regarded as *sayid,* as descendants of the prophet. Although recognition was also accorded to the *syech,* Islamic scholars within the group of the Hadhrami, the status of the *sayid* was particularly high.[20] Lohanda (2001) points to the fact that the particular regard in which the Orang Arab were held by the Betawi was not only based on the former's high religious status but also on the fact that in contrast to the Hadhrami they did not engage in dubious business methods or conduct an aggressive interest policy.

From the colonizers' point of view the Arabs constituted an irritation in several respects. They were successful merchants, many of whom competed with the Dutch on equal terms. Above all they were highly regarded as Islamic scholars and as such represented an obstacle to Dutch efforts to spread Protestantism. The result of this mistrust was that the Arabs suffered particularly from discrimination by the Dutch administration when it came to the issuing of travel and trade permits. In 1918 further immigration from Hadhramaut was banned with the aim of curbing the size of the Arabic population and forcing the Arabs to assimilate.

With the emergence of the pan-Islamic movement at the end of the nineteenth century, Arab protests against such discrimination increased. Drawing on the help of the Turkish consuls who had been stationed in Batavia since 1883, they drew public attention to their grievances. The consuls demanded the right for boys of Arabic descent to study in Istanbul and in some cases issued Arabs with Ottoman passports, which allowed the holders to demand European status. Following the dissolution of the Ottoman Empire, the Dutch authorities found themselves increasingly having to deal with the English, who were now governing Hadhramaut and regarded all Hadhrami as protected British subjects (Gobée and Adriaanse 1959). The leaders of the Arabs in Batavia managed to have the immigration ban lifted on people from Hadhramaut and, through their protests, also contributed to the abolition of the policy of settlement along ethnic lines.

These activities, which not only benefited the Arabic but also the local population, generated respect for the Arabs. The respect accorded to Arabs as Muslims and the integrative effect of Islam in the struggle for independence resulted in the Arabs not being subjected to the kind of discrimination levelled at other nonindigenous groups after independence. Indeed, they were regarded as having participated in achieving independence. This is not to say that all Arabs exhibited an anti-Dutch attitude during the colonial period. A number of them often opposed the policies directed at the *Vreemde Oosterlingen* while at the same time maintaining good relations with the Dutch. A minority among the Arabs Europeanized themselves, took European names and sent their children to European schools.

Until the early twentieth century, the Arab population remained ethnically, socially and religiously divided, and conflicts among the different groups were common.[21] The bulk of those who had not come from Hadhramaut did not remain long in Batavia and did not assimilate. By contrast, the Hadhrami for the most part settled in Batavia, usually married native women and established families. They formed the predominant proportion of Arabs in the city and largely orientated themselves to the Hadhrami classificatory system, which classified people in social and religious terms in accordance with their descent group (van den Berg 1886). There were four classes of Hadhrami: the *sayid, syech, gabili* and *masakin*. The *sayih* were regarded as descendants of Mohammed and were therefore accorded the highest status. The *syech* and *gabili* formed the middle stratum. The *syech* were originally a religious elite in Batavia but due to their low numbers were forced out of this position by the *sayid*. The *gabili* constituted the warrior class, while the *masakin* were people of inferior descent who lived in Batavia as traders, labourers, servants and slaves. These four groups were hierarchically ordered and their dealings with one another were governed by a differentiated set of rules. For instance, marriages were only permitted within the respective group, a rule that manifested social boundaries and made them impermeable. The *sayid* had to be greeted by all others with a hand kiss.

However, this rigid class structure could not be sustained in the long run. It simply did not correspond to the social conditions and requirements pertaining in Batavia. A large proportion of the Arabs worked as traders, a profession which according to tradition belonged to the class of the *masakin*. However, the prosperity often achieved by such traders meant that they became less inclined to show the required level of deference to the *sayid*. For their part, the *sayid* accused the other classes of undermining traditional morality. One consequence of the potential for social advancement open to the lower Arab classes was that the social reality of Arab life in Batavia increasingly diverged from Hadhrami ideology. The different groups increasingly distanced themselves from one another, which amounted to a gulf between the *sayid* and the other groups – a process taking place at a time when the other ethnic groups in and around Batavia were increasingly converging and had long been subjected to processes of creolization.

It is also important to note that within the respective Arab groups a further distinction was made between the *wulaiti* – Arab newcomers – and the *muwalad* – Indo-Arabs who were descended from mixed unions. The newcomers, who predominantly came from Hadhramaut, were more enterprising than longer-term residents of Batavia and employed Peranakan-Arabs – indigenized descendants of Arab-Indonesian unions – who were less commercially successful. The *wulaiti* had limited social ties within Batavia and cultivated contacts with their homeland. Moreover, they were more conservative in matters of religion. By contrast, the *muwalad* spoke hardly any Arabic, for the most part had no ties with Hadhramaut and had adapted themselves to their local environment. The *wulaiti* looked down on the *muwalad,* who from their point of view had become remote from the true faith and the social and cultural habits of Hadhramaut. Although the former endeavoured to induce the latter to return to true Islam, their efforts proved in vain.

At the beginning of the nineteenth century the *Jam'iyyat Khair* (community for the good) was founded, an organization devoted to promoting Arab culture, language and religiosity and to ensuring that the Arab population was fit to meet the challenges of modern life: 'They tried to reconcile the challenges of the new century with traditional values' (Jonge 2000: 151).

One of the aims of this organization was to forge a fruitful link between the advances of Western science and Islam (Abeyasekere 1989: 109). Thus, the school that it founded, although mainly dedicated to religious instruction, also taught modern subjects such as mathematics, geography and English. Non-Arabs were also allowed access to the organization and its school.[22] *Jam'iyyat Khair* organized for young people to be sent to Arabia to continue their education. Teachers from Arabian countries were invited to come to Batavia to spread pan-Islamic ideas and instruct and further educate people in religious matters. The fact that it was the Arabs who as highly respected Islamic scholars campaigned for social modernization, liberalization and democratization resulted in these ideas being taken up by the wider Indonesian population. If the Arabs, with their superior knowledge of Islam, were proposing reforms, then it seemed clear that one could safely follow without violating the laws of Islam.

The split between *wulaiti* and *muwalad* within the Arab population was reinforced by an indigenous teacher, a Sundanese named Surkati, who was attached to the *Jam'iyyat Khair* movement. Surkati rejected the hierarchical concepts predominant among the *sayid*, aspired to social justice and championed an egalitarian form of Islam that saw all Muslims as equal.[23] Although his ideas were strictly rejected by the *sayid*, Sukrati enjoyed great popularity among the *muwalad*, which again led to conflicts within the Arab population. *Wulaiti* sacked their *muwalad* employees, and supporters of Sukrati were attacked and injured. The *sayid* founded a countermovement, *Al-Irshad*. The importance of the *wulaiti* and particularly the *sayid* declined, as did the significance of the classifications made within the Arab population. The number of *wulaiti* became ever smaller in relation to those who integrated and mixed with Indonesians, and the elitist claims of the *sayid* appeared increasingly unfounded. The conflict, which had begun as an interreligious dispute, increasingly developed into a conflict between *muwalad* and *wulaiti*, between the so-called pure Arabs, who held fast to the social, cultural and religious traditions of their country of origin, and the *mulawad*, who saw Indonesia as their homeland and whose traditions had been transformed in the course of their indigenization.

In 1934, the *mulawad*, or Arab Peranakan, founded the *Persatoean Arab Indonesia*, the association of Indonesian Arabs. Their goal was to dismantle the barriers between the different Arab factions and promote the integration of the Arab population into Indonesian society. They also publicly declared that they had become Indonesians. This integration into Indonesian society led to the disappearance of the rigid boundaries between the different Arab groups. The different groups of Arabs in Indonesia became Indonesians of Arabic origin. The commitment to a new national identity resulted in intraethnic boundaries losing their meaning. Moreover, the Arab quarter was overpopulated, and maintaining the social boundaries between groups in spatial terms had become all but impossible. The abolition of the colonial government's policy of ethnically structured settlement, in part the result of efforts by the reformer Surkati and his supporters, finally rendered the system of intra-Arab classification meaningless and at the same time intensified the process of integration into Indonesia society.

Most people in Jakarta today who are of Arabic-Indonesian descent regard themselves as Betawi. Many of them have only a vague notion of the Arabic element in their background. Many Betawi Islamic scholars are still of partially Arabic descent, although this is rarely emphasized. Rather, the incorporation of an Arabic element is seen as underscoring the Betawi's religious reputation. Thus,

Islamic religiosity as a criterion of Betawi identity is often, more or less implicitly, linked with Arabic representations, which are perceived as increasing the value of a group's practice of Islam. Those who perform Arabic songs and dances or sing and dance in the Arabic tradition are regarded as particularly devout. As Dhofier observed:

> [T]he new sukubangsa [Betawi] was identified as Islam. But although the Betawenese are now generally identified as orang Selam (Muslim) ... they can be classified into two distinct groups, i.e. faithful Moslems who practice Islamic Law and Islamic teachings, and another group who are not very faithful to Islam. This distinction becomes apparent by the preference for 'kesenian gambus' (Arabian music) among faithful Betawenese Moslems, and for 'kesenian lenong' (Betawenese drama play and arts) among unfaithful Betawenese Moslems ... (Dhofier 1976: 32).

It seems that in the context of integration through differentiation and diversification the Betawi are exhibiting a more pronounced tendency to emphasize the specifically Arabic dimension of their identity. Some people more than before refer to themselves as Betawi Arab and point out the particularities that this implies. It seems that Betawi culture and identity are undergoing (additional) upward revaluation via their Arabic dimension. On the other hand, some prominent Betawi Arab have become leading figures in radical Islamist groups, like the *Front Pembela Islam*[24] (FPI), which evokes ambivalent reactions concerning their suitability for political office (see Chapter 7).

Tugu: Exotics or Enclave?

At the beginning of the seventeenth century, the Dutch took prisoners of war in what had previously been the Portuguese-occupied territories of Malacca, India and Ceylon. Many of those prisoners were brought to Batavia. They included people who, in the course of Portuguese Christianization, had adopted the Portuguese names of their respective masters and had been released from slavery, which in turn led to their later designation as Mardijker, deriving from the Malayan *merdeka,* meaning 'free'.[25]

In Batavia they were initially made slaves again but were then freed as soon as they had become members of the Dutch Reform Church. As the practice of Catholicism was prohibited, they usually converted quickly, although such conversions tended to have a merely formal character and Catholic and syncretic rituals continued to be practiced. During the seventeenth and eighteenth centuries the Mardijker formed one of the largest groups among the free inhabitants of Batavia and were also referred to as black Portuguese and as Kristen Asli (native Christians) (Haan 1917; see also Knörr 2011). They spoke a creole language that had Portuguese and Malayan origins. Up until the second half of the eighteenth century, i.e., until the demise of the VOC, this language was the lingua franca among those who were neither colonialists nor slaves, but lived as free citizens (*vrijburghers*) in Batavia and the *Ommelanden*.[26] However, as increasing numbers of slaves arrived from eastern Indonesia and other parts of the Indonesian archipelago, the Portuguese element was progressively replaced by the Batavian or Jakartan variant of Malay.

Many of the Mardijker became part of the emerging Eurasian group, which was socially and culturally positioned between Europeans and natives. There were also renowned and wealthy Mardijker, who, on account of their closeness to the colonial rulers, worked in influential positions for the VOC, established themselves as merchants and thus enjoyed a comparatively high social status within colonial society.[27] Other Mardijker later converted to Islam and became part of the group of the Betawi. Towards the end of the eighteenth century only a few Mardijker remained.

In 1661, twenty-three black Portuguese families originating from Bengal and Coromandel were settled in Tugu[28], an area in northeastern Jakarta.[29] The bachelors among them mostly married women from Bali, and their descendants got married within their own group or to Indonesian women who (had) converted to Christianity. In 1678 a Christian church and school were established in Tugu (Da Franca 1970; Abdurachman 1975; Daus 1989).

The Tugu, as this group of black Portuguese became to be known, were oriented more towards the Europeans than towards the native population. Indeed, they differentiated themselves from the latter in many ways – through their religion, language, clothing and socioeconomic status. They often owned rice fields, on which native workers worked for them. During the Japanese occupation (1942–45) many Tugu were murdered or put in labour camps because the Japanese regarded them as collaborators with the Dutch.

In 1945 Indonesian natives planned to destroy the Tugu settlement and murder the Tugu. However, they were prevented by their commander, Haji Maasum, who declared that the Tugu were Indonesians like himself. He is still honoured for this act in Tugu today. Nevertheless, the danger remained that the Tugu's Muslim neighbours, who associated them with the Dutch, would take revenge upon them. The Tugu were therefore resettled in Pejambon (Gambir) in 1946. Many Tugu also fled to the Netherlands, where many of their descendants still refer to themselves as Tugu today. Others returned to Tugu soon after their evacuation.

> [T]he locals' opinion once forced them to evacuate Tugu, in 1946, because everything that had a 'European flavor', like names and religion, were related to the colonizers. The Tugu people who were Protestant and had Portuguese names like Quido, Angelo, and so on took refuge

in Pejambon and Matraman. In their new place, however, people kept assuming they were Eurasian. Tugu village was left empty with no one daring to go back. 'My relatives called us insane when my husband and I decided to go home the following year. But we stuck to our decision. Somebody had to take care of the village; besides, I believed God would help us', the old woman said. Later on the others moved back to Tugu when they felt safe to do so. The movement was completed in the 70s and nowadays their relations with the local Moslems are very good.[30]

Today Tugu is again home to around seventy families (some three hundred people), who, like the Betawi as a whole, were rediscovered by the state (and the public) in the 1960s and 1970s in the search for visible manifestations of tradition and indigeneity in Jakarta. Despite their low numbers, they play a specific role in current processes of identity construction and transformation in Jakarta. Their being explicitly linked with the Betawi is a relatively new development.

Due to its historical significance, Tugu was identified by the government as a cultural reserve worthy of protection in 1979, a fact that went largely unnoticed due to the volume of traffic and construction works in the settlement's immediate vicinity. Although the area is heritage-protected through a decree by the governor, as yet little has been done to maintain it. Apart from the old church and a cemetery there are few reminders of the Tugu – apart from the Tugu themselves. Nevertheless, Tugu is a popular destination for people interested in the history of Jakarta.

The Tugu have always been known for fostering their culture, which is characterized above all by Portuguese, Arabic and Balinese elements. They have emphasized their distinctness both from their Muslim neighbours (who are mostly Betawi) and from the Christian Depok (Asli).[31] Whereas the Betawi distinguished themselves through their distance from purported Westernness, the Tugu emphasized their closeness to Europeanness.[32]

At the end of the last century, the Tugu still wore black clothes and Portuguese hats, and their language still contained many Portuguese words, some of which can still be found in the Indonesian language today. The Tugu continue to celebrate a special New Year's festival, which the Muslim Betawi living in the immediate vicinity refer to as *Tahun Baru Belanda*, the 'Dutch New Year'. This occasion is marked by performances of *Keroncong*[33], a musical form that combines Arabic, Indian and Portuguese styles and is extremely popular well beyond Tugu and Jakarta. The Arabic elements in the music can be traced back to the African Berbers who occupied the Iberian Peninsula between the eighth and fifteenth centuries. They brought the music to Portugal in the early Middle Ages, from where it spread to Portuguese territories such as Goa and Malacca and from there to Java. The most popular and most widespread variant of *Keroncong* is *Keroncong Moresco,* a *Keroncong* variant of African origin (Heuken 2000).[34]

Ali Sadikin, the Governor of Jakarta in the 1970s, put considerable effort into promoting the culture of the Tugu, particularly their musical heritage. Although this music almost died out in the period immediately following independence, it was rediscovered and revitalized in the 1970s and today enjoys great popularity. There is a *Keroncong* school in Tugu, and in 1989 one of the most well-known *Keroncong* bands was invited to The Hague to present its music at the Tong-Tong Fair, a popular Indonesian music event. They played both traditional *Keroncong* as well as music from various regions of Indonesia, which they gave a *Keroncong* beat. *Keroncong* bands play at many Tugu festivals, on official occasions marked by the City of Jakarta and at touristic events.

A week after New Year the so-called *Mandi-Mandi* festival[35] is celebrated, during which the Tugu – above all young people – cover each other's faces with white powder and sing traditional songs. The white powder symbolizes that people forgive each other and that everyone is 'whitewashed' from the past year's sins. This festival is very boisterous and involves the consumption of a lot of food, including a dish called *Pindang Serani*, which translates as 'Christian fish' or 'Christians' fish'.

Until the mid-1990s the Tugu would not have referred to themselves as Betawi; in fact they would have rejected this designation due to the predominance of negative stereotypes associated with the Betawi and due to their being Muslims. In 1997 Saidi wrote of an encounter with a woman in 1994:

> Although they (the Tugu) have already been settled in Jakarta for two hundred years, they still resist being called Betawi. A woman from the Kampung Tugu, Tanjung Priok, a writer who I met at her home in 1993, explained that she was Tugu, not Betawi, because the Betawi were Muslims (Saidi 1997: 24f.).[36]

Although today the Tugu still refer to themselves as Tugu, and some older people as Portuguese, it is becoming increasingly common among them to refer to themselves as Betawi as well, a designation that depends on situation and context and that does not imply that a specific Tugu identity is being questioned. A *Keroncong* musician explained to me:

> We have lived here for hundreds of years. So we are also somehow Betawi, irrespective of religion. We are Tugu and Betawi – Betawi Tugu, so to speak. Our music also developed at that time and there are many similarities between Betawi music and *Keroncong*. *Keroncong* is actually a Tugu tradition, but it is also a Betawi tradition.

It is thus not as if the Tugu were about to set aside their identity as Tugu or their own specific tradition. The additional classification as Betawi is founded on the hope that the claim 'Tugu are Betawi' will attract state support and public recognition that will boost Tugu culture and identity as well.

The fact that the majority of the (Muslim) Betawi argue that being Muslim is a condition of authentic Betawi-ness does not prevent all Christians from referring to themselves as Betawi. Due to the fact that there is an increasing public awareness of the existence of Christian Betawi minorities, the Tugu – particularly younger people – no longer have serious reservations about (also) classifying themselves as Betawi.

The fact that the Tugu play a role within the framework of the promotion of the traditional and indigenous culture of Jakarta has increased their social significance. By classifying the Tugu as a group of the Betawi or as their relatives, the Betawi increase the store of cultural wealth they can draw on. Through the representation of their cultural tradition as part of Betawi culture, the Tugu are finding their own traditions being invigorated and attracting additional public attention. This may also have financial advantages. A significant number of Tugu are now earning at least a part of their income as musicians and music teachers. As one *Keroncong* musician explained to me, 'I think it's good that I can feed my family with my music. That's good, and it's also good that at the same time I'm contributing to the preservation of our traditions.'

The increasing tendency for Tugu to see themselves not only as Tugu but also as Betawi is also connected with the fact that they understand themselves as co-guardians of Jakartan traditions. A Tugu described this responsibility to me as follows:

> We are all Betawi in so far as we are all Jakarta's natives. Our ancestors already lived in Batavia. That's why we all need to work together to preserve our traditions. That's good for everyone who lives in Jakarta. It means that they can be proud of their culture. We also have a responsibility in this respect. All those who are Jakarta Asli are responsible for this.

The use of 'Jakarta Asli' again emphasizes common roots without denying a specific ethnic identity as Tugu.

However, for large sections of the Betawi the fact that the Tugu are Christians remains problematic. On the one hand, it is the Tugu's Christian faith that has influenced their uniqueness in terms of music, rituals and lifestyle. On the other hand, it is also the Christian faith that distinguishes them from most other inhabitants of Jakarta and especially from the Betawi in their surroundings. Formerly the Tugu were therefore frequently designated as Dutch and their villages were referred to as *Kampung Serani*, i.e., Christian *kampong*, by their Betawi neighbours, among many of whom reservations against the Tugu being Betawi still prevail today, as illustrated by the following quotes:

> The Portuguese who live here are not Betawi. They are Christians.
>
> They can't be Betawi because they are Christians. If they were Muslims they could be Betawi.

On occasion, one encounters more politically coloured arguments: 'But they were always on the side of the Dutch [*orang kompeni*] and also adopted their religion. How could such people be Betawi, tell me that?'

Also among the Tugu, reservations against being classified as Betawi persist, especially among older people. It is apparent – and characteristic of many groups with creole backgrounds – that a distinction is made between an ethnic and a transethnic link with the Betawi. The transethnic link, in contrast to the ethnic link, is primarily founded on cultural and social commonalities and not on shared origins. A well-known Tugu activist explained to me, 'We also feel ourselves to be Betawi but we are not *suku bangsa* Betawi. We are simply the big Tugu family. We have a lot in common but we have different roots; we are different stocks of people.'

Many of the more influential (Muslim) Betawi (Kota) – who seldom live in this area – see it as expedient to attach as many people (and groups) in Jakarta as possible to the Betawi, as they regard this as potentially increasing their own political influence. They thus often find themselves in a dilemma. The majority of the Betawi consider being Muslim an ethnic criterion of being Betawi. However, extending the category Betawi to as many people as possible and avoiding any suspicion of promoting one's own ethnic minority over others serves the Betawi's political mobilization in the urban and multiethnic context of modern Jakarta. In this connection it makes sense to point to the way power is structured and maintained in the Javanese context. Although the Betawi are not ethnic Javanese, they live in a social and particularly in a political sphere that is primarily shaped by (traditional) Javanese structures, according to which power is won and legitimated by integrating opposites and differences rather than doing away with them (Mulder 1996).

As pointed out already, the Tugu, in contrast to the Betawi, have long emphasized their affinity with European culture, their high level of formal education and their character as civilized Christians, thereby distinguishing themselves not only from the Betawi but from indigenous Indonesians in general. The fact that a majority of the Tugu preferred to emigrate to Holland rather than stay in Indonesia in the face of the hostilities directed against them illustrates the distance that existed between them and other Indonesians. For quite some time after independence had been achieved, the Tugu were not recognized as genuine Indonesians but linked with the colonial rulers and, as such, discriminated and persecuted. By contrast, the Betawi were linked with the colonial rulers not as collaborators but as their slaves and servants. Whereas in the period following independence, this also seemed an unpopular heritage, the discovery of the Betawi potential for shaping a traditional and indigenous profile for Jakarta as well as a transethnic Jakartan identity made it possible for this heritage to be recontextualized accordingly. Although the Betawi emerged in the colonial context and have origins that to a large extent lie beyond Jakarta, their Jakartan and Indonesian indigeneity has rarely been contested. Their social distance to the colonial masters, their rejection of modern ways of life and their Muslim faith facilitated their retrospective public transformation from former slaves and servants to opponents of the colonizers and fighters against colonialism.

The different conceptualization and perception of the Betawi (as a whole) and the Tugu with respect to their indigeneity and heritage reveal that a society's interpretations of origins (particularly of creole groups) largely depends on the social contexts in which they emerge. The relationship between an emerging creole group and a given indigenous population as well as the ways in which this relationship is communicated and substantiated determine whether an emerging creole culture and identity will be able to develop not only ethnic but also transethnic reference within an ethnically heterogeneous society. Where a particularly small group is concerned – as in the case of the Tugu – the formation of transethnic links can be matter of a group's survival. It seems that the Tugu can only survive if they (also) become Betawi. Through their link with the Betawi they acquire not only a status as members of a larger group – the Betawi – but may also share the transethnic dimension of Betawi-ness in terms of culture and identity.

Nowadays, many Tugu explicitly refer to their link with the Betawi and to the mixing of the Tugu with the indigenous population in general. This emphasis on proximity to the indigenous population is also founded on the fact that the experience with their own otherness has for the most part been a painful one, and hence, with the fear that an emphasis on difference may provide grounds for further discrimination.[37]

Whereas some older Tugu still refer to themselves as Portuguese, most young Tugu reject this self-designation. A young Tugu living in the Tugu area said to me: 'We are not Portuguese. We can't even speak Portuguese. We have mixed with everyone here. We are Tugu, but actually we are like the Betawi – except for the fact that we are Christians. But we all believe in the same God.'

Reference to being mixed with the local population is thus not associated with a notion of having lost one's identity as a Tugu. On the contrary, the emphasis on a link between Tugu and indigeneity – also via the Betawi – strengthens the identity of the Tugu as it becomes a share of something larger, namely Betawi-ness, and thereby of Jakartan indigeneity and tradition.

The fact that little remains of the language and architecture of the Tugu is seldom bemoaned. By contrast, the significance of Tugu music, songs and stories is emphasized. It is often explained that change is not something to be feared as long as there is a collective memory of a shared origin and history. For instance, a *ketua RT*[38] in Tugu, a man of advanced years explained to me:

It's not really important whether every house here looks like a typical Tugu house. Times change. We have mixed with the natives. In the end there were not many of us. I think it is much more important that we know where we come from and that we have a shared history. Then it's not painful when times change. We have been mixing for so long that we have also lost our language. The others did not speak our language and we were in the minority.... We are mixed and we now speak the language that everyone speaks here. There are a number of Tugu endeavouring to revive the Tugu language, but since there are no longer any native speakers this project seems doomed from the outset.

One might think that a few hundred Tugu in a city of Jakarta's size hardly merit attention when it comes to identity-related processes. However, because the Tugu are able to contribute something unique to the fund of traditions that can be drawn on in Jakarta, they are accorded a comparatively high level of significance irrespective of their low numbers. As (integrated) diversity is believed to increase the prestige and potential power of an ethnic group – particularly one with heterogeneous origins – it is in the interest of the Betawi as a whole to integrate minorities close to them without denying their specificities. Due to the creole context of their development and their existence within an ethnically heterogeneous society, the culture and identity of the Betawi must express intraethnic heterogeneity to be able to exert a transethnic effect and gain social significance beyond the boundaries of the Betawi. There is thus no danger at present that the Tugu will be absorbed by the Betawi of the inner circle in the sense that their Tugu identity will be swept under the carpet because this would merely add a few hundred Betawi to the existing Betawi. The promotion and incorporation of the Tugu only makes sense from the Betawi point of view if the Tugu enrich the internal diversity of the Betawi as a whole, hence, if Tugu-ness becomes one distinct feature of wider Betawi-ness. After all, unity in diversity requires diversity to be able to represent unity.

Kampung Sawah: The (Christian) Betawi in the Paddy Field

Kampung Sawah[39] lies in Pondok Gede on the border to Bekasi in eastern Jakarta. It is (or has been until recently) surrounded by paddy fields that separate Kampung Sawah from the surrounding areas. Around 60 per cent of the population here are Muslim and 40 per cent are Christian (with somewhat more Catholics than Protestants).[40] The Muslims found in Kampung Sawah are seldom Betawi. The houses in Kampung Sawah are scattered between gardens of the durian and rambutan that the area is known for.[41]

The Christians in Kampung Sawah chiefly refer to themselves as '(Orang) Kampung Sawah' and are also designated as such by others. However, a link has meanwhile been forged between the Kampung Sawah and the Betawi.

The Christian Kampung Sawah were privileged under the Dutch. They were given land, formal education and jobs as government officials. Like the Tugu, they were subject to discrimination following independence. When Kampung Sawah was attacked in 1945, many of its inhabitants suffered violent deaths. Those survivors who nevertheless remained in Kampung Sawah increasingly adapted to the local conditions of life but retained their Christian faith. Many of the inhabitants, however, fled to other cities and to Keramat Raya, the Christian centre of Jakarta, from where they spread to other parts of the city, often establishing small Christian communities. In 1980 several families founded an association that functions as a network for people from Kampung Sawah who today live in different districts of Jakarta. One of the association's goals is to preserve the culture of Kampung Sawah. An older man, a member of this association, explained the situation as follows:

> We people from Kampung Sawah are now very scattered – in Jakarta but also in other Javanese cities. So we have to organize ourselves in order to remain in contact and in order to preserve our own culture. For example, *Keroncong* music. That's a type of music introduced by Christians. We need to make that clear, because today many people play *Keroncong* and have no idea that it is a Christian tradition.[42]

In 1994 a large part of the population of Kampung Sawah were removed from the settlement due to government appropriation of the land. In 1996 most of them were allowed to return following a protracted legal dispute. Today the settlement has two mosques, one Catholic and one Protestant church. Unlike in the cases of the Tugu and the Depok, Christianity was not primarily introduced by Christian immigrants but by indigenous residents who converted during the colonial period (Shahab 1994). Marriages between Muslims and Christians are not unusual, but conversion to Christianity of one of the spouses usually takes place in such cases.

Their place of residence and their Christian faith are key criteria of Kampung Sawah identity, more so than their connections with the Betawi. However, the Kampung Sawah I met often complained that due to their faith they were not recognized as Betawi by many Muslim Betawi. A rice farmer said to me: 'Whoever says we are not Betawi should come here and see how we live. Then they would see we are Betawi.'

The Christians in Kampung Sawah clearly differentiate themselves from the Christian Tugu and Depok Asli, small numbers of whom also live in or nearby Kampung Sawah. They claim that the latter are far more modernized than the Kampung Sawah and that, contrary to themselves, particularly the Depok Asli (who they sometimes derogatively refer to as 'Belanda Depok') would have a reputation for looking down on their Muslim neighbours. A woman from Kampung Sawah explained to me: 'The people from Depok are very different from us. They think they are better. They see themselves as Dutch and often still speak the language. We've never done that.' It is often mentioned that the Kampung Sawah have a closer relationship with their Muslim neighbours than with the Christian Tugu and the Depok Asli: 'The Belanda Depok and the Tugu are different from us. We are more similar to our Muslim neighbours than them, even if they are Christians. We live in a village environment [*secara kampung*] and are not as European in our lifestyle' (woman from Kampung Sawah, thirty-nine). The few Tugu living in Kampung Sawah are said to belong to one family. Their contacts with their Muslim (and Christian) neighbours appear to be less intense than among the Tugu in Tugu.

The fact that the Christians in Kampung Sawah keep a distance from their fellow Christians is appreciated by their Muslim neighbours. Shared antipathies towards certain others seem to have a unifying effect also in Kampung Sawah and decrease the significance of religious differences among those who share them. In conversations I had with people in Kampung Sawah it was emphasized that there had not been any significant religious conflicts for a long time.

In terms of the processes being discussed here, the Kampung Sawah have so far played a subordinate role. However, particularly among those Kampung Sawah who live in the more urban areas of Jakarta, there is increased engagement with the relationship between Betawi and Kampung Sawah identity. A woman who left Kampung Sawah many years ago told me:

> We are Kampung Sawah and we are Betawi. I actually only realized I was Betawi once I had moved away from Kampung Sawah. That's when I realized that the Betawi in Jakarta are like us. They use the same words to refer to their relatives and they speak like us.[43]

Generally, it seems, that up to now a sense of commonality is primarily constructed in terms of the recognition of cultural similarities and not in terms of common origins or descent. However, it has been noted by some Kampung Sawah that they may attract more attention when associating themselves with the Betawi. 'The Betawi are being promoted. I think we should also be promoted because we are really also Betawi. We need to make that clear to the people,' a young man who had then left Kampung Sawah a year ago told me.

A hotly debated and contested issue has been a bylaw passed by the City Council concerning the establishment of Srengseng Sawah – the district in South Jakarta, which Kampung Sawah is part of – as Jakarta's Betawi village (officially inaugurated in 2001). In its annotations the bylaw demands that residents should embrace a Betawi way of life, including a community life deeply rooted in Islamic values. Opponents to the bylaw – among them many Betawi – stated that linking the Betawi exclusively with Islamic values would not reflect Betawi reality. The debate that ensued focussed on the question to what extent the Betawi were to be linked (exclusively) with Islam and many voices pointed out that there were in fact Christian, Hindu and Buddhist Betawi, too. As well, reference was made to the open-mindedness and tolerance of Betawi culture which would be betrayed by establishing a purely Islamic Betawi village. Setu Babakan (located) in Srengseng Sawah has meanwhile become a popular Betawi site, which is dedicated to the preservation of Betawi culture. I have not witnessed any debates concerning its Islamic character in recent years.

It remains to be seen whether the Kampung Sawah as a group of people will associate themselves more closely with the Betawi. It remains to be seen whether they will be co-opted by the more urban Betawi to contribute to the diversification of Betawi culture and identity – after all, the Kampung Sawah could bring back (memories of) the paddy field to the Betawi – as long as there is a paddy field left, that is.

Bangsawan Betawi: About the Invention of a Betawi Aristocracy

It is only recently that some research has been conducted on an alleged Betawi aristocracy, the so-called *bangsawan* Betawi. Due to the absence of source material and the marginal nature of my own research in this area, the following should be regarded as preliminary.

In 1613 the Dutch established their first fortified settlement in the form of a goods and trading station in Jayakarta – later Batavia and Jakarta – on the Ciliwung River. At the time the western part of Java – including Jayakarta – was under the control of the Sultanate of Banten.[44] Conflicts had arisen between Banten and Jayakarta because Banten was experiencing a socioeconomic decline as the result of political unrest while Jayakarta was prospering due to flourishing trade and payments made by the Dutch and English for their right to establish settlements. In February 1619 Prince Jayawikarta was deposed by Prince Ranamanggala of Banten and banished to Tanara to the west of Batavia, because he was considered being too closely aligned with the English. Banten favoured trade with the Dutch and already had a history of strained relations with the English who had settlements in Banten. In May 1619 Dutch troops destroyed Jayakarta, including Jayawikarta's palace. The troops from Banten who now ruled Jayakarta directly offered barely any resistance. In principle, they welcomed the Dutch presence since it offered protection from the powerful army of Sultan Agung of Mataram, who controlled Central Java and threatened Banten. The indigenous population was driven out of Jayakarta – which provided the roots of the myth that was later to emerge.

There are contradictory reports as to the whereabouts of Prince Jayawikarta at this time – according to the official version he was exiled to Tanara, but there are other reports that he based himself in Jatinegara Kaum to organize attacks against the Dutch. It is evident that many of those driven from Jayakarta settled in Jatinegara Kaum (which was soon after renamed Batavia), including members of Banten's leading aristocratic families.[45] Today the long-established residents of Jatinegara Kaum still speak a Sundanese dialect that originates from Banten. Abdussomad (1997) identifies linguistic and cultural commonalities between the so-called (Orang) Sunda Banten and the old-established residents of Jatinegara Kaum and points particularly to the linguistic parallels between these two groups in terms of kinship terminology. The link between the inhabitants of Jatinegara Kaum and the Sunda Banten is also witnessed by the many gravestones there bearing the names of aristocrats who were among those driven from Batavia (Heuken 2000). Whereas it is easy to comprehend that Jatinegara Kaum is up to date considered a node of anti-colonial resistance and a refuge for the Sunda Banten aristocrats driven from Batavia, the question remains how the aristocratic Sunda Banten in Jatinegara Kaum turned into a Betawi aristocracy in Jakarta – and why.

The first public mention of an aristocratic class of the Betawi was at the beginning of the 1980s. The proponent of the aristocracy thesis, Gunawan Semaun, was then vice president of *Iwarda,* an organization that had been founded in 1954 as *Mangkudat Iwarda,* a community of descent within the group of the Betawi Pinggir. *Mangkudat Iwarda* is an acronym for *Masyarakat Pemangku Adat Ikatan Warga Djakarta Asli,* which roughly translates as 'Society for fostering the traditions of the Jakarta Asli'.

The politicization of this organization can be traced back to the early 1980s, when a number of Betawi (above all Betawi Kota) tried to convince their fellow Betawi to support the ruling party *Golkar.*[46] One Betawi member of *Golkar* drew attention to *Mangkudat Iwarda* and proposed using the organization to mobilize support for *Golkar* (Shahab 2000). In 1981 the organization was renamed *Iwarda.* Because *Iwarda* was now to function as a Betawi and Jakartan organization active at the level of national politics, I suppose this renaming was meant to situate *Iwarda* as a Betawi (and Jakartan) organization rather than a particular Betawi descent community, which *Mangkudat Iwarda* was known to be.

Gunawan Semaun, the vice president of *Iwarda,* soon attracted attention by, on the one hand, claiming to be a *bangsawan* Betawi and, on the other, propounding the existence of an aristocratic class of Betawi. He and his supporters were not met with approval by the majority of the organization's members and were excluded from it. In 1986 these ex-members founded *Al Fatawi*[47] *Mangkudat,* which propagated the existence of the *bangsawan* Betawi and increasingly provided their message with ideological underpinnings.[48]

The ideological foundation of *Al Fatawi Mangkudat* is *Kitab al Fatawi,*[49] the 'Writings of the Fatawi', which are said to have been begun in 1552 and completed in 1954 (Shahab 1994). The writings are made up of three parts – the *Babu Tarik* dealing with the history, the *Babu Adat wal Adat* dealing with the legal system and the *Babu Silsilah* dealing with the genealogy of the Fatawi.[50]

These writings are used to give evidence to an aristocratic stratum of Betawi – the *bangsawan* Betawi – who are claimed to be the descendants of the *Fatawi*, i.e., religious and secular intellectuals who are differentiated from ordinary Betawi of mixed origins. In the view of this aristocracy the lack of recognition accorded to them by ordinary Betawi must be traced back to the fact that the latter come from low, mixed, non-aristocratic origins and are largely unaware of their historical genesis or find it unpleasant to consider.

> There is an aristocratic class; there are religious and secular intellectuals; and there are merchants and laborers. It should be noted that most of the Betawi who manifested themselves in the 1980s are descendants of merchants, so that they look at the *bangsawan* Betawi with scepticism.[51]

It is claimed that (the ancestors of) the ordinary Betawi cooperated with the Dutch colonial rulers. Only the Fatawi and their entourage who fled to Jatinegara Kaum are regarded as never having accepted the rule of Batavia.

Today the *bangsawan* Betawi are made up of five extended families that are said to be descended from five princes who all ruled in Jayakarta.[52] Extravagant genealogies are used to prove aristocratic descent and illustrate that the heirs of the aristocracy are in no way descended from slaves or others in the service of the colonial rulers. The *bangsawan* Betawi from Jatinegara Kaum see themselves as the actual (and worthy) original inhabitants of Jakarta. They distinguish themselves from the ordinary Betawi by emphasizing their aristocratic origins and their untarnished reputation in matters of colonialism. As one such old *bangsawan* Betawi told me:

> The Betawi are a construct of colonialism. We were already in Jakarta before them and were driven out by the Dutch. However, we didn't run away but settled nearby in Jatinegara Kaum. Our origins are Sundanese, but we are above all Jakarta Asli – more than the Betawi.

Whereas previously this group presented themselves as Jakarta Asli of aristocratic and Sundanese origins, they now claim to be the aristocratic class of the Betawi.

> We in Jatinegara Kaum are Betawi if this is referring to the fact that we are the original inhabitants of Jakarta [*orang asli Jakarta*] – the descendants of the *Fatawi*. We are the real original inhabitants of Jakarta, because we were already here prior to the colonial period and later fought against the colonial rulers. The other Betawi only came into being later and they are descended from slaves and workers. We are the true Betawi, the Jakarta Asli.

The *bangsawan* Betawi disseminate their theses and theories in articles and columns in various daily newspapers (*Sinar Pagi, Berita Buana, Pelita*). Whereas in the 1980s they emphasized their own group and its aristocratic origins, it has now become more important to publicly question the legitimacy of those responsible for the revival of Betawi-ness. They accuse *Dinas Kebudayaan,* the cultural department of the Jakartan government, of basing its promotional policies and publications only on colonialist sources rather than availing itself of genuine Betawi sources.[53] They claim that events are being promoted that distort Betawi traditions and run counter to the Islamic faith of the true Betawi. They refer to LKB,[54] the cultural association of the Betawi, as 'Betawi à la Batavia', because it is responsible for alienating people from the original Betawi traditions. They see its members as descendants of followers of the colonial rulers. The *bangsawan* Betawi claim to reject all cultural and religious practices that in their view have been polluted by colonialism and external influences. The state television broadcaster (TVRI) and the Department for Museums and History[55] of the DKI Jakarta, which produce programmes on Betawi culture, are accused of ignorance in matters of 'true Betawi-ness and Jayakarta' and of showing programmes that offend the sense of honour of the 'Jayakarta family' (Shahab 2000: 204–6). Accordingly, they regard only those forms of expression of Betawi culture as genuine that are compatible with their ideas of a pure Islam. All other forms are regarded as mixed and corrupted.[56] Whereas the Betawi Kota regard the year 1975, or more precisely the workshop on research into Betawi culture[57] that took place that year, as a prelude to the revival of Betawi culture, the *bangsawan* Betawi see this event as the beginning of the destruction of Betawi culture.

An essay by Abdussomad (1997) bears the title 'Jatinegara Kaum: the oldest kampung in Jakarta inhabited by Jakarta Asli who are not Orang Betawi'.[58] The title implies that Jakarta Asli are normally to be considered Betawi, but that this does not apply in the case of the people in Jatinegara Kaum. The author emphasizes that the people in Jatinegara Kaum are genuine and old Jakartans but not Betawi.[59] The people in Jatinegara Kaum, he goes on to explain, see themselves as Jakarta Asli but not as (ordinary) Betawi, who they reject on the grounds of their link with colonialism. Saidi (1997) argues that these people emphasize differences between the Betawi and their own group, although due to cultural commonalities there is also the potential for foregrounding the latter.

The context of the Betawi's emergence, which was shaped by colonial repression and (subversive) rebellion against it, as well as the postcolonial experience of social discrimination have shaped an outlook among the majority of the Betawi that is highly sceptical of any emphasis on social hierarchies and against the cultivation of aristocratic sensibilities. The surfacing of a Betawi aristocratic class is therefore usually dismissed as an absurdity, as illustrated by the following responses by Betawi whom I asked for their opinion of the *bangsawan* Betawi:

> Betawi and aristocracy – they don't fit together; it's a contradiction in terms. The Betawi are poor people: some belong to the middle class. But when a few people now claim they are aristocratic Betawi – that's just ridiculous. Betawi as aristocrats... [laughs].
>
> Aristocratic Betawi? That's just rubbish. Aristocratic Javanese I can accept. But aristocratic Betawi? No, they don't exist. Anyone who says so has no idea about the Betawi.
>
> Someone told me that he was a *bangsawan* Betawi and I was only an ordinary Betawi [*Betawi biasa saja*]. I just laughed and said, 'So what does that mean? Are you my king or what?'

The *bangsawan* ideology is unable to gain influence because it is the ideology of a minority that cannot find support among the great majority of the Betawi since it implies their debasement. Although the different groups of Betawi are becoming increasingly prepared to recognize each other as true Betawi in the interest of appearing as an internally diversified unity, they reject the existence, let alone integration, of an aristocratic class. It seems that the *bangsawan* Betawi are increasingly becoming prisoners of their own aristocratic conceit. They do not want to be ordinary Betawi, but at the same time want to benefit from the public attention the latter are being given. The project of their own Betawi-ization by means of the aristocratization thus seems to be in vain.

'Fatawi' versus 'Batavia': Et(hnon)ymological Disputes in Jakarta
The fact that the *bangsawan* Betawi associated themselves with the Betawi at all also seems surprising given that they fundamentally rejected the designation Betawi due to the association with Batavia – the name the Dutch gave the city that had previously been called Jayakarta. Batavia is associated with colonialism, repression and slavery, whereas Jakarta is (audibly) derived from Jayakarta and is therefore positively associated with both precolonial and postcolonial times. However, in the context of the project 'How can one be an (aristocratic) Betawi without being a Batavian?' a way out of an apparent dilemma has been found, namely, the invention of an alternative etymology of the ethnonym Betawi. The *bangsawan* Betawi now claim that the term Betawi is not derived from Batavia, as generally assumed, but from Fatawi, the Indonesian term for Islamic scholars – who they claim were also forefathers of the *bangsawan* Betawi. Thus, thanks to an alternative et(hnon)ymology, they point out that the *bangsawan* Betawi are 'Betawi à la Fatawi' and not, like the ordinary Betawi, 'Betawi à la Batavia'. The dissemination of their 'knowledge' about the origin of the term Betawi remains a key concern of the *bangsawan* Betawi. They claim that deriving the term Betawi from Batavia is part of a comprehensive, colonialist falsification of history that aims to transform the anti-colonial natives expelled from the city of Jayakarta

– the Fatawi-Betawi – into colonial creatures of Batavia in the interest of providing a legitimation of Dutch colonial rule: 'So, the word Betawi is not derived from Batavia, because Batavia has been the enemy of the ancestors of the Betawi people ever since the Dutch occupation. Remember that the Betawi are not the product of the colonial government.'[60] The claim that Betawi is not derived from Batavia but from Fatawi enables them to claim Betawi identity without having to situate themselves in the colonial context of Batavia. The purported true Betawi (and their scattered descendants) are accordingly those from Jayakarta who fled to Jatinegara Kaum: the (merely) so-called Betawi are Betawi à la Batavia – people of mixed origins who collaborated with the colonial rulers and their contemporary successors. It is hardly surprising that those characterized and classified in this way show little enthusiasm for recognizing an aristocratic class of so-called better Betawi, who seem intent on disparaging them.[61]

Batak Going Betawi: Or, What Is a Batak Betawi?

As has been pointed out previously there are individuals and groups that adopt an identity as Betawi in Jakarta and increasingly discard their original ethnic identity. There are the so-called Betawi Sunda or Sunda-Betawi,[62] a category of people that in the course of historical creolization became Betawi while retaining a Sunda dimension of identification. However, this Sunda dimension is not an independent, second identity that exists alongside the Betawi identity or relativizes the latter's meaning. This is evident in the following statement: 'They are the Betawi who are very similar to the Sunda because there were many Sunda among them when they mixed. But they are Betawi, not Sunda.' Hence, this is not a case of dual ethnicity but one in which Betawi identity is differentiated by means of referring to one particularly important ethnic origin.

In contemporary Jakarta, there is also another identity-related process taking place in the course of which an original ethnic identity is equipped with an (additional) Betawi dimension. The original ethnic identity is transformed by means of Betawi-ization. In contrast to the Betawi Sunda case, it is not the category Betawi that is differentiated by means of another – for example, Sundanese – identity, but the original ethnic identity which is differentiated by means of the category Betawi. As a consequence, these groups do not become a specific sort of Betawi – as seen in the case of the Betawi Sunda – but a specific Betawi sort of some other ethnic identity.

While in Jakarta, I came to hear of the so-called Batak Betawi and was told that there are groups of people of Batak background who organize themselves as Batak Betawi. However, I was never pointed to a possible contact with such a group so was never in a position to verify the existence of the Batak Betawi as a collective phenomenon. Although I met people who told me they were Batak Betawi they were not aware of a collective institutionalization of their identity either. However, this is not to imply that this phenomenon does not exist. In a city such as Jakarta it is simply impossible to encounter all identity-related processes that are taking place – all the more so when the processes concerned are (as yet) marginal. The descriptions provided by some of my informants seemed plausible enough to suggest that processes of Betawi-ization of Batak identity may take place on more than an individual level. If such processes are in fact occurring, they would – albeit on the outer edge of the outer circle of the Betawi – involve neither processes of conversion as already described nor the provision of the original Batak identity with a merely transethnic notion of Betawi-ness. It would involve a process of Betawi-ization of the original Batak identity. It is interesting to note that the informants who told me about this Batak Betawi phenomenon not only saw this process as proof of the increasing attractiveness of the category Betawi but also interpreted it as amounting to a growth of the Betawi.

Against the background of the social upgrading of the Betawi and due to the fact that many people feel little connected to what is being communicated to them as their place of (ethnic) origin by their parents or grandparents, I consider it likely that processes are taking place in the course of which groups sharing the same ethnic identity are transforming the latter by endowing it with a Betawi dimension, thereby likely trying to increase its authenticity. However, as yet these processes do not seem to have much social significance nor are they widespread. It is not unlikely that Betawi activists in particular may feel inclined to overestimate the significance of such processes by interpreting individual processes of Betawi-ization as social processes.

Notes

1. *Kota* = city; *tengah* = middle, centre; *pinggir* = periphery, here: Betawi living on the outskirts of the city; *udik* = rural, provincial, thus those living in the rural environs; derogatory connotation, implied boorishness, poor manners and a lack of education. Cf. Saidi (1994, 1997) who uses linguistic, cultural and origin-oriented features to classify different groups whose Betawi identity is disputed as either Betawi or non-Betawi. However, for the most part he does not consider emic ascriptions.
2. For figures from the years 1978 and 1989 see Shahab (1994). According to these data more than half of the Betawi Tengah surveyed in 1989 had higher professional positions, either as owners of large firms (35 per cent) or more senior civil servants (29 per cent). The size of the survey sample is not indicated.
3. The Betawi Kota were (and are) occasionally further differentiated with reference to their type of residence and designated accordingly as *Orang Kampung(an)* or *Orang Gedong(an)*, i.e., as residents of a *kampung* or as residents of modern houses. *Gedong(an)* = building; it refers to larger modern residential and commercial buildings.
4. *Bamus:* Acronym for *Badan Musyawarah Masyarakat Betawi* = Betawi Consultative Assembly. *Bamus* unites more than sixty Betawi organizations under one umbrella. The number has grown significantly in recent years as has the number of organizations that include Betawi in their names without being registered with *Bamus*.

5. These associations are so numerous that any selection presented here would appear arbitrary. This applies to the constantly expanding number of Betawi associations as well as to other ethnic associations. It also applies to the different forms of organization that are developing on the basis of shared professional, social, religious and cultural interests.
6. Cf. Coakley (2003: 9): '[A] group's territorial claims become stronger as (1) the group increases as a proportion of the total membership of "its" territory and (2) the proportion of the total membership of the group within this territory increases.'
7. The two best known *pesantren* in Jakarta are, to my knowledge, *Athariyah* and *Asyafiiyah*.
8. Cf. Ramelan (1977), who suggests that state actors need to recognize the key position of the *kiyai* because the latter can convince their communities of state programmes as well as organize resistance against them.
9. By contrast, Christian Betawi living in peripheral areas (see further down) do not appear to have such missionary ambitions, which would likely cause potentially violent opposition by more radical Muslims.
10. *Ora* (Javanese, also common in Jakarta) has the function of negating adjectives, verbs and nouns.
11. Probonegoro (1987) and Lohanda (1989) describe performances/rituals expressing the belief in different spirits.
12. On the (historical) relationship between communism and the nationalist movement in Indonesia, see Kahin (1952).
13. This information was supplied to me by two (former) residents of the district (both of them Betawi).
14. Pekojan: a word of Persian origin meaning 'trader'. In this context it refers to a residential quarter inhabited by Indian merchants. Today it is located between Jalan Bandengan Selatan and Jalan Pekojan in northwestern Central Jakarta.
15. People with Arab-Berber origins were originally referred to as Moors, i.e., as 'mouro' (Portuguese, meaning 'Muslim'). This was the term used in Batavia to refer to Islamic Indians who had come to Batavia in the seventeenth and eighteenth centuries (Jayapal 1993; Lohanda 2001).
16. At the beginning of the nineteenth century, Raffles (1817: I: 63) counted '400 Moors and Arabs' in Batavia.
17. Figures for 1930 show 5,231 Arabs, for 1900 2,245, for 1885 1,448, and for 1859 312 (Jonge 2000). Jonge has taken these figures from various censuses and historical reports. Castles (1967) puts the number of Arabs in 1815 at 318, in 1893 at 2,842, although it should be noted that in 1893 Moors and Arabs were included in one, namely, the Arab category.
18. For a more detailed discussion of the commercial activities of the Arabs and their social consequences see Abeyasekere (1989).
19. See van den Berg (1886). He refers to the fact that numerous Arabs lived in these areas as prosperous settlers.
20. On the differentiated perception of the Arabic population by the Betawi, see Brondgeest (1927).
21. Jonge (2000) provides a description of the different groups, the causes of conflicts and the way they were dealt with.
22. Cf. Mandal (2002). He argues that although the schools of the *Jam'iyyat* were open to all Muslims, they were mainly attended in Batavia by Arabs.
23. For details of Surkrati's ideas and goals see Affandi (1976).
24. On the background of the FPI and its activities, see *Refugee Review Tribunal* (2009). See also the FPI's website at http://fpi.or.id/.

25. *Merdeka* originally derives from the Sanskrit *maharddhika*. A historical description of Portuguese influences in Jakarta can be found in Da Franca (1970). For a more current discussion of these groups in the seventeenth century see Niemeijer (2000); see also Heuken (2000); Knörr (2011).
26. See Lohanda (2001), who provides a description of the different groups and the social structure of Batavia linked with them. Details of the different Portuguese-Asian groups in Southeast Asia are provided by Daus (1989).
27. A number of examples can be found in Lohanda (2001).
28. The *Prasasti Tugu* (monument of stone), which was found in the Kampung Batu-Tumbuh near present-day Tugu and which has been in the national museum since 1911, originates from the Hindu kingdom of Tarumanegara (fifth century A.D.). The monument is a memorial stone commemorating the construction of a canal by Hindu monks. It was only later that it provided the name for the area in which it had been found, and this term was subsequently increasingly used to designate the black Portuguese living there; see Heuken (2000).
29. For more detail on the origins and history of the Tugu, see Heuken (2000). For a comparison with other Christian groups, see Kurris (1996). In this later work the groups of the outer circle dealt with here are also referred to as Betawi.
30. These statements are documented in records held by the library of the Indonesian Heritage Society in Jakarta. The author remains unknown.
31. This distinction is not reflected in the statistics on the ethnic distribution of the Jakartan population listed by Castles (1967) in which the Tugu and Depok people are treated as one group (with just under a thousand members). This amalgamation may have been based on their common Christian faith and their perceived proximity to European culture.
32. This brings to mind other creole groups, who, like the Tugu base(d) their claim to superiority over the native population above all on their Christian faith, their affinity with European civilization and their high level of formal education (e.g., the Krio of Freetown, Sierra Leone, see Knörr 1995, 2007a, 2010b; Cohen 1981).
33. *Keroncong* is also one of the instruments used to play this music. It is a small guitar-like instrument with five strings. The name is based on the type of sound the instrument makes. Other instruments making up a *Keroncong* band include: guitars, *macinas* (a type of mandolin), flutes, violins, string bass and tambourines.
34. See also Da Franca (1970); Abdurachman (1977).
35. *Mandi* (Indonesian) = to bathe; the repetition (*mandi-mandi*) serves to exaggerate the meaning in the sense of bathing in white powder as a form of purification.
36. My translation. The original Indonesian is as follows: 'Meskipun sudah lebih dua abad menetap di Jakarta, tetapi merekan enggan disebut orang Betawi. Seorang ibu dari Kampung Tugu, Tanjung Priok, yang penulis jumpai di rumahnya pada tahun 1993 mengatakan bahwa dirinya adalah orang Tugu, bukan orang Betawi, karena orang Betawi itu Islam, katanya.'
37. In this respect, the situation of the Tugu is similar to that of the Chinese in Jakarta; see Chapter 5.
38. *Ketua* = leader, head; *RT* = acronym of *Rukun Tetangga* = neighbourhood community, the smallest administrative unit in Jakarta. A *kelurahan* includes different *RT*.
39. *Kampung Sawah* = literally translated: paddy field village. It is the name of a residential settlement in eastern Jakarta surrounded (although now less and less) by fields used for rice farming.
40. Shahab (1994) supplies the following figures: 53.7 per cent Muslims, 25.5 per cent Catholics, 20.8 per cent Protestants. Since 1994 the proportion of Muslims is likely to have increased.

41. *Durian* is the prickly fruit of the *durio* or *zibet* tree (*Durio zibethinus*) whose name is derived from the Malayan or Indonesian word *duri* (prickle, thorn). It is also referred to as a stink fruit. *Rambutan* (*Nephelium lappaceum*) is a tropical tree from the soaptree plant family (*Sapindaceae*). It is related to the lychee tree (*Litchi chinensis*). The name of the plant is derived from the Malayan word *rambut* (hair) and refers to the thick bristles on the fruit.
42. The people in Kampung Sawah claim that *Keroncong* music is a purely Christian tradition and cultivate it as a particular cultural asset.
43. Shahab (1994: 141) notes: 'Besides the Betawi language, these people [Kampung Sawah] also use Betawi kinship terminology.... All these terms, *abah, mak tua, empok* are identified in linguistic literature as Betawi terms. They also recognise *lenong, tanjidor, topeng, wayang* – the Betawi arts – as part of their arts.' It should be noted here that some of the kinship terms are also used by people other than the Betawi and that the artistic forms referred to – in particular *wayang* – are seen by other groups as their own – as generally Indonesian or as typically Jakartan artistic forms.
44. A historical map of the territorial divisions of the time can be found in Latif and Lay (2000).
45. On the genealogies of the families concerned and the history of Jatinegara Kaum, see Abdussomad (1997).
46. *Golkar:* acronym for *Partai Golongan Karya* = Functional Group Party. *Golkar* is the former hegemonic party during the era of *Orde Baru*.
47. *Fatawi:* derived from the Arabic *Fatwa* = legal pronouncement. In this case the reference is to the ruling house of Banten.
48. Another, more worldly goal of the *bangsawan* Betawi is the return of the *Istana Jipang*. According to the *bangsawan* Betawi this house was built in 1619 by Prince Wiranta Yudha, who had been driven from Jayakarta by the Dutch and had fled to the area now known as Pal Merah. There he built the house in question, which today is still owned by a Chinese family. A *bangsawan* Betawi family formed a community of heirs (*Pusaka Wihara*) and since the mid-1930s has been fighting a legal battle for the 'return' of the house.
49. As far as I know, these writings are not available in published form. I obtained a copy of large parts of this work through personal contacts.
50. *Babu* = chapter; *tarik* = chronicle, history; *adat* = common law, cultural (legal) system; *silsilah* = genealogy, family tree.
51. From an article produced by the association *Al Fatawi Mangkudat* in *Pelita*, 18 April 1986.
52. These are said to be the princes (*Pangeran*) Wijayakrama, Ahmad Jayawikarta, Adimerta, Kartawirja and Mertakusuma, who are collectively termed *Kepangeranan Jayakarta*.
53. 'For sure, most of the researchers who talk about the history of Jayakarta only copy from the literature written by Dutch authors. Although what they mean is Jayakarta, what they actually write is Batavia ...' *Sinar Pagi*, 25 July 1989, translated by Shahab and cited in Shahab (2000: 205f).
54. LKB: *Lembaga Kebuyaan Betawi* = Betawi cultural institute.
55. The Indonesian name for this authority is *Dinas Museum dan Sejarah*.
56. In this respect they resemble the Betawi Pinggir, whom Shahab (1994) assigns the *bangsawan* Be-tawi to. Most Betawi Pinggir who I spoke to disputed the existence of an aristocratic class among the Betawi. Many were familiar with the *Al Fatawi Mangkudat* but disputed the aristocratic character of its members. They tended to see the organization as a conservative, Islamic association of Betawi who refer to the nativeness of their practiced traditions. This may have to do with the fact that the emphasis on the aristocratic element has been declining.

134 *Creole Identity in Postcolonial Indonesia*

57. This workshop was devoted to the resuscitation of Betawi traditions and was instigated by (Javanese) Governor Sadikin, who is seen as an advocate of Betawi culture.
58. My translation. The Indonesian title is as follows: 'Jatinegara Kaum: Kampung tertua di Jakarta penduduk Jakarta asli yang bukan Betawi.' In the essay Abdussomad describes the lifestyle and history of this group.
59. Interestingly, the title in the table of contents of the essay is a little different from that in the book. In the former case, 'yang' is replaced by 'tapi' (thus, instead of 'who are not Betawi' – '(who) *however* are not Betawi'. 'However' underscores the impression that this is a notable phenomenon and implies that genuine Jakartans are normally Betawi.
60. *Sinar Pagi,* 24 June 1986, cited in Shahab (2000: 205).
61. There are other – non-aristocratically inclined – Betawi promoters who also derive Betawi from Fatawi. Their concern is to replace the colonial context of the genesis of the Betawi with a (more) indigenous context. Accordingly, Jatinegara Kaum is regarded as an area in which many of those settled who were expelled from Batavia by the Dutch. In the course of the processes of mixing among ethnic groups during the colonial period, the Betawi came into being. This view also seeks to counter the idea of the Betawi as a product of colonial Batavia. However, it does not claim an aristocratic class of Betawi.
62. These groups are called Sunda Betawi in English, but Betawi Sunda in Indonesian. Both terms are common in Jakarta. In both cases Betawi is linguistically differentiated by Sunda, not vice versa.

Chapter 5
Betawi versus Peranakan

Conceptual Disentanglement

Indonesian citizens of Chinese origin are officially referred to as Warga Negara Indonesia Keturunan Tionghoa (WNI), or as (Orang) Tionghoa.[1] Colloquially – and to some extent derogatively – they are sometimes referred to as Orang Cina or non-Pribumi.[2] Although there are other so-called non-Pribumi in Indonesia, the term is above all used to refer to the Chinese (Dhofier 1976: 10), and there Chinese who have internalized this designation and use it to refer to themselves (Heryanto 2001: 100). However, since the fall of the Suharto regime in 1998 the careless and depreciative labelling of Indonesians of Chinese origins has become more objectionable.

The Chinese are internally differentiated on the basis of their expressed and perceived degree of indigeneity or exogeneity. Until well into the nineteenth century all Chinese who had converted to Islam were referred to as Peranakan (Lohanda 2001),[3] an indication of the level of significance attached to the conversion to Islam as a criterion of indigenization. Later, this designation was extended to cover all Chinese born in Indonesia as well as the descendants of Indo-Chinese unions.[4] The term Peranakan was thus used, on the one hand, to indicate Chinese (or Chinese-Indonesian) descent and, on the other hand, to differentiate Chinese of indigenous and Indo-Chinese descent from Chinese, who were born in China and who neither settled in Indonesia permanently nor married into the native population. The use of Peranakan foregrounds the (comparative) indigeneity of those referred to as such, thus distinguishing them from those designated as Totok.

Peranakan thus denotes people with historically exogenous (Chinese) origins who have become indigenized – i.e., Indonesianized – via processes of mixing with one another and with the native population. This process involved creolization in so far as ethnic mixing, ethnicization and indigenization took place. However, in the case of the Peranakan, the Chinese dimension of identification was transformed and Indonesianized, but – due to the large number of Chinese and their relatively high socioeconomic status – not replaced (as in the case of the Betawi). Peranakan identity – Chinese identity in the contemporary Indonesian context – refers to Chineseness as an ethnic identity within Indonesia; it is not a national identity that refers to China as homeland. Particularly during the past ten years this process has been boosted in that the Indonesian government has implemented new laws that officially acknowledge the Indonesian identity and citizenship of Indonesians of Chinese descent.

In contemporary Indonesian society, culture and identity play the major roles for the internal differentiation of the Chinese. Chinese whose major source of identification is Indonesia are referred to as Peranakan; Chinese whose major source of identification is China – or who are suspected of prioritizing their Chinese over their Indonesian identity – are sometimes still referred to as Totok (Tan 2008).[5]

> The term 'Peranakan' itself has created a lot of confusion. Most writers have used it to refer to Indonesia-born Chinese, regardless of their cultural background.... However, some writers ... and the Indonesian Chinese themselves, consider that to be born in Indonesia does not automatically make a Chinese a 'Peranakan'.... It is true that generally Peranakan Chinese were Indonesia-born, but not all Indonesia-born Chinese are Peranakans. A Chinese, who is born in Indonesia, is still a totok, if he or she is Chinese-speaking and China-oriented (Suryadinata 1992: 2).

In this chapter I shall concentrate on the relationship between the Betawi and the Peranakan – or Indonesians of Chinese origin. When speaking of the Chinese I refer to Chinese identity as an ethnic, not as a national ascription (like Suryadinata 1992). In identity discourses in Jakarta (and Indonesia), the relationship of exogenous and indigenous elements of origin and identification play a significant role. Because the Chinese in Jakarta have indigenized themselves not only by becoming Peranakan, but also by becoming Betawi, and because indigeneity within Jakarta corresponds not only with Indonesian but also with Betawi identity, the discourse around Chinese identity also operates in relation to Betawi culture and identity. The boundaries between Peranakan and Betawi are fluid, and it is often the situation and the context that determines whether one presents oneself or is perceived as Peranakan or Betawi. Various forms of identifications have emerged that link the Peranakan and the Betawi in manifold ways.

For instance, certain groups are referred to as Hitachi – an acronym for *hitam tapi Cina*, meaning 'black but Chinese'. Those designated as such are conceived of as 'black', i.e., as looking like the (Indonesian) Betawi,[6] but at the same time are 'known' to be (ethnic) Chinese. The designations Betawi Tionghoa and Cina Betawi are also used. They emphasize Betawi-ness while also signifying the latter's Chinese dimension. Differentiations are also made with reference to specific areas of settlement and certain indigenous groups that have historically mixed with the Chinese.

Cina Benteng: The First Peranakan

Contacts already existed between Chinese and Indonesian kingdoms in the ninth century, with the Chinese establishing a number of important ports on the northern coast of Java (Groenevelt 1880). Many Chinese converted to Islam, married into aristocratic dynasties and thus gained access to the ruling classes. Over the course of several generations these marriages between Chinese men and Indonesian women gave rise to Indo-Chinese groups.[7]

Even before the Dutch seized Jakarta, the eastern bank of the Ciliwung River was settled by (Muslim) Chinese who cultivated rice and brewed *arak* – a distilled rice spirit.[8] The land was granted to them by Pangeran Wijaya Krama, the ruler of a part of the Sultanate of Bantam, who the Dutch referred to as *Coninck van Jakarta*. In 1611 the Dutch acquired land near this settlement and constructed a small factory at the mouth of the Ciliwung River. Several years later they constructed Benteng, the first Dutch fort on the river's eastern bank. The indigenous inhabitants soon began referring to the Chinese settled in the area as *Cina Benteng*, a name they still retain.[9] They are regarded as the first Peranakan in Jakarta.

Between Privilege and Expulsion: The Chinese in Batavia and Early Postcolonial Jakarta

After the Dutch seized Batavia in May 1619 increasing numbers of Chinese flooded into the city. The Dutch governor general, Jan Pieterszoon Coen, who had already spent years in the East Indies, was convinced that with their commercial prowess the Chinese was the group best suited to bringing prosperity to the city.[10] The Europeans in Batavia relied on the goods brought from East Asia to Batavia by the Chinese both to serve the needs of the colony's inhabitants and for further export to Europe. The Chinese in turn shipped local Indonesian products to China (Abeyasekere 1989). Coen therefore took pains to convince the Chinese living in neighbouring coastal regions to settle in Batavia. Soon after, Chinese also began arriving in Batavia from Hokkien in southern China, along with a smaller number of immigrants from Canton. For the most part they were merchants, who brought their own coolies. Chinese also worked in and around Batavia as architects, shipwrights and canal builders, in the fishing industry and as artists and artisans. Between 1619 and 1739 their numbers increased from a few hundred to some four thousand within Batavia and around ten thousand in the city's surroundings (Blussé 1986).

The new Peranakan, those Chinese who were born in Batavia under Dutch colonial rule, mostly married native women, above all (Balinese) slaves, in the early days of settlement. As Hindus the Balinese were not governed by any restrictions regarding the preparation and eating of pork. However, following the abolition of slavery and the conversion of many Chinese to Islam or – in the case of close contact with the Dutch colonial rulers – to Christianity, ethnic origins ceased to play a significant role in the choice of spouses.

Most Peranakan either became part of the emerging group of the Betawi in the course of a few generations or maintained a distinct identity as Peranakan. Although the latter were oriented to the Indonesian lifestyle due to increased mixing with the local population, it retained a reference to the Chinese origins of the men.

The relationship between Chinese and Betawi culture and identity is thus a multifaceted one with a long historical tradition. Since the initial phase of Dutch colonial rule, which was also the period in which a Betawi culture and identity developed, Chinese and Betawi culture continued to influence one another. In the course of the creolization processes that took place in Batavia and the *Ommelanden* many features of Chinese culture were absorbed into the culture of the Betawi and many Betawi features into Chinese culture, as seen in rituals such as wedding ceremonies, dance, music, religion and language.[11] Chinese influences can be observed, for instance, in *Cokek*, a dance accompanied by a *Tanjidor* orchestra, as well as in *Lenong Betawi*,[12] a type of folk theatre that emerged in the 1930s, in *Topeng Betawi*, a masked dance, and in Betawi marriage ceremonies.

Categorizations applied by the colonial regime created a boundary between the Chinese and the Indonesians that was manifested in the form of privileges and disadvantages. An important reason for the special status accorded to the Chinese lay in their ongoing trading relationships with China. Whereas the Dutch accorded the Chinese particular privileges in the field of trade and commerce, other *vrijburghers,* the free citizens of Batavia, were severely restricted in their trading activities due to the monopoly of the VOC. As a result the mid-seventeenth century saw protests by non-Chinese *vrijburgher* who felt that Dutch policies were placing them at a disadvantage. On the other hand, from 1620 onwards the Chinese were the only citizens forced to pay a head tax (*hoofdgeld*) on their presence in Batavia. However, this meant that they were permitted to exploit their networks and trade freely over the entire Indonesian archipelago and beyond. In return the Dutch gained a welcome source of revenue in the form of head and profit taxes as well as leasing charges levied on the Chinese.

> In the period of 1619–85, the interests of the Company and the Chinese colony of Batavia were evenly balanced: both were engaged in the pursuit of optimal profits from the overseas trade. Because the Batavian inter-archipelago trade depended so much on the Chinese trade, the Chinese colony was given some latitude within the operating structure of the East India Company. What was good for the Batavian Chinese was, at that time, good for Batavia in general (Blussé 1986: 95).

When establishing the colony in 1619, the Dutch colonial rulers also introduced the office of the Chinese *kapitan,* to whom the Chinese had to pay their taxes and who thus functioned as a connecting link between the Chinese settlers and the colonial government. In 1685, due to the substantial increase in the Chinese population, additional Chinese district wardens – *chineesche wijkmeester* – were appointed (Lohanda 2001: 283, 304).

Within Batavia itself the interests of the colonial rulers and the Chinese largely complemented each other. The situation was different in the *Ommelanden*. The administrative and cooperative structures that served Dutch and Chinese interests within Batavia did not extend to the areas outside the city.[13] Whereas the Chinese within Batavia cooperated closely with the Dutch, the Chinese who flooded into the areas around Batavia in the late 1600s and early 1700s mostly worked as labourers on sugar plantations that almost exclusively belonged to Chinese landowners (*potchias*) (Lohanda 2001). These areas were not equipped with the administrative structures organized along ethnic lines that had been established in Batavia – including the institution of the ethnic *kapitan*. Batavia's Chinese *kapitan* had no influence in the *Ommelanden* and there were no *wijkmeester*. Taxes were collected by the – usually corrupt – Dutch sheriffs, who, if appropriately remunerated, were prepared to overlook substantial numbers of Chinese heads or to grant settlement permits (*permissiebriefjes*), thus freeing the *potchias* from the

Figure 5.1. Glodok, Chinese quarter – end of the nineteenth century (Picture No 10113239/ JAVA/DJAKARTA 1881/Djakarta: the Chinese quarter/Mary Evans Picture Library).

required head tax.[14] As a result it was all but impossible to control the influx of economic migrants into the plantations in the environs of Batavia.

When the sugar price fell drastically in the middle of the eighteenth century and sugar mills had to be closed, many Chinese labourers became unemployed and survived by turning to all kinds of illegal activities. To counteract their criminal activities, prevent further immigration and get rid of as many unemployed Chinese as possible it was decreed that Chinese without residence permits were to be deported to Ceylon. When rumours spread that Chinese were being thrown overboard during the passage to Ceylon, the Chinese in the *Ommelanden* armed themselves and attacked Batavia. In the ensuing battles and massacres the Chinese (above all from the *Ommelanden*) faced an army composed chiefly of European and Indonesian soldiers. In the course of the struggle some ten thousand Chinese lost their lives, including many women and children as well as Chinese in Batavia who had joined neither the *Ommelanden* Chinese nor the Dutch. The massacres resulted in the death of a majority of the Chinese population and an initial collapse of trust between the Dutch and the Chinese. The office of Chinese *kapitan* lost its prestige. The incumbent *kapitan* was jailed and later banished into Moluccan exile. The Chinese from the *Ommelanden* accused him of corruption, idleness and even involvement in the attack on Batavia, where in reality he had exercised little influence. The remaining Chinese were no longer permitted to live inside the city walls and were resettled in Diestpoort (present day Glodok in northwest Jakarta).

The loss of the Chinese soon proved economically disadvantageous for Batavia, and to reactivate trade the settlement of new Chinese was already permitted in 1741. These arrived in large numbers, and trade and commerce soon began to flourish again. In 1743 a new Chinese *kapitan* was appointed.

At the beginning of the nineteenth century the Dutch relocated the colonial administration and the residences of its officials to *Weltevreden*[15] to the south, which today forms the centre of Jakarta. Many Chinese remained in the area of what is now Glodok. Others moved into the areas previously inhabited by the Dutch, which were now increasingly settled by people of highly diverse origins. The Chinese intensified their activities in the areas of trade and commerce and extended their spatial reach. As a result there was a reinvigoration of the interethnic contacts between Chinese and the other inhabitants of the city that had suffered due to the banishment of the Chinese to the Chinese quarter. At the same time, spatial separation meant that contact was weakened between Europeans and all other groups. As their prosperity increased many Chinese sent their children to Western-oriented schools in order to prepare them for careers in international trade (Lohanda 2001).[16]

The beginning of the independence movement and growing public dissatisfaction with the Dutch colonial regime coincided with repeated attacks on the Chinese, who were seen as representing and collaborating with the Dutch. Hatred of the Dutch was repeatedly vented against those who were (supposedly) close to them but were more vulnerable than the Dutch themselves. Nevertheless, up until 1965 Jakarta did not see any large-scale riots against the city's Chinese inhabitants.

Until well into the 1960s contacts between Chinese and other inhabitants of Jakarta were manifold. Chinese festivals provided the entire population of Jakarta with an opportunity to celebrate. For instance, the Chinese celebrated *Imlek* (Lunar New Year) with their neighbours regardless of which ethnic group the latter belonged to. Chinese New Year was always celebrated with a large public festival, and on Chinese New Year's Eve cultural events were held in which all population groups participated. Fireworks, *Barongsai* (lion dance), *Tanjidor* and *Cokek* performances along with martial arts displays and circus performances attracted a large, ethnically heterogeneous public.

> In the 1950s, everybody in town – Chinese families, Betawi people, members of the Arabic and Indian communities – would flock to Glodok and Harmony in downtown Jakarta to attend this merry event, especially during Cap Go Meh, the celebration 15 days after the new year. … For the young, it was a time for affairs of the heart. A Javanese boy might meet and fall in love with a Chinese girl. It was very common at that time (Widiadan 2000).

The Chinese also took part in the celebrations marking *Idul Fitri* – the end of Ramadan. Social interaction between Chinese and other ethnic groups in Jakarta were thus generally a normal part of life.[17]

The Repression of the Chinese during the Suharto Era

In 1965, Suharto – who was major general at the time[18] – held communist China in part responsible for the failed coup attempt against President Sukarno and branded the country's Chinese as unpatriotic. The so-called *Orde Baru* – the New Order – was established, which involved measures to limit the influence of the Chinese and punish the Chinese for their alleged support for actions aimed against the government. All Chinese – whether Peranakan or Totok – were (derogatively) classified as non-Pribumi (or tidak asli), i.e., non-native. Non-indigenous groups, including the Peranakan and Chinese with Indonesian citizenship, were not considered part of the Indonesian nation unless they were absorbed into the indigenous population. They were subjected to severe discrimination and arbitrary measures in particular between 1965 and 1968 (Turner 2003). They were given identification cards that made reference to their Chinese origin, and Chinese who applied for passports were required to show not only their birth certificate and personal identification but also needed to document their citizenship and the adoption of an Indonesian name. Chinese schools were closed. Chinese media and the teaching of Mandarin were largely prohibited. Schools and universities were not allowed to admit Chinese students beyond a particular Chinese quota. The importation of Chinese print media was strictly prohibited (Heryanto 2001). At the end of the 1970s Confucian weddings and public ceremonies were also banned. The declared aim of all these measures was the complete assimilation of the Chinese: '[P]ribumi Indonesian leaders consider Indonesian identity as a complete abandonment of ethnic Chinese identity or "Chinese cultural elements" and adoption of what they perceive as an indigenous Indonesian identity' (Suryadinata 1992: 4). The Chinese were not regarded as integrated as long as they continued to practice Chinese culture:

> We can no longer tolerate the existence of Chinese temples, nor can we tolerate *petilasan-petilasan*[19] which smell Chinese. We will restore everything to asli. Do accept our measures ... Celebration of Chinese New Year need not to be continued, except by those Chinese who are aliens (Major-General Sumitro, cit. in Suryadinata 1992: 42).[20]

What was regarded as appropriate for indigenous ethnic groups was denied the Chinese: 'Pluralism has been applied by pribumi Indonesian leaders to their fellow pribumis, but not to the Chinese minority' (Suryadinata 1992: 4).

The Chinese were thus expected to assimilate completely and abandon Chinese culture and language. However, due to their enormous economic significance they could not simply be ignored as citizens. As a result especially the more influential among them were assured of their membership of the Indonesian nation – although this entailed strict avoidance of reference to the Chinese aspect of their identity. The following report on an event held in 1980 – which Simbolon described as historic in 1991 – provides a taste of the state-promoted *Pancasila* ideology.[21]

> [M]ost of the participants belonged to the predominant ethnic group in the nation's economic life, the *non-Pribumi*.... The atmosphere ... reflected the strong determination of all participants to dismantle the 'historical burden' of ethnic differentiation, only a year after the nation had been rocked by serious ethnic issues as the result of a major presidential decision to give various economic advantages to *Pribumi* (Simbolon 1991: 24).

The same event was reported in the Indonesian magazine *Informasi* as follows:

> Spontaneous resounding handclapping was the expression of their deep sense of relief every time a speaker greeted them as the equally natural children of this motherland. Every time it was uttered 'dear compatri-

ots', they felt as if they were refreshed with the 'magic water' of our Nusantara. On the fully programmed Sunday, they were spiritually invigorated by their solemn recognition as brothers and sisters, made by the government's high officials of the Indonesian Republic.[22]

The chief function of such more or less publically staged, emotionally charged incorporations of the *non-Pribumi* was, of course, to ensure that Chinese capital remained in the country.

Whereas on the one hand the Chinese were supposed to become Indonesian, on the other they suffered discrimination at the hands of those they were supposed to assimilate to. They were thus expected to become Indonesian while being denied all the privileges associated with that status. Even the official designation of the Chinese as Orang Cina, which was reinstituted in 1967, was calculated to discriminate against them. Orang Cina is regarded as a derogatory and politically incorrect term, because, among other reasons, it conjures up associations with the *kapitan* of the colonial period. It was for this reason that it was replaced at the beginning of the twentieth century with Orang Tionghoa – an Indonesian form of the term used by the Chinese themselves.[23]

The Chinese were also banned from political life under Suharto (Turner 2003). Although there had been Chinese members of previous governments, over the more than thirty years that Suharto was in power not one of his ministers was Chinese. Furthermore, during the Suharto era there were no Chinese army generals or high state officials (Heryanto 2001; cf. Anderson 1990).

The exclusion and discrimination suffered by the Chinese meant that for thirty-two years they were forced to conceal their Chinese identity. However, the repression of the Chinese did not result in cultural and social assimilation but rather the opposite. Because the practice of Chinese culture was not permitted in public, it was transferred to the private sphere. Speaking of impressions retained from his youth and his parents' experiences, a Chinese man told me, 'Those with the best chances were the ones who were not recognized as Chinese; so everyone who didn't look too Chinese tried to conceal their Chinese origins and pass themselves off as something else.'

Recent Developments: 'Free the Dragon' versus 'Be(com)ing Betawi'[24]

In May 1998 violent street battles erupted in Jakarta after the army had fired on protesting students calling for the resignation of Suharto, who they had long held responsible for economic decline, corruption, nepotism and the lack of democracy and the rule of law. The civil unrest that these protests triggered particularly affected the Chinese. Many of their houses and businesses were set ablaze and destroyed by rioting gangs. Chinese and people regarded as Chinese were attacked, injured, killed and raped.

The ongoing social unrest – in combination with the persistent economic recession and increasing demands for democratization and liberalization – ultimately led to Suharto's removal from power. As a consequence of *reformasi, liberalisasi, demokratisasi* and *desentralisasi* the repression of the Chinese has since abated. In 2000 Suharto's successor – Abdurrahman Wahid – rescinded the presidential decree 14/1967 by which Suharto had established the social exclusion of the Chinese. The discriminatory measures relating to passport applications were abolished.[25] Several laws have been implemented in recent years that acknowledge the equality of all ethnic groups, including the Chinese. In 2006, the legal separation of Indonesians into indigenous and non-indigenous groups was abolished, and hence, the Chinese have been allotted the same rights as native Indonesians. The abolition of state discrimination is also seen as helping eliminate discrimination against the Chinese and avoid further riots.

Since the formal abolition of discrimination against the Chinese, Chinese culture and identity have been increasingly revived. Apart from the public (re-)appearance of Chinese (folk) culture and the public staging of important Chinese events, there are now Chinese language media and Chinese television and radio broadcasters. Chinese New Year has been recognized as an official holiday and is openly celebrated by Chinese Indonesians and other Indonesians alike. Public signs can be written in Chinese, and Confucianism has been recognized as an official religion. A Chinese village has recently been built at the Taman Mini Indonesia.

My impression confirms that of Turner and Allen, who argue that a) since the fall of Suharto Chinese culture has been undergoing a public revival (in media, literature, education, etc.) and that b) while commentators often declare their opposition to discrimination against the Chinese, they explicitly refer to the latter's close ties with Indonesia (Allen 2003; Turner 2003; cf. Knörr 2008a, 2009b). In the context of the (public) revival of Chinese culture and identity, the latter are performed and portrayed as (ethnic) dimensions of Indonesian culture and identity. The revitalization of Chinese culture in Jakarta is for the most part an interethnic and transethnic affair. The Chinese promote their culture as a means of stepping again onto the public stage and contributing to the city's image as a cosmopolitan city and the national capital of all Indonesians. As an older Chinese activist explained to me:

> The Chinese who do that want to reestablish contacts – as they were before – with all people in Jakarta through their festivals. We aren't doing this for the Chinese but for all people in Jakarta. We are happy when everyone takes part. We are part of Jakarta, part of Indonesia.

Many people in Jakarta welcome the fact that people of Chinese descent are again able to openly foster their own traditions. The current revival of the Chinese is accordingly seen in a mostly positive light. However, this applies primarily to the kind of cultural enrichment described above that is seen as adding colourful tradition to the urban image of Jakarta and as accessible to everyone.

In spite of the liberalization of political and social life and the revitalization of Chinese traditions associated with it, many Indonesians of Chinese origin still prefer not to emphasize their Chinese identity. There is still fear particularly among older Chinese that stressing Chinese identity could again raise questions

Figure 5.2. 'Free the Dragon' (cover from *Jakarta Kini*, edition November 2000).

about the status of the Chinese as Indonesian citizens. Chinese who foster traditions and publically support the revival of Chinese culture therefore often emphasize that this does nothing to alter the fact that they are Indonesians. As one young Chinese man explained:

> Chinese who have been born and have grown up in Indonesia quite obviously see themselves as Indonesian citizens, not as Chinese. They feel just as Indonesian as the Sundanese and Javanese do, because this is their country. So when we celebrate our New Year traditionally, we do this just as other ethnic groups cultivate their own customs. That doesn't make us any less Indonesian.

When charting the development of the relationship between Chinese and Betawi culture and identity in Jakarta, it becomes apparent that the repression and banning of Chinese culture during the Suharto era coincided with the state's support for and the rise of the Betawi, who, as pointed out already, have been strongly influenced by the Chinese. The Betawi with their heterogeneous origins thus somehow functioned as a (temporary) asylum for and host of Chinese culture, which could, in Betawi garb, appear as a dimension of indigenous culture. Not being considered Chinese, it was not feared to serve anti-national or subversive interests.

However, the Chinese dimensions of Betawi culture could not offer sufficient consolation to those Chinese who did not feel they belonged to the Betawi. An old woman who described herself as Peranakan explained to me:

> I know that the Betawi have many Chinese customs or customs that have Chinese elements. But they are nevertheless Betawi because they are from the Betawi, they belong to the Betawi. That's why although I can see the Chinese in Betawi culture I can't feel it, because I am not a Betawi. I am Chinese, Indonesian Chinese, but not Betawi.

The revival of the Chinese, which took off only after the fall of Suharto, hence, much later than the revival of the Betawi, is also allowing for the (re-)discovery of commonalities between Chinese and Betawi culture. Some years ago I encountered a small Chinese New Year's celebration in a side street in Kebon Sirih, in Central Jakarta. Most people living here are Betawi or Chinese. A lot of people stood watching and participating in the small procession, including many of the local Betawi. I made a remark to a young woman in the crowd about many Betawi participating in these Chinese New Year's celebrations, and she said: 'Yes, we like it, too. And it's also a bit like the Betawi *ondel-ondel* processions' – i.e., the processions chiefly made up of costumed and masked dancers that are organized in particular for Jakarta's birthday. Another older woman told me, 'I think it's

Peranakan Festival
What's On

The Chinese Indonesian Peranakan Festival kicks off with a series of seminars on 31 Oct-2 November at LIPI Building, Jl Gatot Subroto, covering a huge range of topics based around the influence of the Chinese in Indonesia - from the role of Chinese women to feng shui. There will also be a dinner and cultural show.

For more information, or registration (public fee rp300,000), contact the Mitra Museum Secretariat at Menara Batavia 11/F, Jl KH Mas Mansyur, tel 574 7569-70, fax 574 7569.

end of January 2001
Performance: Wayang Orang by Peranakan Chinese Artists
Gedung Kesenian, 380 8283.

end of January 2001
Exhibition: Chinese nuance in Indonesian Fine Arts
Museum Seni Rupa and Keramik, Kota. 690 7062.

end of January 2001
Exhibition: Peranakan Chinese Cultural Heritage
Museum Sejarah, Kota. 692 9101.

end of January 2001
Exhibition: Maritime Trading Between China and Indonesia
Museum Bahari, Pasar Ikan 669 3406.

end of January 2001
Exhibition: Peranakan Chinese Art in textiles and accessories (includes decorative and ceremonial cloth and a fashion show)
Museum Tekstil, Pusat. 560 6613.

end of January 2001
Exhibition: Puppets and show of wayang potehi
Museum Wayang. 692 9560.

plus ....
Performance: Peranakan Chinese Traditional Music and Dances (Museum Sejarah, Museum Tekstil, LIPI Auditorium, Teluk Naga Tangerang); Food Festival; as part of the exibitions and TV talk show.

Figure 5.3. Programme of Peranakan Festival, Jakarta 2001.

good that it's happening again and that's why I'm watching. It is a good thing when all groups can experience their culture.'

The relatively recent revival of Chinese culture and identity is now taking place simultaneously with the meanwhile long established revival of the Betawi. In connection to these concurrent processes, discourses are engaging with the complex and in parts ambiguous relationship between the categories Peranakan and Betawi. These discourses refer to both the Jakartan and the Indonesian context; they concern processes of (mutual) inclusion and exclusion and evoke ambivalent responses.[26]

While many Chinese have joined the Chinese revival, the increased prestige and influence of the Betawi has led many others to claim Betawi rather than Chinese or Peranakan identity. During the Suharto regime and also in its aftermaths, an increasing number of Chinese have designated themselves as Betawi and have also become members of Betawi associations. These are often people of Chinese descent who have grown up in Betawi environments, who are related to Betawi, speak the Betawi dialect and have always been socially and culturally closer to the Betawi than to other Chinese. As one young woman said to me: 'I haven't actually ever felt like I was really Chinese, more Betawi. My friends are Betawi. I speak Betawi, not Chinese. My parents have always insisted we are Chinese. But I see things differently now and say, I am Betawi.'

The emergence of the Peranakan and the Betawi has been accompanied by a process during which both have incorporated features of the respective other. The boundaries between the Peranakan and the Betawi are fluid and dependent on situation and context in many ways. In areas that have long been inhabited by both groups, there have emerged those who are referred to as Cina Betawi or Hitachi – 'Hitam tapi Cina'. The groups concerned are made up of descendants of old-established Peranakan who live mostly on the outskirts of Jakarta and in Tangerang. Although their lifestyle, social status and appearance make them seem Betawi, their Buddhist or Confucian religion makes them appear as Chinese. As a result they are sometimes seen as Chinese Betawi, sometimes as Betawi Chinese and sometimes as both.

> Thus the *Cina kampung*[27] are closer to the indigenous people than to other Chinese and it is difficult sometimes for outsiders to differentiate physically between *Cina kampung* and indigenous people. ... The most obvious difference between the Cina Betawi, either those who are in Jakarta or those who are in Tangerang, and the other Betawi in general is in their religion. Most of the Cina Betawi are either Buddhist or Confucianists (Shahab 1994: 146).[28]

> Among the peranakan Chinese living in Java are the so-called Cina-Betawi (Lohanda 2001: 31).

People who see themselves as Betawi of Chinese descent often point out that their sense of belonging is undermined by the lack of recognition accorded them by Islamic Betawi. Two women I spoke to summed up this situation as follows:

> I am Betawi but not Islamic. I'm a Buddhist Betawi. There are many Betawi who therefore do not recognize me as genuine Betawi. That's a pity but that's just the way it is.

> We have always fostered Betawi traditions – even more than the *Orang Kota* who say we are Chinese. Formerly the Betawi also had a bad reputation. That is why I usually only said where I lived, that is, where I came from. It was bad to be Betawi and bad to be Chinese. Today it's okay to be Betawi. However, there are many Betawi who say we are not Betawi because we are not Muslims. They say we are actually Chinese. I don't really feel Chinese although I am a Buddhist and my ancestors were partly Chinese. I think I am Betawi.

Recently (February 2013) some Indonesian Islam leaders have publically declared the celebrations of the Chinese New Year (*Imlek*) – which is now a public holiday in Indonesia – as *haram* (forbidden) for Muslims. They have urged Muslim Indonesians not to partake in the celebrations and Chinese Indonesians not to invite the latter. However, most public reactions as well as attitudes expressed in personal communication give the impression that such demands are perceived as backward and as not compatible with Jakarta's and Indonesia's heterogeneity in terms of culture and religion. As well, they evoke bad and unwelcome memories and fears of anti-Chinese riots, of massacres and repression not merely among Chinese Indonesians but among the majority of Jakartans. Currently it seems to be the conservative Islam leaders who are rejected for their demands rather than the Chinese who celebrate *Imlek* together with their Muslim compatriots.[29]

Although the Cina Betawi, or Hitachi, are not in themselves a new phenomenon, the emphasis on their Betawi-ness is a more recent development. The Hitachi has become, so to speak, a Chitahi – 'Cina tapi hitam' – a Chinese who is actually a Betawi. A man who I asked why he considered himself a Betawi whereas his brother described himself as Peranakan explained: 'In Indonesia it is better to be Betawi than to be Chinese. Do I look Chinese? No. Am I rich like a Chinese person? No. Thus, I am Betawi. When my brother says he is Peranakan, that is perfectly alright, but I feel myself to be Betawi.'

The valorization of the Betawi and the associated public engagement with their culture has led to a growth in Betawi consciousness within those groups whose identity is situated between the Betawi and the Chinese. The traditions of Gambang Keromong, Lenong and Cokek that have at some stage been declared by the state to be Betawi traditions are (also) practiced by the Chinese, and those who feel themselves to be both Betawi and Chinese are quick to point to the affirmation of their Betawi-ness by state institutions. A man who claimed both Betawi and Chinese identity told me: 'Even the Governor says that Gambang Keromong and Cokek are part of Betawi culture. And we practice both. That means we are also Betawi. It doesn't matter whether we are Muslim or not. It's about culture and tradition, not religion.'

The fact that Chinese and Betawi forms of artistic expression exhibit many similarities due to their mutual influence on one another and that for a long time Chinese culture could only be expressed in a Betawi disguise facilitates a contextual ascription of ethnic belonging. A woman explained to me:

> In the past our ancestors came to Indonesia from China. But they married native women and became Indonesian. However, they retained their religion. We are Betawi because our culture is more Betawi and we speak Bahasa Betawi. But we are also Chinese, Peranakan, because our faith is Confucian and we have Chinese ancestors. We are both.

It is still generally difficult for anyone to be accepted as Betawi without being a Muslim. This is true for people of (partly) Chinese identity too. If such a person wants to be recognized as Betawi in an area mostly inhabited by Muslim Betawi, then that person will have to convert to Islam. As this young man explained:

> I feel closer to the Betawi than to the Chinese. So I have to convert to Islam. If that means I am not allowed to eat pork anymore then I won't eat pork. My parents didn't like that at first but they understand that it is better for me this way. My girlfriend is half Betawi, half Sunda, and

we would like to marry in the Islamic tradition. It's better that way and simpler.

Today many Chinese also 'convert' to Betawi-ness by converting to Christianity, usually to Catholicism. Formerly, many Chinese passed themselves off as Menado, as the latter are said to look like the Chinese but, unlike the Chinese, are considered native Indonesians. Today, becoming Betawi seems like a more attractive alternative to many in that it goes along with a greater degree of authenticity, as the following statement by a man in his thirties shows: 'I have grown up here alongside the Betawi. The Betawi are more similar to me than the Menado. What do I have in common with people from Menado apart from the fact that I look like them?'

The acquisition of Betawi identity increases the authenticity and public recognition of one's national identity as Indonesian. As a woman of Chinese descent who referred to herself as Betawi explained to me, 'If you are Betawi, it is clear that you are Indonesian. But if you are Chinese, whether you are Indonesian is not clear at all.' The assumption of an identity as Betawi offers the possibility of belonging to an unambiguous Indonesian category of people (without necessarily having to convert to Islam) who are at the same time considered native Jakartans. It is now being increasingly recognized not only in the private but also the public sphere that there are also Christian (and other religious) minorities among the Betawi. However, despite the fact that it may also slowly be becoming easier to claim Betawi identity while being a Buddhist or Confucianist, the latter two are still closely associated with being Chinese. This means that it is easier to assume an identity as Betawi by way of a conversion to Christianity. With regard to religious customs and obligations, such a conversion is less problematic for the Chinese than a conversion to Islam, which would be a requirement for the adoption of most other ethnic identities. Christians are allowed to eat pork and do not have to interrupt their daily business activities for prayer five times a day. Converting to Islam would not permit having an altar in the home or to take part in traditional Chinese ceremonies. Eating in the home of one's (non-Islamic) parents would not be allowed due to the danger of crockery coming into contact with pork. Praying in the home of one's parents would be prohibited as there may be a dog around. Buddhist rituals and Chinese daily habits are thus more compatible with Christianity and Catholicism in particular. Catholicism attaches great significance to altars and saints, permits dogs in the house and the consumption of pork. It is also less associated with the Dutch colonialists. Above all, conversion to Catholicism is not subject to the level of monitoring as conversion to Islam is. As one young man put it:

Had I converted to Islam I would now be checked constantly. People would want to see whether I was behaving according to the rules of

Islam. Most people here are Muslims, and they would know that I have not always been a Muslim. Being Catholic doesn't come along with these sorts of problems. No one comes to check on people, and I can practice my religion more freely in the way that seems right to me.

Chinese 'converts' are often people who have separated or distanced themselves from their families or the Chinese milieu. Many no longer want to be classified as Chinese because of the discrimination they have experienced in the past. In some cases entire families convert and become both Betawi and Christians. They usually emphasize that from their point of view the Betawi are not to be characterized by the fact that they are Muslims but by the fact that they are the original inhabitants of Jakarta. Indeed, this applies to many Chinese as well. One female convert stated that 'the Betawi emerged from a whole range of different groups of people. These included many Chinese. So you don't have to be Muslim to be Betawi. The majority of the Betawi claim this simply because most Betawi are in fact Muslim. But this is not a must.'

The revival of Betawi-ness, which is being pushed forward and represented by the Betawi Kota, is also being accompanied by an increasing public awareness that being Betawi is not necessarily synonymous with a lack of education, modernity and urbaneness. This change in attitude facilitates the adoption of Betawi identity. As one young man who claimed both Chinese and Betawi identity rather emphatically put it, 'It simply isn't the case that the Betawi are people who do not send their children to school and just sit around in the mosque. Maybe that is what the Betawi Kampung are like, but it certainly doesn't apply to the Betawi Kota.'

For the majority of Chinese who live in the Chinese districts of Glodok and Mangga Dua the option of conversion does not readily present itself. Anyone who looks Chinese and lives and works in a district dominated by Chinese is likely not to be considered Betawi and would not gain anything from be(com)ing Betawi. Rather, it would likely lead to exclusion. It is precisely here, on the site of so many past attacks, that Chinese solidarity is considered significant. Moreover, rootedness in Chinese identity is more pronounced here due the limited close contact with non-Chinese.

In the course of the decline in discrimination against the Chinese and against the background of a general liberalization, an increasing number of Peranakan are reconsidering the Chinese dimension of their identity. In some ways the Chinese revival is experienced as a countermovement to the Betawi revival. A young man said to me:

> Many Chinese Indonesians are poor. Many here have Chinese origins but are referred to as Betawi because they look like Betawi and are poor. But actually they are Hitachi or Cina Benteng. They are Chinese because

they came from China back then. They are Chinese Indonesians – in the same way as one can be Javanese Indonesian or Betawi Indonesian.

What is at stake here is the assertion of Chinese identity as one of the ethnic identities indigenous to Indonesia, the Peranakan's claim to recognize the (indigenous) Chinese as a *suku bangsa* within the framework of the state doctrine of *Bhinneka Tunggal Ika* – 'Unity in Diversity' (cf. Unidjaja and Gunawan 2004).

There are also many Chinese who prefer adopting an identity as Jakarta Asli rather than as Betawi. Ascribing oneself to the category (Orang) Jakarta Asli is particularly popular among people who see themselves as native Jakartans without, in ethnic terms, allocating themselves either to the Betawi or some other ethnic category of people. For Chinese Indonesians, who have been denied equal civic rights for decades and whose identification with Indonesia has been mistrusted, emphasizing indigeneity and national identification is particularly important. It has become more accepted in recent years that the Chinese in Indonesia should be regarded as a native ethnic group (*suku bangsa*) rather than a foreign national one. However, many Chinese still ascribe themselves to groups and categories of people beyond the Chinese to stress their Indonesian indigeneity. They do so mostly in a fashion whereby they supplement rather than substitute their Chinese/Peranakan identity. In Jakarta, many Chinese nowadays stress their (also) being Betawi – as described above – many others go for the Jakarta Asli option instead.

Responding to my question as to whether he was Betawi, one young man of Chinese descent said, 'I am not Betawi because my ancestors were Chinese, not Betawi. They did not integrate themselves into the ethnic group of the Betawi. We are not Muslims and we do not practice Betawi culture. But we are Jakarta Asli. Jakarta is our home. Just as it is the home of the Betawi.'

There are still Chinese (as well as other Jakartans) who continue to associate the Betawi with backwardness and therefore continue to reject affiliation with them in ethnic terms, as indicated by the following statements:

The Betawi are different. They are strict Muslims and have little interest in modern education and modern professions. They have very specific traditions that don't really mean anything to me. However, like the Betawi I am a Jakarta Asli, because my ancestors already lived here and I was born here.

I am Orang Jakarta. I was born here and grew up here. I work here and my whole family is here. My friends and my business partners are here. You ask whether I am Betawi. No, Betawi are people who practice Betawi traditions, speak their own dialect and have rather old-fashioned attitudes. I am modern and educated. I am Orang Jakarta, Jakarta Asli.

More recently, the category Jakarta Asli has come to offer the possibility of connecting one's Chinese identity with Jakartan indigeneity – the possibility to represent oneself as indigenous *and* Chinese, that is. Being Jakarta Asli on top of being Chinese underscores a person's rootedness in Jakarta while not denying his or her Chinese identity. As one young man explained to me, 'As a Jakarta Asli I am a native [*orang asli*] of Jakarta, and thus also an Indonesian. After all, Jakarta is the capital of Indonesia.'

The Betawi's Appetite for Incorporation

The revival of the Chinese also creates additional competition in the field of identity politics in Jakarta. It is not surprising that particularly the Betawi experience the Chinese revival as a challenge. This is particularly so among Betawi activists and among representatives of the state who have been promoting Betawi culture and identity for long.

As pointed out already, Chinese and Betawi culture in Jakarta are strongly influenced by one another. However, Betawi culture and identity, having a creole background rooted in heterogeneous origins, has the larger potential for incorporation and a higher degree of flexibility in interpreting who and what is Betawi. Whereas Chinese culture in Jakarta has been influenced (mostly) by the Betawi, heterogeneity of origin is a constitutive criterion of Betawi identity. As a creole culture and identity, the latter has the far greater potential to interpret its origins and links according to situational demands. Against this background, Betawi activists in particular are attempting to counter the *Chinese* revival of Chinese culture and identity with a *Betawi* revival of Chinese culture and identity. From their point of view Chinese-ness should be promoted and enhanced as one particular dimension of Betawi culture and identity rather than as a separate culture and identity.

Although there are fears and reservations regarding the Chinese revival among other Jakartans as well, they have a specific meaning for the Betawi and for the relationship between the Betawi and the Chinese.

Particularly those Betawi who are concerned to draw as many people as possible into the Betawi camp by interpreting Betawi-ness in a broad rather than narrow fashion often perceive the revival of the Chinese as an irksome rival movement. Many Betawi seem uncomfortable with the idea that the revival of the Chinese might be stealing their show. Public events staged by the Chinese as well as their increased political involvement have been attracting a great deal of attention, particularly because the Chinese had been banned from staging their culture and from taking on political mandates for so long.

Many politically active Betawi would rather include the (Peranakan) Chinese in the Betawi camp. They fear that the current revival of the Chinese is encouraging Indonesians of Chinese descent to embrace Chinese-ness and withdraw from the circle of those who might (potentially) be counted as Betawi. Some Betawi activists go so far as to generally interpret the Jakartan Chinese as 'actually Betawi'. They do this by pointing to the fact that most Jakartans of Chinese origin are descendants of people who had already settled in Jakarta hundreds of years ago. One Betawi activist explained this to me as follows: 'The Chinese were here just as early as those groups from which the Betawi emerged. Some Chinese quickly became Betawi, while others retained their identity as Chinese or Peranakan. But in principle they are also Betawi: Chinese Betawi, but Betawi.'

It is argued that the attachment to Jakarta is as strong among the Chinese as among the Betawi. It would therefore make sense for the Chinese to see themselves as Betawi rather than as a separate group of Chinese. A DKI Jakarta official made a similar point: 'We should promote Chinese culture in the same way as we promote Betawi culture. However, it should not be promoted as a separate culture but rather as part of Betawi culture, as Jakartan tradition.'

It is often emphasized that Betawi-ization would make Chinese identity more evidently Indonesian, an attitude that implies that this would otherwise not be the case. It is thus insinuated that Chinese and Indonesian identity are not as compatible as Betawi and Indonesian identity. No Betawi would consider demanding of the Javanese in Jakarta to abandon their ethnic identity and henceforth live as Betawi because it is taken for granted that the Javanese are a *suku bangsa*, an ethnic group of Indonesian origin. The Chinese, on the other hand, are not accorded this status as naturally. According to the Betawi argument, their incorporation into the Betawi category would manifest their belonging to the group of native Jakartans, and thereby their belonging to Indonesia whereas insisting on a separate Chinese identity is likely to (re-)establish their status as foreigners. To lend plausibility to their identity as Indonesians, so the message goes, the Chinese should identify themselves primarily as Betawi rather than indulging in Chinese-ness. At the same time it is argued – more or less explicitly – that the Chinese themselves would be to blame for not being recognized as genuine Indonesians should they continue to separate themselves from the Betawi. This attitude is illustrated by the following comments by a prominent representative of the Betawi:

> I don't understand it. On the one hand the Chinese have always wanted to be recognized as Indonesians, and now some of them are doing everything they can to be recognized as Chinese instead. Chinese news, Chinese radio broadcasts and so on. If they want to be recognized as Indonesians then they would be better off identifying themselves as Betawi. After all, they have been here just as long as we have.

In spite of the professed closeness of the Chinese and the Betawi, the use of 'as us' indicates that a distinction is being made between 'we' (Betawi) and those who are *like* 'us', but not identical to 'us'. The historical proximity of the Chinese and the Betawi is enlisted as an argument for promoting the incorporation of the Chinese into the group of the Betawi and for interpreting (Indonesian) Chineseness in Jakarta as 'actually Betawi', as a dimension of Betawi-ness. Many such Betawi emphasize the degree of mixture that has occurred among the Betawi and the Chinese and to justify the latter's incorporation as Betawi, as evident in the following statements:

> The Betawi of course have mixed origins. And many Chinese are mixed and have been for a very long time. They are therefore actually Betawi, even if they also have Chinese blood. We Betawi are the product of mixing.

> Of course these people are Betawi. At that time many Peranakan were also part of the Betawi, as were other ethnic groups. The Betawi have mixed origins. I mean, look at these people. They aren't Chinese, they are Betawi.

However, there are also Betawi who are in favour of a distinct revival of the Chinese. In an interview, a member of the Indonesian Institute of Sciences (LIPI)[30] argued that the suppression of Chinese culture had been a mistake and counterproductive to the proposed assimilation of the Chinese. She went on to say: 'Culture could be used as a tool for Chinese-Indonesians to interact socially with the local culture and its people, which in turn would also lessen the likelihood of any possible conflict' (Widiadan 2000). Although this statement implicitly denies Chinese culture and Chinese people local status, Chinese distinctness is not denied its position within an Indonesian context of ethnic and cultural diversity.

Concerning the public representation and appearance of contemporary Chinese culture and identity, parallels between the pre- and the post-Suharto era are evident. As before, it is above all those Chinese feeling at home in Jakarta and Indonesia who provide a public face of Chinese culture. Although Chinese events are now being staged in mainly Chinese quarters as well, their growing popularity is based on the fact that Chinese culture and identity is represented and communicated as a dimension of Jakartan and Indonesian culture and identity – whether directly linked with Betawi-ness or not.

Notes

1. *Warga Negara Indonesia Keturunan Tionghoa* = Indonesian citizen of Chinese origin.
2. *Pribumi* = natives.
3. Although as a rule the term Peranakan is used to denote Indonesian of Chinese origin, it is also sometimes used to distinguish other indigenized people and groups of exogenous origin (Arabs, Indians) from non-indigenized people and groups whose exogenous origin continues to be their primary source of identification.

4. Raffles (1817: 74): 'There are no women on Java who come directly from China; but as the Chinese often marry the daughters of their countrymen by Javanese women, there results a numerous mixed race which is often scarcely distinguishable from the native Chinese. The Chinese on their arrival generally marry a Javanese woman, or purchase a slave from the other islands. The progeny from this connexion, or what may be termed the cross breed between the Chinese and Javans are called in the Dutch accounts *Peranakans*.'
5. One of the first works to deal explicitly with the problem of distance between Chinese and Indonesians is by Skinner (1963); see also Bertrand (2004).
6. Compared with Chinese, Indonesians are regarded as dark, as *hitam* (black).
7. Descriptions of this Muslim-Chinese population in Java can be found in Ricklefs (1984); cf. Lombard (1989).
8. For a detailed description see Lohanda (2001).
9. Remarks on these Chinese settlements can be found in 'Chronologisch Geschiedenis van Batavia, geschreven door een Chinees', *Tijdschrift voor Neerlands Indië* Vol. 1, 1842: 62.
10. Coen stated: 'Daer is geen volck die ons beter dan Chineesen dienen' – 'There is no people that serves us better than the Chinese' (cited in Haan 1935: Vol. 1: 10).
11. Many Chinese influences are also evident in local traditions in other parts of Indonesia.
12. Lenong Betawi features wooden puppets used as actors. It also exhibits strong Sundanese influences. See Grijns (1976) on Lenong in the environs of Jakarta.
13. A detailed description and analysis of these structures is provided by Blussé (1986).
14. Blussé (1986) describes the exposure of such wheelings and dealings.
15. *Weltevreden* (from Dutch) = well content. This name was given to the settlement by the colonial regime due to the fact that it was cleaner, more sparsely settled and less prone to flooding than northern areas and because it had a lower number of indigenous inhabitants.
16. A description of Chinese life in Batavia around 1900 from a European point of view can be found in Ponder (1988).
17. The relationship between the Chinese and the Indonesian in various fields of art is described in Blussé (1991); see also Tan (1991), who deals with the problematic designation ethnic Chinese in this context.
18. Sukarno transferred most of his power to Suharto in 1966. In 1967 Suharto was named acting president and in 1968 he was formally elected president.
19. *Petilasan-petilasan:* rituals, performances, customs.
20. The quote was originally printed in the daily newspaper *Berita Antara*, 5 January 1967. Sumitro was commander-in-chief of Brawijaya Division and later chief of staff of the Operational Command for the Restoration of Security and Order.
21. For a more detailed discussion of Indonesia's state ideology see Chapter 6.
22. *Informasi*, 1 April 1980: 12, cited in Simbolon (1991: 24).
23. Coppel and Suryadinata (1970: 106); Suryadinata (1992: 42f). Tan emphasizes that this designation also points to the fact that the Chinese are still seen as foreigners and as an integrated whole (1991: 119).
24. Parts of this chapter have been published before, see Knörr (2009b), cf. Knörr (2008a).
25. The new political and legal developments relating to the state's dealings with the Chinese are detailed by Freedman (2003).
26. On the current relationship between ethnic and national identity among the Chinese in Indonesia see also Purdey (2003).
27. *Kampung* refers to the village environment in which these people live.
28. The ambivalence concerning the classification of the Hitachi or Cina Betawi as (more) Betawi or Chinese is also apparent in the relevant literature. For instance, Allen (2003:

393) classifies the Hitachi as Betawi when she writes: 'Many Betawi (indigenous Jakartans) are known as "Hitachi", which stands for "Hitam tapi Cina" (brown-skinned Chinese).'
29. This information was obtained through the media and in conversations with Indonesian informants well after my actual field research and shortly before this book went into press. See, for example, 'Indonesia Islam Leaders Stir Row over Chinese New Year', *JakartaGlobe,* 10 February 2013 (http://www.thejakartaglobe.com/news/indonesia-islam-leaders-stir-row-over-chinese-new-year/570697) .
30. LIPI: abbreviation of Lembaga Ilmu Pengetahuan Indonesia.

Chapter 6

Orang Betawi versus Orang Indonesia

The Connection between Ethnic Diversity and National Unity

Pancasila and *Bhinneka Tunggal Ika* as Core Principles of National Identity

When Indonesia achieved independence in 1949 it had been under colonial rule for 350 years. Java had been the centre of Dutch colonial power and retained its central role after independence. Because there had been no Indonesian state prior to the colonial period, a common Indonesian identity had yet to be created: 'In conclusion it can be said that the *systematic* production of Indonesian tradition only began 30 years after Indonesian independence when the *Pancasila* were declared by decree to be the binding doctrine of state' (Moosmüller 1999: 40). Moosmüller's conclusion is based on his study of the construction of ethnic and national identity in Indonesia. In his view, whereas in the course of the struggle for independence different groups – namely the Javanists, communists and Islamists – had found common ground in 'anti-colonial hatred' and 'vague ideas of political independence', it became increasingly clear following the end of colonial rule that 'no common national path existed' (ibid.).

Since independence the term Indonesia has referred to the territory of the former Dutch colony *Nederlandsch Indië*. Indonesians only adopted this term for themselves and 'their' country at the end of the nineteenth century, when a select number of them studied at Dutch universities and became acquainted with Western theories of the nation-state (Avé 1989). The Indonesian independence movement was thus initiated by students who had previously seen themselves as inlanders, as natives of the Dutch colony of *Nederlandsch-Indië*. In Dutch 'exile' these students had realized they were Indonesians, members of 'one people' – *satu bangsa*[1] – people who shared a common history, language, territory and culture. Indonesia, a concept originally created by European anthropologists and linguists denoting 'all peoples of the archipelago and adjoining territories that belong to the same language family and which are linked by historical and cultural commonalities' (Moosmüller 1999: 35)[2] thus provided the concept of a unified Indonesia for those who launched the struggle for their country's independence and from whose ranks the postcolonial rulers of the nation would emerge. National unification was a condition for the achievement of independence because it was only unity that could forge an Indonesia that was large and strong enough to push out the Dutch once and for all.

In *Nederlandsch-Indië* the early years of the twentieth century saw the establishment of various organizations that, although differing in terms of political and religious orientation, all promoted national unity and called for independence. However, apart from the goal of national independence they had little in common – Javanists and Islamists, poor and rich, city-dwellers and peasants had divergent notions of what an independent Indonesia should look like.

It was Sukarno who was finally able to assume leadership of the Indonesian independence movement by founding the Indonesian National Party (*Partai Nasional Indonesia*, PNI) in 1927 that brought the diverse groups together under one umbrella. Although Sukarno belonged to the Javanist camp, he worked with political activists from other regions of Indonesia and supported the establishment of Bahasa Indonesia rather than Javanese as the national language. His policy of *NASAKOM* – the insinuating (and acronymic) linking of nationalism (*Nasionalisme*), religion (*Agama*) and communism (*Kommunisme*) – was based on ideas he derived from Javanese mysticism.

However, once independence had been achieved the unity that had been so hard-won was lost, and Sukarno was unable to keep the different wings of the party from quarrelling with one another. In 1965 the conflicts culminated in a bloody power struggle between the communists and the nationalist military.

Sukarno, who had been president of Indonesia since 1945, was succeeded by Suharto in 1967. Suharto remained in power until 1998 and made modernization and economic progress his chief priorities. He gave the military more power and pursued an anti-communist and (until the end of the 1980s) anti-Islamic policy, thereby improving relations with the West, which had suffered under Sukarno, and gaining Western support in the form of World Bank loans.[3]

In the late 1970s the lack of social and economic progress resulted in mass protests, above all by students. Furthermore, Islamic opposition to the regime was on the increase. The government responded to this social unrest by attributing it above all to a lack of national consciousness and solidarity. In 1978 measures introduced to counteract this perceived deficit included the adoption of a 'manual for the realization and implementation of the *Pancasila*'.[4] The *Pancasila*, which became the central doctrine of the Indonesian state, consisted, in brief, of five major principles, symbolized in the *Garuda Indonesia*, the coat of arms and national emblem of Indonesia:[5]

- *Ketuhanan Yang Maha Esa* (symbolized by the star): Belief in the one all-powerful God (monotheism)

- *Kemanusiaan yang adil dan beradab* (symbolized by the chain): A just and civilized humanity
- *Persatuan Indonesia* (symbolized by the banyan tree): The unity of Indonesia
- *Kerakyatan yang dipimpin oleh hikmat kebijaksaan dalam permusyawaratan/ perwakilan* (symbolized by the bull's head): Democracy, based on Indonesian village democracy
- *Keadilan sosial bagi seluruh rakyat Indonesia* (symbolized by the rice and cotton): Social justice for all Indonesians

These principles had already been adopted in the preamble to the constitution in 1945. As part of the New Order – *Orde Baru* – that characterized Suharto's thirty-two-year regime, they were to be disseminated as a national doctrine and used to guide political practice and ideological orientation in all state institutions such as government authorities, schools and universities. In 1985 the *Pancasila* doctrine was declared the most important principle to govern all mass organizations and parties: 'Suharto firmly indicated that the basis of the state was

Figure 6.1. *Garuda Pancasila,* Gunkarta (photographer) via Wikipedia Commons, picture taken at the National Monument (Monas), Jakarta (n.d.).

final and *Pancasila* was the only legitimate ideology.... Adherence to *Pancasila* became compulsory for all social and political organizations in the mid-1980s' (Bertrand 2004: 38). This emphasis on the *Pancasila* as the only legitimate ideology had much to do with the concerns of those in power regarding stability and security in the face of what was perceived as a fragile national unity.

The almost mystical meaning that is often attributed to the *Pancasila* is based above all on the way in which Sukarno had originally explained their origins. These origins, it was claimed, lie in Indonesia's precolonial history and more precisely in the fourteenth-century kingdom of Majapahit. The *Pancasila* thus seem to be a 'return of the wisdom, legal conceptions and mores from the golden age of the Javanese kingdom of Majapahit in the fourteenth century' (Moosmüller 1999: 38). The evocation of Majapahit follows from the nonexistence of Indonesia as a precolonial entity: 'There was no precolonial precedent of Indonesia, which is why it could never have been created on the basis of a reality or an idea of older political entity' (Hubinger 1992: 4). The popularity that the doctrine of the *Pancasila* came to enjoy is essentially founded on the precolonial indigeneity attributed to it that lends it a certain anti-colonial charm and an almost mythical power independent of the respective postcolonial rulers.

> I dug out five jewels that were buried deep in the soil of history. Due to foreign oppression that had lasted 350 years the five gleaming jewels had disappeared into the Indonesian soil.... I am not the creator of the *Pancasila*. The *Pancasila* were created by Indonesian history itself. I merely dug the *Pancasila* out of the soil of the Indonesian nation (Sukarno, cited in Wandelt 1988: 22).[6]

By deriving the *Pancasila* from Javanese mythology and not presenting them as his own creation, Sukarno conferred them with a quality that transcends time and sets the doctrine above the divergent ideologies of various social and political groupings. It is disputed among scholars whether the propagated ideals of *Pancasila* also accord with precolonial traditions. However, whether the *Pancasila* are based in precolonial traditions or in postcolonial constructions of precolonial traditions has been of little relevance for their social meaning and political efficacy.

The efficacy of the *Pancasila* doctrine as a unifying national principle has always suffered when it has been too closely linked with particular political ideologies. When in 1959 Sukarno linked nationalism, religion and communism (*NASAKOM*) to form a new doctrine of statehood he also proclaimed that every deviation from this ideological trinity would be against *Pancasila* and thus hostile to the state. In doing so he met with resistance from the anti-communist military – which ultimately led to his downfall. His successor, Suharto, consequently depoliticized the *Pancasila* by positioning them more clearly in the context of Javanese *kebatinan* mysticism and by declaring *kasunyatan,* the 'highest wisdom', to be their fundamental core that could be achieved through the practice of *kebatinan*. In simple terms, *kasunyatan* involves surmounting contradictions and differences between material and spiritual life by means of an intuitive understanding (*rasa*) of the hidden, inner core of one's own being (*batin*), which has its origins in *Hyang Sukma*, the all-embracing God (Mulder 1996). According to this concept the external world reflects a transcendent order within which each individual must occupy a certain position. *Rasa* is able to lead the individual to the position that has been prescribed for him. Once a person has taken up this position he is able to fulfil the tasks associated with it and thus in turn increase his intuitive, emotional power (*rasa*) and consolidate his personality (*batin*).

This principle is suited to providing direction to the individual on how to live his life, but it can also function as a source of guidance for an ethnically, culturally and religiously heterogeneous society in which it is necessary to overcome ruptures based on difference without suppressing diversity. Just as by means of *rasa* the individual is able to find his respective position within the world and thus strengthen both his personality as well as the whole, so too can the different Indonesian groups find their position within the totality of the Indonesian nation of which they are part. Thereby they may strengthen their own – ethnic, religious, cultural – personality as well as the Indonesian nation as a whole. Or, in Suharto's famous words: 'We should let our differences blend in perfect harmony like that of the beautiful spectrum of the rainbow.'

It is no secret that despite the *Pancasila,* this 'beautiful rainbow' did not materialize during the Suharto regime. Rather, the highly generalized principles of the *Pancasila* were construed to serve different ideologies and legitimate divergent political interests and practices.

> There was a time in the history of the republic, when the banner of revolution was raised and politics enthroned as the sole commander. This was done in the name of *Pancasila*. But then, when development replaced revolution, and economics instead of politics was regarded as the saviour, this too was done in the name of *Pancasila*. There was a period when the people believed that nationalism, religion and communism could be synthesized into one spirit, called the spirit of *Nasakom* ... because *Nasakom* was understood as the crystallization of *Pancasila*. But under the authority of *Pancasila* also *Nasakom* was cursed, the Communist Party banned, and Marxism prohibited (Darmaputera 1988: 146).

Despite the many profound political changes the *Pancasila* continue to be considered important principles of the Indonesian state and society. The lack of the *Pancasila*'s social and political implementation and the fact that they were made to function as legitimating the abuse of power, is usually not blamed on the *Pancasila,* but on those (formerly) in political power.

In connection to this book's theme, it is the national motto of Indonesia – *Bhinneka Tunggal Ika*/Unity in Diversity – that is of special interest. It is inscribed in the *Garuda Pancasila* (*Pancasila* eagle), the national symbol of Indonesia (written on the scroll gripped by the Garuda's claws). Apart from being the national motto, the unity of Indonesia/*Persatuan Indonesia* is also one of the principles of the *Pancasila* (represented by the banyan tree). Unity (in Diversity) is thus the major principle and concern of Indonesian nation- and statehood.

According to the Javanese conception *Bhinneka Tunggal Ika* was first used in a religious poem (*Sutasoma*) by the philosopher Mpu Tantular, who lived in the kingdom of Majapahit during the fifteenth century. In this poem he formulated a doctrine that connects Hinduism (symbolized by Shiva) and Buddhism (symbolized by Buddha) in such a way that their unity is based in and strengthened by their difference (Santoso 1975).

Bhinneka Tunggal Ika is such a powerful notion also because it combines contemporary social and political needs – namely to achieve national unity in an extremely heterogeneous society – and (presumably precolonial) Javanese ideals of (reaching) consensus and one-ness. In the context of the country's extensive heterogeneity it is a matter of national survival to uphold *Bhinneka Tunggal Ika* as a social and political ideal. Consensus is also an ideal that shapes the life of the individual as well as that of the group beyond the political sphere. As already mentioned, this ideal of unity is likely to have been developed in the postcolonial *aliran kebatinan* as *kebatinan* mysticism. Although the notion of its precolonial genesis may thus be a postcolonial construct, this does not detract from its contemporary significance.

The Betawi as a Representation of *Bhinneka Tunggal Ika*: On the Meaning of 'Diversity of Origin' for 'Unity in Diversity'

The Betawi play a particular role in the context of the construction and representation of national identity. This is above all due to the fact that Betawi culture and identity have a creole background and, based on that, may serve as categories of both ethnic and transethnic identification. The fact that against a background of heterogeneous origins the Betawi have in the process of creolization developed a collective identity as a *suku bangsa* and as such are also being regarded as the indigenous population of Jakarta – the national capital – has connected indigeneity and heterogeneity in a way that symbolizes (and thereby serves) nation-building and national identity in postcolonial Jakarta and Indonesia in specific ways.

The Betawi are particularly suited to providing support for the claim that ethnic diversity does not need to inhibit the emergence of common identity. To employ the terminology of Indonesian state ideology: the Betawi can serve as a particularly germane representation of *Bhinneka Tunggal Ika* – of 'unity in diversity'. The Betawi emerged from different ethnic groups and Betawi culture and identity includes different dimensions of these origins while at the same time transcending them. The Betawi represent and symbolize shared identity against a background of ethnic heterogeneity. As such, the Betawi can be regarded – and publically communicated and displayed in relation both to Jakarta and to Indonesia – as a model for forging common identity on a background of diversity. The Betawi provide an ethnic embodiment of the national principle of *Bhinneka Tunggal Ika*. They represent as an ethnic group what Indonesians are supposed to represent as a nation.[7] As a (Javanese) statesman explained to me, 'The Betawi show all Indonesians that people can be of different origins and at the same time develop a common identity. We can learn a great deal from the Betawi.'

In Jakarta *Bhinneka Tunggal Ika* is significant for the construction of shared identity with reference to Jakarta and Indonesia. The Betawi function as representations of local (i.e., Jakartan) and national (i.e., Indonesian) identity – with local and national identity being in particularly close interaction in Jakarta due to the fact that Jakarta is at the same time a locality/town and, as capital city, the major representation of the nation. In the words of the (Javanese) statesman mentioned above: 'The Betawi have roots that are as mixed as people in Jakarta. And they are like Indonesia, with its many ethnic groups [*suku bangsa*]. The Betawi are a real symbol of *Bhinneka Tunggal Ika*.'

The Betawi themselves, above all those in the urban and political centre, also like to present themselves as a representation of 'unity in diversity'. As one of their activists put it to me, 'We are like *gado-gado*[8], composed of mixed ingredients but as a whole a tasty and unique dish. Just like Indonesia – many people of different origins, who are all Indonesians. The Betawi are what Indonesians should be – different but united.'

Official publications by the City of Jakarta found on the Internet, in tourist bureaus and hotels also state a connection between the heterogeneity of Jakarta and the heterogeneity of Indonesia, and between *Bhinneka Tunggal Ika* and the Betawi, who are portrayed as an (ethnic) representation of both Jakartan and Indonesian diversity.

> Indonesia's cultural diversity is celebrated in the national motto '*Bhinneka Tunggal Ika*', meaning 'Unity in Diversity'. One manifestation of this tenet of Indonesian national identity is the government's efforts to give equal precedence to the development of traditional art forms from each ethnic group in Jakarta. In Jakarta, the Orang Betawi – the natives of the city – are considered to be the hosts of these cultures, having emerged from the melting pot of races, ethnic groups and cultures of Indonesia in the 19th century.[9]
>
> Jakarta is a city of contrasts; the traditional and the modern, the rich and the poor; the sacral and the worldly, often standing side by side in this

bustling metropolis. Even its population gathered from all those diverse ethnic and cultural groups, which compose Indonesia, are constantly juxtaposed present reminder of the national motto; Unity in Diversity. … The ethnic of Jakarta called 'Orang Betawi' speaks Betawi Malay, spoken as well in the surrounding towns such as Bekasi and Tangerang.[10]

The uniqueness of the Betawi, which is above all founded on the heterogeneity of their origins, is complemented by their indigeneity, which provides the foundation for their being comprehended and promoted as a host of all people resident in Jakarta.

This unique group of people, today known as 'Betawi', represents an amalgamation of Javanese, Sundanese, Balinese, European and Arab culture influences, to name a few, all of which contributed to a unique expression in architecture, design, textiles, cuisine and theatre.… As the nation's capital, Jakarta is able to show all the several of art forms of all regions and ethnic groups in the archipelago. And to realize this idea in line with the motto 'Bhinneka Tunggal Ika' (Unity in Diversity), the regional government feels obliged to develop all traditional art forms as equitably as possible with the local Betawi art forms as host heading the rest.[11]

The Betawi, in this view, provide patronage for all ethnic groups as well as for their respective (traditional) cultures. The Betawi as well as Jakarta are conceptualized as melting pots and amalgamations. Moreover, the Betawi are also presented as the initiators of the 'Jakartan melting pot':

Being at the crossroads of one of the busiest sea routes in the world, as well as the hub of inter-island shipping, has made Jakarta a cultural melting pot. This process began in the 17th and 18th century, when the unique and colorful Betawi people of Jakarta evolved as an amalgamation of the Javanese, Sundanese, Balinese, Arabic and European influences here.[12]

Just as Betawi-ness serves as a unifying link for Jakartans of different ethnic identities, so should Indonesian-ness serve as a unifying link for Indonesians of different ethnic identities. To borrow from Suharto's phrase cited above: just as the Betawi emerged as the result of transcending differences, so should Indonesians strive to transcend differences to realize the *Pancasila* vision of a perfect rainbow. The Orang Betawi are, thus, a symbol of the Orang Indonesia 'en miniature'.

Jakarta, long before known as the port and the trade city, is a city where various nations gather and contribute their culture. No wonder the

> Betawi culture is the blend of the Arabic, Chinese and Portuguese culture since the Jayakarta era.... The external influence gives a role in forming the custom, art and culture, and even the architecture of the Betawi house.... Unlike the other traditional house architectures in Indonesia, the Betawi traditional architecture welcomes the external influence.[13]

As this statement demonstrates, the heterogeneous origins of the Betawi are also associated with a particular openness to external influences that is portrayed as a characteristic feature of the Betawi and of Jakarta, a feature that supposedly distinguishes both from other groups and cities.

Also, Betawi cuisine is used to connect diversity of origin with unity in diversity. For instance, Jakarta hosted an event called 'Heritage Food in Heritage City 2004'. Describing the aim of the event at a press conference, the committee chairman of the Jalansutra Club, which has dedicated itself to the cultivation of traditional cuisine, stated: 'We want to show that many ethnic groups, like the Chinese, Indians, Dutch, Arabs and Portuguese, were key influences of Betawi culture' (Aurora 2004). Apart from providing an opportunity to sample traditional Betawi foods, the event staged many artistic performances that also referred to the Betawi's diverse origins – for example, Chinese-influenced *Tanjidor* concerts and *Barongsai* dances, Indian *Tabla* and Sundanese-influenced *Lenong Betawi* performances.

National Meanings of Betawi Indigeneity

As has already been pointed out, an ethnic group requires that a territory is ascribed to it to gain social recognition, just as, conversely, it is through its ethnicization in the sense of its ascription to an ethnic group (or a combination of ethnic groups) that a territory becomes a social site. However, in Jakarta only the Betawi) relate to Jakartan territory in an ethnically ascriptive manner. There are no areas that are inhabited more or less exclusively by particular ethnic groups and, although many people identify with their respective residential areas, these areas are not considered the land of, for example, the Batak or the Sulawesi. Ethnic traditions are certainly fostered in Jakarta. For instance, (ethnic) Javanese living in Jakarta cultivate Javanese traditions, however, without restricting these to exclusively Javanese territories. Although Javanese weddings, for example, often take place at specific sites, such as specific hotels, these hotels do not thereby become exclusively Javanese territories. The possibility of expressing one's own ethnic identity in terms of territories is thus largely absent in Jakarta. However, an increasing number of Jakartans now see their primary ties as being with Jakarta and less with a region of origin outside the city. As explained earlier on, Betawi-ness, due to its creole background and heterogeneous roots, can serve to bridge this void by providing a link across ethnic groups who can identify with their respective ethnic shares in Betawi-ness. They may relate to Betawi-ness in an ethnic and transethnic manner according to their respective identity-related and circumstantial needs. The creole nature of Betawi culture and identity facilitates both ethnic and transethnic identifications with Jakarta well beyond the group of the Betawi. How does this affect the connection between Betawi-ness and national identity in Jakarta?

The valorization of the Betawi and their being promoted both as the city's indigenous population and as the hosts of the national capital by state institutions has increased the Betawi's identification with Jakarta as a city per se and as the nation's capital in particular. Already in 2001, when thousands of Indonesians from East Java threatened to storm Jakarta to prevent – if necessary by force – the overthrow of 'their' President Wahid (who came from East Java), the Betawi organized militias to defend the city against the intruders.[14] They were permitted to do this by the police force on the condition that they only carried traditional weapons. While hundreds of tanks and thousands of soldiers and police filled the streets and guarded parliament buildings, groups of Betawi wearing traditional costumes and carrying traditional weapons presented themselves as the indigenous counterparts of the state forces. They publicly declared – in the press and on radio and television – that as Betawi they felt it was their duty to defend their city. An interesting aspect of these declarations was the repeated assertion that Jakarta belonged to the Betawi and that the Betawi therefore had to ensure that Jakarta's entire population as well as the city's guests could feel safe. When asked why the Betawi were defending Jakarta in this way, one of these so-called warriors told me:

> As Betawi we have the duty to defend our city. The city belongs to us and therefore we must ensure that no outsiders destroy the city and its reputation. We also want foreigners to feel safe here. This is important for the whole of Indonesia, because Jakarta is the national capital. Most foreigners live in the capital. We are the native inhabitants [*penduduk asli*] of the capital and therefore we are defending it. But everyone else can also help.

The Betawi thus appeared both as defenders of 'their' city and – therefore – as defenders of national interests. Their status as the indigenous population of the national capital determined their status as guardians of both local and national interests. As one old man explained to me:

> We are the natives here. That is why we are Jakarta's hosts, so to speak. And Jakarta is our capital city as well as being the capital city of all Indonesians. We are the Betawi and this is the home of our people. Since Jakarta is the city of the Betawi and Jakarta is the capital of Indonesia we

Figure 6.2. Betawi warriors in founding year of the Forum Betawi Rempug (FBR), (this picture appeared in *The Jakarta Post,* 16 February 2001).

as Betawi must defend Jakarta – because it is the city of the Betawi but also because it is the capital of all Indonesians.

Others were also impressed by the Betawi's engagement – more in terms of the level of commitment that was being shown than by the actual defensive potential on offer, which was seen as rather low. As one passer-by commented, 'In one way it's funny to see them turning out in their war uniforms. But I think it's a good thing. It shows that they are really standing up for Jakarta and for everyone living here.'

The increasing social acknowledgement of the local and national significance of the Betawi and their promotion by state institutions have also increased identification with the state among many Betawi or at least led to a decrease in their sense of alienation from it. This particularly applies to the Betawi Kota, who are positioned in the political and urban centre of the Betawi. Their increased commitment to greater participation in political life at both a local and national level presupposes engagement with the state and communication with state institutions. State promotion of the Betawi over more than forty years has emphasized their local and national significance for Jakarta as a city per se and as the nation's capital. Outsiders are viewing the Betawi contribution to local and national matters in increasingly positive terms. Although stigmatization of the Betawi still exists, its significance and discriminatory potential have been qualified by positive ascriptions.

Betawi-ization versus Javanization of the National Centre

The promotion of Betawi culture by state institutions in Jakarta was, in part, also a reaction to criticism of the enforced Javanization of the Indonesian archipelago.[15]

> [I]t is widely felt that the efforts of the central government to foster a national Indonesian identity are in reality a plot to further Javanese political control. Being Indonesianized is equated with being Javanized, with the result that people hold firmly to their own ethnic cultures so as not to be submerged in what they perceive as a Javanese mainstream (Bruner 1974: 274).

As long as the Betawi were being promoted primarily in terms of tradition and folklore and as long as they were not making demands of a more political nature, this promotion was more of a political boon than a burden for the majority Javanese ruling elite. The political effects of their promotion could only materialize in the course of democratization and as the result of the decentralization of power. We will return to this later.

The identification potential offered by the dominant and primarily Javanese variant of urban life in Jakarta – 'this very vital Javanese-Indonesian mongrel culture' (Mulder 1996: 156) – was for a long time restricted largely to members of the urban middle class (which includes many Javanese). As a result of the link that has existed between the Javanese and political power for several decades many people in Jakarta still find Javanese identity, even in its Jakartan variant, to be unsuitable as a source of identification. By contrast, Betawi culture and identity until recently has remained relatively free of political connotations. Moreover, the Betawi accommodate cultural features of the different ethnic groups residing in Jakarta and for the most part belong – like most people in Jakarta – to the working class. This common social status has been an important factor in providing a potential for transethnic identification. Within Jakarta, Betawi-ness thus offers many people of non-Javanese descent – as well as many poorer Javanese – a welcome alternative to Javanese-influenced urban culture. For example, the Betawi-style wedding already referred to has become increasingly popular among non-Betawi, particularly among people who do not have links to a specific ethnic culture outside Jakarta. A young woman I met in Jakarta who classified herself as Sundanese and Orang Jakarta and who was planning her marriage to a man from Sumatra explained to me: 'Betawi style is Jakarta style. It's not so posh, it's not so super-traditional, not so Javanese, you know what I mean? Betawi style is more like Jakarta; it's more fun and everyone can participate. It's not so exclusive. Anyone can copy the Betawi-style.'

For their part the Betawi commonly emphasize the distinction between the genuine Betawi wedding ritual, which only 'genuine' Betawi are able to conduct, and the copy. However, as a rule, they are also proud that 'their' ritual is finding increasing approval outside their own group and is being preferred even by many urban Javanese to the – internationally famous – Javanese wedding ritual.

More recently, while this book is going to press (and too late to go into detail), the new Governor of Jakarta, Joko Widodo (himself a Javanese originating from Surakarta, Central Java)[16] has instructed civil servants (including teachers) to wear traditional Betawi clothes on Wednesdays to promote Jakarta's distinct identity, a policy he intends to apply to students, hotel and mail employees in the near future. Shortly after this regulation had been put in place, the day of Betawi attire was changed to Fridays to account for male civil servants' habit to wear specific clothes to perform their Friday prayers, clothes that resemble the traditional Betawi outfit and that can easily be exchanged for the latter on Fridays.[17]

Betawi Contra *Orang Kompeni:* Postcolonial Constructions of Anti-colonial Heroism

In the context of the increased linkage of the Betawi with national identity the Betawi have also been (retrospectively) attributed a greater social and political role in the struggle against colonial repression. In the early postcolonial period the Betawi were largely excluded from public consciousness and socially stigmatized due to the fact that they were a reminder of colonial repression and slavery and associated with a lack of education and modernity. However, since the early 1980s the attempt has been made to give them an anti-colonial profile that emphasizes their significance for postcolonial Jakarta and Indonesia. On the one hand, they are presented as the guardians of cultural and religious tradition and identity during Dutch rule, an achievement, it is argued, that benefits all Indonesians today. On the other hand, they are credited with subversive and heroic conduct against the Dutch colonizers.

In this context, different forms of anti-colonial activities are (retrospectively) Betawi-ized. Much that was once characterized as Sundanese or Javanese – or simply as indigenous, Indonesian – resistance is today classified as Betawi. It has been as it were retrospectively 'discovered' that 'it was (almost) always Betawi' – as one Javanese explained to me – who during the colonial period contributed, in the form of small acts of heroism in Batavia and its environs, to safeguarding the native while at the same time unmasking the oppressors and putting them in their place.

The integration of the Betawi in the Indonesian context of anti-colonial resistance does not have a great deal to do with their actual role in the political struggle for independence towards the end of the colonial period. Indeed there were only few Betawi among the educated elite who actually brought about the overthrow of the colonial regime and took power in the postcolonial period. The narratives of heroism that have been publically communicated since the 1980s are based less on the great heroism of a figure like Mohammad Husni Thamrin than on the little heroes of everyday colonial life and the subversive, spiritual and martial activities that represented their rebellion against the repression and exploitation suffered at the hands of the colonial rulers and their allies.

The exclusion of the Betawi from public consciousness and the fact that they were pushed to the periphery of early postcolonial society in Jakarta was in large part due to the attitudes of early postcolonial elites. Subsequently it was above all state institutions on the local level that identified the potential offered by the Betawi to the process of forging a national identity. They discovered their symbolic value for the concept of unity in diversity and their suitability for the role of protectors and guardians of indigenous Jakartan identity and tradition. As a result the Betawi – as the indigenous inhabitants of the present-day national capital – have been attributed an active anti-colonial role and, thereby, more national significance. According to these narratives, the Betawi already defended the (future) national capital, the capital of all Indonesians, during the colonial period, waging a struggle against the foreign occupiers for the people of Indonesia.

The Betawi themselves – and in particular the activists among them – are also endeavouring to cast their ancestors as heroes of everyday colonial life to historically enhance their national significance but also to legitimate their demands for more political power. They therefore promote narratives of Betawi heroism both within their own organizations and in the context of public events and scholarly as well as journalistic media. In 2002, as part of its efforts to contribute to the public, anti-colonial profile of the Betawi, the Department of Culture and Museums of the Province of Jakarta[18] organized a literary competition for teachers. As in the case of the *None dan Abang Jakarta* pageant, all teachers were permitted to take part regardless of their ethnic origins. The aim of this literary competition was to raise public awareness of the Betawi as (anti-colonial) heroes. Accordingly, the only works accepted for the competition were those that took as their themes protagonists and stories from the *Cerita Rakyat Betawi* – the Stories of the Betawi (Ali 1993) and already indicated this subject matter in the titles.

The *Cerita Rakyat Betawi* consists of stories about the most renowned Betawi heroes and their actions and experiences in the (colonial) surroundings in which they lived. Each story concludes with a summary and evaluation by the author Rahmat Ali, a native of East Java who has collected the stories and published them in book form.

Figure 6.3. A *jago* in action, cover of Ali's *Cerita Rakyat Betawi I* (1993) (illustrator unknown).

In these stories the stereotype of the poor, uneducated and rather awkward Betawi is countered by the image of the Betawi hero who retains his feistiness even in the most adverse circumstances. Although the Betawi are cast in the *Cerita Rakyat Betawi* as (poor) members of the common folk, they achieve heroic status through their actions. As a consequence they are admired by all and often feared, above all by the despised colonial rulers. The organizers of the literary competition hoped that Jakartan teachers' works on the heroes of the Betawi would help disseminate a different, more positive image of the Betawi and their culture. When I spoke with the chairman of the competition committee, who is a well-known scholar and promoter of the Betawi, he explained the prerequisites for entry in the competition as follows:

> The essays must have literary value and be properly bound. They must deal with Betawi themes and make reference to these themes in their titles. For example, a title might mention Si Pitung, Si Angkri, Pangeran Syarif, Si Jampang.... The entrants can select from the wealth of stories concerning the individuals named and discuss them. A possible theme would be, for example, 'Si Pitung – enemy of the *kompeni*'.[19]

The competition aimed at making a connection between the Betawi and anti-colonial engagement. The Betawi's anti-colonial attitude and the courage they showed in the struggle against the Dutch was to be emphasized. As one committee member put it:

> It is important to show that the Betawi played a very important role in the triumph over colonial domination. They struggled against the Dutch in their own way, often subversively, and thus contributed to their ultimate defeat. This is something the people have to know – in Jakarta and throughout Indonesia.

The organizers also emphasized the significance of the Betawi's preservation of their own culture under the conditions of colonial oppression. One of the initiators of the competition explained:

> The art and culture of the Betawi are an important element of Jakartan art and culture. The Betawi have preserved their culture under particularly difficult circumstances. Their culture is an important part of our national treasure. We have to take care that it is not suppressed by the many people coming from outside Jakarta.

For this reason, he went on to explain, a particular aim of the competition was to encourage teachers to engage with the Betawi as the natives of Jakarta. Because as teachers they were responsible for instructing children and young people they were in an ideal position to spread knowledge of the significance of the Betawi: 'With this competition we want to encourage Jakarta's teachers to engage with traditional Jakartan culture. We want them to recognize the values that are embedded in our culture, particularly in the stories of the Betawi.'

Certainly most of the teachers I interviewed in the course of my research were taken with the idea. In essence they echoed the arguments made by the initiators. The most important issue, as they saw it, was the need for children and young people in Jakarta to become acquainted with the history of Jakarta and its indigenous culture:

> The culture of the Betawi is the traditional culture of Jakarta, and that is why all those living here have to be acquainted with it. When people live here a long time, over many generations, they reach a point where their own culture fades. It is better when people become acquainted with the indigenous culture, the culture of the place where they are living. Then people feel at home.

A number of critical voices were also heard, both from Betawi and from others. However, criticism was directed less at the idea of a literary competition dealing with the culture of the Betawi than the chosen subject, the *Cerita Rakyat Betawi:*

> I think it would be better if it wasn't about the *Cerita Rakyat Betawi,* at least not exclusively. Those are stories about heroes and really more for children. I'd rather deal with real literature or with the history of the Betawi – how they lived and things like that.

One Betawi expressed his annoyance that the kind of engagement with the Betawi being promoted by the governor was always about things from the past, old traditions, old music, old dances:

> After all, we're living today, and we Betawi don't always want to be treated as if we were remnants of the Stone Age. If they only promote this kind of thing then the image of the Betawi will never change. On the one hand they say they want to keep our culture alive. On the other they act as if we were already dead. But we're not.

By connecting the Betawi and their heterogeneous origins with anti-colonial heroism, the organizers also wanted to point out that heterogeneity can indeed lead to community and solidarity – and even heroic forms of them. As a teacher explained to me:

> The Betawi of course emerged from different ethnic groups – people who all came to Jakarta from different regions. But their history shows that it can work, that people can grow together and don't have to fight against each other. And there were even real heroes among the Betawi, who contributed to the struggle against the colonial rulers and helped the poor people win their rights. These essays should reflect this.

The heterogeneous origins of the Betawi and the process of their creolization are linked with Betawi heroism to function as an argument supporting the unity in diversity doctrine, which, as the example of Betawi heroism is to convey, cannot only work out but may even bear heroic fruits. The fact that many so-called Betawi heroes were not actually Betawi when they acted heroically is not seen as contradicting this concept, rather the opposite. As one young man pointed out, 'The Betawi were the poor people, but they did not let themselves be beaten. There were also others who acted courageously. But most of them became Betawi too, because they lived here.' The heroization of the Betawi is intended as a means of generating stronger identification with Jakarta among Jakartans – with Jakarta per se and with Jakarta as the national capital. If some Betawi heroes were not yet Betawi, but became Betawi in the course of their heroic activities, then this may in fact increase the potential for a more general identification with Betawi heroism.

The social backgrounds of the heroes, who – like the majority of school children in Jakarta – usually came from poor backgrounds, were also emphasized, thereby highlighting the glorious effects of solidarity among the indigenous population. One participating teacher told me:

> These great men were small people, had no Western education and no money but were poor like most other indigenous people here. But for this reason people were on their side. This can teach us that it is more important to act in the interest of everybody than to think egotistically and focus only on one's own advantage. Most people in Jakarta are poor too. The pupils can learn that one can achieve something even if one is poor.

The 'great' men among these 'small' people were the *jago*, most of whom came from Marunda on the northeastern edge of present-day Jakarta. They play an important role in the (re-)construction of the anti-colonial history of the Betawi that serves to underpin the Betawi's national significance.

Jago refers to a person who is an expert in the art of *pencak silat*[20] – an Indonesian and Malayan form of martial arts that comprises spiritual and technical skills and different developmental stages. A *jago* is equipped with particular magical and physical strength that gives him great confidence in his fighting prowess

(Onghokham 1984: 327). Physical strength, courage and the mastery of magical forces are thus the major qualities of a *jago*.

> [J]ago has various meanings, including 'rooster older than 12 months', 'main candidate in an election'; 'front runner', 'champion'; and 'the favorite to win'. Generally speaking, a jago is regarded as someone to be respected by his community because of his gifts or talents, a person with posture and social status, somewhat like a prize rooster. Exactly where and when this expression originated cannot be confirmed (Maryono 2001: 1).[21]

In the traditional Javanese context the *jago* was the protector of his village, while his physical and spiritual abilities also enabled him to exercise influence on local political decisions. The *jago* was thus always an ambivalent figure – he could deploy his special abilities to provide protection and bring about justice but also to spread fear (Schulte Nordholt 2002). The task of the *jago* in the colonial context was not restricted to the struggle against the foreign oppressors and stealing from the rich. He also had to distribute a part of his booty – at least ideally – among the poor. Whether he measured up to this ideal, whether he served the interests of local groups or those of the authorities depended on the prevailing distribution of power (Onghokham 1984).

During colonial times the majority of the land was in the hands of wealthy landowners, who held estates on which the Betawi lived as tenants under the supervision of overseers. These tenant farmers were obliged to hand over a large part of their harvest to their landlord; they had no civil rights and were consequently subjected to various types of chicanery. The Betawi were not permitted to own their own land or establish village collectives and were subject to strict supervision by the overseers of the individual private estates, the *particuliere landerijen* established in 1620. These circumstances form the background of the significance accruing to the *jago* in colonial Java, particularly in and around Batavia. (Abeyasekere 1989). The *jago* took the place of an organized police force and to a certain extent protected the landowners, overseers and villagers from one another (Slamet-Velsink 1998). In return they were granted certain privileges, such as exemption from taxes and compulsory labour services. The payment of protection money was not uncommon either (Boekhoudt 1908).

The taxes and levies the Betawi had to pay, the chicanery they had to endure and the mostly inefficient structures of the colonial system of village administration in the *Ommelanden* were the major factors in strengthening the influence of the *jago*. Where community representatives – *lurah* – did exist they usually had only very limited influence. The supervision of landowners by the colonial administration existed for the most part only on paper, and the *sherifs* stationed by the administration in the *Ommelanden* were not in a position to counteract the power of the landowners or the formation of powerful criminal gangs. These gangs, known as *rampok* or *garong*, were usually commanded by a *jago*. The *rampok* lived in various settlements, which profited from their raids and to which they offered a certain level of protection from landowners and other *rampok* (Cribb 1991).

In the course of the twentieth century the Betawi in Marunda mixed extensively with the Sundanese and Makassarese living in the area. As a result, they still speak a particular Betawi dialect today.[22] According to legend the area owes its name to a *jago* by the name of Ronda who is said to have robbed and killed a wealthy Chinese merchant and was then hunted down by Dutch landowners who threw him in the Glodok jail (Heuken 2000). There were also female *jago*, such as the renowned *Si Mirah*, the 'lioness of Marunda'. She was also an expert in *pencak silat* and defended the local population against raids by neighbouring *jago*.

Future *jago* were trained by experienced *jago*, who among other things instructed their apprentices in the techniques of robbery. Trainees were also taught by a religious teacher, a *kyai*, who provided them with general religious knowledge as well as specific skills, like the art of making oneself and others invisible (*ilmu panglimunan*) or invincible and unbeatable (*ilmu kekebalan*). A *jago* candidate also learned the techniques of *pencak silat* and self-defence. The material and physical power of the foreign colonial rulers was thus set against the magical, spiritual and physical powers of the local *jago*. Although the *jago* was permitted to take from the rich he was obliged to use as little violence as possible. Ideally, violence was only to be used to defend oneself or to prevent the suffering of others. In the collective and idealized memory the *jago* was a person with an intense feeling of solidarity with the oppressed community of which he was a member. A *jago* utilized his physical and mental skills to defend the rights of the so-called 'little people', the *wong cilik*.

The most famous and in the context of the anti-colonial profiling of the Betawi the most prominent and revered *jago* in Batavia was Si Pitung:

> Betawi folklore has an abundance of heroes ... but the most famous of all is Si Pitung – the archetypal Betawi champion – a pious Moslem, an expert in traditional martial arts (pencak silat), loyal, respectful without being subservient, down-to-earth, simple and a defender of the poor against oppression and injustice (Koesasi 1992: 6).

The Si Pitung House in Marunda is up to date a place of pilgrimage for those interested in Jakartan history even though it is unclear whether Si Pitung ever lived there and whether it was the base from which he planned his operations.[23]

According to the legend Si Pitung was a kind of Indonesian Robin Hood operating at the end of the nineteenth century. In fact, he is often referred to as the *Robin Hood Betawi* today (van Till 1995: 465; Ali 1993: 7). He supposedly began his career after having been robbed of money earned by selling his father's goat.[24] As revenge he then robbed a wealthy landowner in Marunda, Hadji Sapiudin, an ethnic Bugi who was infamous for exploiting the local population. After Si Pitung was captured by *schout* Hinne, the Dutch chief constable of Tanah Abang, he and his friends managed to escape from the jail in *Meester* as a result of Si Pitung employing his magical powers. Despite a bounty of 400 guilders being placed on Si Pitung's head, he continued to rob the wealthy and killed two policemen.

The name Si Pitung is said to derive from *pituan pitulung*, which roughly translates as 'Pitung's group of seven' (Mertokusumo 1977). These seven accomplices are supposed to have dressed identically to confuse Si Pitung's enemies and lend him an aura of invincibility and ultimately immortality – an aura that was to endure beyond his death. The stories of his (physical) death are accordingly very varied. There are still Betawi today who believe that Si Pitung is still among them waiting for an opportunity to rise against their oppressors and punish them for their injustices.

Si Pitung has evidently been undergoing a process of increasing Betawization. While he is now revered as a local and national hero of the Betawi, according to older legends he was in fact a Sundanese who came to Batavia from Cirebon. However, according to all the legends now in circulation, his parents already had Betawi names (Bung Piung and Mbak Pinah), and he was born in a village in Rawabelong (now Palmerah in the western inner-city area of Jakarta).[25]

Since the Betawi have heterogeneous origins, the designation as both Sundanese and Betawi – especially in an historical context – is usually not perceived as contradictory by either the Betawi or the Sundanese. As a Betawi explained to me, 'Si Pitung was Sundanese. But he was Betawi because he lived in Batavia. Thus he was first Sundanese then Betawi.' And a Sundanese told me: 'The Sundanese who came to Batavia often became Betawi. Some Sundanese remained Sundanese and became Betawi as well. And others simply remained Sundanese.'

The first film about Si Pitung was made in 1931. However, it was in the 1970s that Si Pitung achieved significant popularity, namely when state promotion of the Betawi began. Books were written, films were made and Si Pitung was immortalized on stamps. Since then the Si Pitung museum has also enjoyed great popularity.

In a number of the films devoted to Si Pitung a connection is made between Si Pitung as Jakarta's most famous *jago*, the Betawi more generally and anti-colonial and nationalist attitudes and actions in particular. One example is *Si Pitoeng* from 1970, which apart from the usual portrayal of Si Pitung as an Indonesian Robin Hood ridicules Dutch efforts to capture him. In this latter respect the focus is above all on the infamous *schout* Hinne, who is presented as an incapable and clumsy police officer continually having the wool pulled over his eyes by the local population regarding Si Pitung's whereabouts. In the film *Banteng Betawi* (*The Bull of Batavia* or *The Betawi Bull*) the good collaborators of Si Pitung are contrasted with the evil collaborators of the Dutch, the latter being charged with responsibility for Si Pitung's death. Si Pitung appears at his most nationalistic in the film *Si Pitung Beraksi Kembali,* which can be roughly translated as *Si Pitung Returns* or *The Resurrection of Si Pitung*. In this film, which was made by Chinese Indonesians, Si Pitung is depicted as a national hero par excellence. He becomes the teacher of a group of revolutionary youth who rebel against the colonial rulers. In response the army burns down a *kampung*. One of Si Pitung's supporters is shot as he is climbing a flag pole to tear down the Dutch flag. As he falls he tears off the blue lower part of the (Dutch) flag, leaving the upper, red and white (Indonesian) part waving in the wind: 'Si Pitung's depiction as a hero fits in well with the modern period of merdeka (freedom, independence), and this is what attracts large crowds to the cinemas' (van Till 1995: 465, ref. to Damardini 1993: 144.). In the words of an old Betawi:

> I'm proud of Si Pitung because he was a Betawi. He fought against the Dutch and showed them that we would not simply accept oppression. He contributed to the liberation of Indonesia and helped us to save face. I have seen Si Pitung films and they have moved me deeply and made me proud to be a Betawi.

Jago still play an important role in Betawi folk theatre, *Lenong Betawi,* where Si Pitung usually appears as a down-to-earth Betawi, a devout Muslim and a fighter for justice. In the *Cerita Rakyat Betawi* he is presented as a former hero of the Betawi and as an Indonesian Robin Hood who, although a robber, used his loot in the cause of justice.[26]

The celebration of Si Pitung, particularly during the 1970s, was not confined to the Betawi, and his heroization was also promoted by the city authorities then. However, in the 1980s, when it became more obvious that the Suharto clan was enriching itself at the cost of Indonesian people, Si Pitung sank into oblivion. Heroizing an avenger of the poor seemed too dangerous politically.

The Chinese also profess an admiration for Si Pitung, and some are generous sponsors of *Lenong* performances that feature Si Pitung. Exhibiting support for Si Pitung (and thus with the Betawi) also functions as a means of positioning themselves on the side of the oppressed and of counteracting the image of the Chinese as oppressors of the native population and former collaborators of the colonial regime. A Chinese expert on Si Pitung and promoter of *Lenong* performances, explained to me:

> Si Pitung was a Betawi just like the Chinese who were then living in Jakarta were Betawi, Peranakan-Betawi. Si Pitung opposed the colonial

rulers and their collaborators. The Peranakan-Betawi were also oppressed by the Dutch and suffered under their rule just as much as the Betawi and all other Indonesians. That is why I like Si Pitung and why I think it's important that we always remember him.

Identification with Si Pitung thus allows the Chinese to assert their own Betawi and Indonesian identity: 'The Chinese may have used their interest in Si Pitung to prove that they were real Betawi and genuine Indonesians' (van Till 1995: 481).

Jago booty is also claimed to have been used for the construction of mosques, although there are at the same time voices expressing doubts that this was really the case. Given that the preservation of Islam during the colonial period is regarded as an act of preserving the native in the face of the foreign – namely the Christian faith of the Dutch colonizers – the (purported) construction of mosques financed by money looted by *jago* associates the latter – and thus the Betawi – with an anti-colonial and indigenous ethos. Whether or not Si Pitung and his peers actually financed the construction of mosques, this claim contributes to the retrospective legend-formation around the *jago* in terms of their anti-colonial and nationalist attitude. The claim that Si Pitung was educated in a *pesantren* – an Islamic boarding school – also supports the investment of the *jago* – and the Betawi – with an Islamic, and thus indigenous, anti-colonial ethos.

In contrast to their idealized public image, the role of the *jago* was an ambiguous one. *Jago* not only protected the native population and provided them with financial support, they also robbed them. Due to the magical powers attributed to them they often enjoyed not only a special status in their respective communities but also protection from the authorities, who feared them. The power afforded by *pencak silat,* which was traditionally intended to aid the achievement of perfection and the protection of existential values, was thus often used to acquire material wealth: '[T]he jago were mostly in the service of those who were able to reward them, i.e. not the common people but elite elements' (Slamet-Velsink 1998: 35; cf. Schulte Nordholt 1991). During the colonial period the ideal of *pencak silat* as a repository of sacred powers and values was thus suspended when *jago* collaborated with the rulers and functioned as intermediaries who did not protect the poor but contributed to their exploitation. As Maryono put it in a public lecture in 1997:

> Although the oral, written and visual tradition of the *jago* character has it that he is a defender of the rights of the poor and the powerless ... against the oppression of the Dutch, ... [the] *jago* were also employed by the local and colonial authorities, becoming an extension of the colonial system, whereby their mastery and use of the martial arts was put to suppress and control the same *wong cilik* they were supposed to defend.

Current efforts to cast the Betawi as anti-colonial and nationalist heroes have focused only on the positive aspects of the *jago* phenomenon during the colonial period while ignoring their negative impact.

The Betawi of the present have preserved many aspects of the *jago*. For instance, the practice of *pencak silat* is still an important criterion of their identity, and a certain martial disposition is still regarded as typically Betawi. It was this disposition that was, for example, given expression in the actions taken to protect Jakarta from the invasion by East Javanese in 2001, when Betawi were seen in traditional fighting outfit. As in Batavia the Betawi fought – albeit above all symbolically – with simple weapons but with a high degree of mental and moral commitment.

Betawi heroes have also been referred to in connection with economic restructuring demands by the International Monetary Fund (IMF) in return for loans to Indonesia. Some Indonesians argued that accepting these demands meant subservience to the IMF and the West. Referring to the historical *jago* they insisted that Indonesians should, like the *jago* of colonial times, insist on their independence and self-reliance rather than give in to foreign demands.

The Betawi-ization of the colonial *jago* is a postcolonial phenomenon and reflects contemporary interests both on the part of the Betawi and of those in power. The Betawi-ization of the *jago* has contributed to the Betawi being cast as anti-colonial heroes who participated in the struggle against colonial oppression and the liberation of the country from the colonial system. The anti-colonial significance attributed to them in this way allows them to function as a symbol of postcolonial nationhood.

Orang Betawi and Orang Indonesia as Interconnected Categories of Identification

The attempt to construct a powerful symbol of national identity in Jakarta has largely been drawing on the creole background of the Betawi by referring to their heterogeneous origins, their ability to create a common and indigenous identity against a background of diversity and their anti-colonial composure. It is the confluence of these ascriptions that allows Orang Betawi and Orang Indonesia to function as closely interconnected categories of ethnic, local and national identification.

In this context creoleness, as the result of historical processes of ethnogenesis and indigenization taking place against a background of ethnic diversity, serves above all as a symbol of the major state motto, namely *Bhinneka Tunggal Ika*, unity in diversity.

The postulated and widely recognized indigeneity of the Betawi to Jakarta serves to situate indigeneity and authentic tradition within the nation's capital. Due to their heterogeneous origins Betawi culture and identity allow for ethnic and transethnic identification and are not seen as (significantly) detracting from the importance of Jakarta's non-Betawi residents' culture and identity. In combination of their diversity of origins and their emergence as a *suku bangsa* in colonial times the Betawi can function as a symbol of unity in diversity and nationalism both with regard to Jakarta and Indonesia. The fact that Jakarta is also the nation's capital lends Betawi traditions an additional national dimension.

Before their promotion by state institutions the Betawi were classified as a group with little sense of national identity. They were regarded as a group uninterested in issues that did not exclusively concern them, as a group that did not identify to any significant degree with state institutions and indeed often opposed them. This situation has changed significantly as a result of their being promoted by the state.

Particularly as a result of the postcolonial construction of the Betawi's anticolonial stance and the Betawi-ization of anti-colonial activities the Betawi are now being retrospectively attributed a greater significance in the national context than before. They are now cast as subversive antagonists of the colonial rulers and defenders of the interests of the little people of indigenous provenance. As such they are presented as participants in the struggle against colonialism and the achievement of national independence. As guardians of indigenous tradition in a foreign-dominated, colonial environment they are portrayed as having significantly contributed to the preservation of indigenous traditions even in the most adverse circumstances, traditions that, in being located in the national capital, are also conceptualized as a national asset belonging to all Indonesians.

Notes

1. *Satu bangsa* (Indonesian = one people) was also one of the most important mottos of the liberation struggle.
2. Cf. Earl (1850); Logan (1850). Both were the first to use the term, which was subsequently adopted by anthropologist and linguists.
3. One of the measures produced by Suharto's anti-Islamic policy involved increasing the number of Javanese Catholics in the military. In the long term even Suharto was unable to exclude Islam from political and public life. Its role as a unifying force at all societal levels was simply too significant and its exclusion from social life was opposed by too many people, including highly influential individuals; see Bertrand (2004).
4. The Indonesian title is *Pedoman Penghayatan dan Pengamalan Pancasila.*
5. For a discussion of these principles see for example Drake (1989).
6. The irony of the Javanist viewpoint lies in the fact that its interpretations of precolonial culture and religion often draw on knowledge accumulated above all by Dutch scholars. Today we know that considerable parts of this knowledge were based on constructions that served to confirm structuralist theories in terms of certain shared structural cores. A focus of research had been native classification systems relating to different areas of life – such as physical environment, cosmology and social organization. The core elements declared as being characteristic of the Indonesian region were sociocosmic dualism, recep-

tiveness toward and integration of foreign cultural elements, dual filiation and asymmetric connubium; see J.P.B. de Josselin de Jong (1977); cf. P.E. de Josselin de Jong (1988); see also Carey (1980); Sutherland (1994).
7. On the relationship between ethnicity and nationalism in Jakarta see for example Simbolon (1991).
8. A typical Betawi dish consisting of various vegetable and peanut sauce.
9. http://www.indo.com/destinations/betawi.html.
10. http://www.indonesia-tourism.com/jakarta.
11. This quotation is from the old website of the DKI Jakarta (http://www.dki.go.id). It has meanwhile been replaced by a new one (http://www.jakarta.go.id), which also includes sections on the Betawi.
12. This quotation is from the old website of the Jakarta Chamber of Commerce and Industry (http://www.kadin.or.id/webpages/kadinjkt.htm), which is not any longer in operation.
13. See footnote 11.
14. These militias were, at least partly, to become the *Forum Betawi Rempug* (FBR) founded in 2001; see also further down.
15. The reference here is to ethnic Javanization.
16. See also Chapter 7.
17. See Tambun's article in *JakartaGlobe* (2013).
18. In Indonesian: *Dinas Kebudayaan dan Permuseuman Propinsi DKI Jakarta*.
19. His expression in Indonesian was *Si Pitung – musuh kompeni*.
20. *Pencak silat* is a form of self-defence involving the use of sticks and hands. It has different regional and ethnic variants. The philosophical and moral foundations and goals of *pencak silat* are based on the conviction that people are individuals within a physical world, social beings within a social group and a group within a larger universe of God's creation. On this basis, *pencak silat* offers a means of developing individual, social, universal and religious values and producing individuals whose lives are shaped by piousness (*takwa*), sensitivity (*tanggap*), courage and purposefulness (*tangguh*), a sense of justice (*tanggon*), creativity and sincerity (*trengginas*).
21. Cf. Slamet-Velsink (1998), who points out that *jago* have different designations in different local contexts.
22. On the history of Marunda see Surachimat (1985).
23. On the different, contradictory statements regarding the origins and residence of Si Pitung see van Till (1995); cf. Abeyasekere (1989); Lombard (1990).
24. The complete story of Si Pitung is included in *Cerita Rakyat Betawi* (1–7).
25. I have found only one essay (written by a member of the *Indonesia Heritage Society* prior to an excursion to Marunda) in which Si Pitung is described as Sundanese by birth. However, no sources are supplied.
26. In the final summary of his compilation of the Si Pitung stories Ali concludes: 'As an erstwhile hero of the Betawi Pitung is actually recognized as a robber but as one who used the spoils of his raids to help the needy. He is the Robin Hood of Indonesia' (Ali 1993: 7). The original Indonesian reads: 'Pitung sebagai tokoh kisah Betawi masa lampau memang dikenal sebagai perampok, tetapi hasil rampokan itu digunakan untuk menolong orang-orang yang menderita. Dia adalah Robin Hood Indonesia.'

Chapter 7
Betawi Politics of Identity and Difference

Betawi Goes Politics: The First 'Betawi untuk Gubernur' Campaign

The increased level of social recognition nowadays enjoyed by the Betawi owes much to their promotion by the state. This has also led particularly the more urban Betawi becoming less alienated from the state and its institutions. At the same time the Betawi have increasingly realized the political potential inherent in their creole background and perceived indigeneity within the Jakartan context. In recent years the growing self-confidence and increased public recognition of the Betawi have also been accompanied by demands for greater Betawi participation in politics, particularly at the level of the DKI Jakarta. Such demands have come not only from the Betawi themselves. By 1999 at the latest, an increasing number of those supporting this cause began to set their sights on getting a Betawi elected to the post of governor of Jakarta. This in turn led to the launching of the first *Betawi untuk Gubernur* campaign in 2002.[1] From this time onwards the Betawi, among them many Betawi Kota and members of the influential middle and upper classes, threw their support behind Fauzi Bowo, the Betawi candidate for governor.

The first *Betawi untuk Gubernur* campaign (2002) proved problematic for many Betawi insofar as supporting the election of a Betawi governor also meant opposing the reelection of the (then) incumbent (Javanese) governor, Sutiyoso, who had supported the promotion of the Betawi while in office. He also cultivated a certain Betawi touch by allowing himself to be addressed as Bang Yos,[2] the Betawi form of address for a man, rather than as *Mas* Yoso, the Javanese term. In part this habit was interpreted by the Betawi as an expression of his respect for them but was also ridiculed and interpreted as mere ingratiation.[3] However, from the outset Betawi commitment to the election of a governor from their own ranks posed a dilemma, as it seemed to contradict the Betawi's acknowledgement of the man who had done much to increase their kudos. One Betawi activist explained to me: 'I would like us to elect a Betawi governor, but ideally without endangering the reelection of Sutiyoso.' However, supporting the election of a Betawi governor and thus the defeat of Sutiyoso was ultimately made easier for the Betawi by a series of political scandals that beset the incumbent in the run-up to the election and by his close association with Suharto and the *Orde Baru*.

Moreover, political machinations in the final weeks before the election resulted in increasing criticism of Sutiyoso for purportedly splitting the Betawi vote in order to ensure victory.

It is important to be aware that in 2002 the governor was not elected directly by the people of Jakarta, but by the city council. At the time the city council comprised 85 representatives from eleven different parties. Each faction could – alone or in coalition with one or more other factions – nominate one pair of candidates for election as governor and deputy governor. The winning pair of candidates was then elected by councillors in a secret ballot. Fauzi Bowo, the Betawi candidate, who did not belong to any party, had registered himself early on as a candidate for the governorship and had been seen as a front-runner for several months. However, he then unexpectedly withdrew his candidacy and instead accepted the position as Sutiyoso's prospective deputy. By having a Betawi as a candidate for the deputy governorship, Sutiyoso clearly hoped to improve his own chances of reelection as governor. Sutiyoso thus brought a Betawi on board primarily to remain at the helm himself. However the majority of the Betawi found this solution unsatisfactory – after all there had already been a Betawi deputy governor before. The reasons for Bowo's change of mind were not revealed, but he did make his decision after it had become known that vote-buying had made Sutiyoso's reelection – and therefore the election of his deputy – very likely. Sutiyoso and Fauzi Bowo won the election as foreseen and were inaugurated as city governor and deputy governor. In 2007, Fauzi Bowo succeeded Sutiyoso and was elected as the first Betawi governor in the first direct election ever to take place in Jakarta.[4]

Particularly in the run-up to the 2002 election for governor – which I had the chance to observe and follow in Jakarta and which in many ways turned out to be the heyday of Betawi politization after the fall of Suharto – many people in Jakarta debated over the question as to whether a Betawi should become governor or not. The reasons expressed for supporting or opposing a Betawi taking this office reflect the ambivalent meanings associated with the Betawi as a group and with Betawi as category of identification. They also reflect the complex relationship between the categories of Orang Betawi and Orang Jakarta and their relationship with the category of Orang Indonesia. I could only follow the run-up for the 2007 election from afar and during one relatively short visit. However, I got the impression that while the discourses and arguments had not changed much, they took place in a more relaxed atmosphere. The political situation was more unwound, and it seemed quite clear that a Betawi, namely Fauzi Bowo, would finally make it this time. In the following I shall focus on the major discourses taking place in the run-up of the elections in 2002 and 2007. Most of the empirical data were obtained during the 2002 run-up to the election, but, as I have pointed out, the arguments as such had not changed much during the 2007 campaign.

Indigeneity in the Production of Authenticity and Commitment

Since the fall of the Suharto regime, new laws on regional autonomy have been implemented to reshape the relationship between the state and the provinces and to give local populations within the provinces greater self-administrative powers. Against the background of the decentralization of political power, local populations are now in a better position to assert themselves and demand more political influence (Aspinall and Fealy 2003; cf. Benda-Beckmann and Benda-Beckmann 2001). Decentralization is also a measure aimed at decreasing the dominance of the Javanese, particularly beyond Java. In Jakarta as well, these developments increased demands to elect a Betawi governor. As a high-ranking member of *Bamus* explained:

> It is no secret that the Javanese have been politically dominant since Indonesian independence and that other groups regard this to be unjust. Electing a native of the city, that is, a Betawi, as governor in the national capital would send a positive signal that there is a preparedness to ensure a greater degree of local and regional impact on the political level.

Because the Betawi are regarded as the indigenous population of Jakarta and as the group most readily identified with Jakarta, it was often also argued that they would therefore also be the most likely ones to improve living conditions in 'their' city:

> The Betawi love their city more than all those who merely live here but have their roots elsewhere. That is why the Betawi should provide the governor. This will make it most likely that the governor conducts politics in the interest of Jakarta, because it would be his city. ... The ties to their land will give them the strength to govern Jakarta in Jakarta's best interest (Sundanese man in his early thirties).

Particularly for many of the poorer people in Jakarta it seemed more likely that a Betawi governor would do more to combat poverty than would a Javanese (Sutiyoso) who had already been in power when Suharto and his cohorts were enriching themselves at the cost of their compatriots. The fact that the majority of the Betawi belong to the poorer section of the population also facilitates social identification with them irrespective of ethnic affiliation. An older *bejak*[5] driver told me:

> The Betawi are mostly poor like the majority of people in Jakarta. They know what it's like to be poor. I hope that a Betawi governor would do something for the poor people, that he would ensure that they

are better off rather than simply make sure that he and his family are comfortable.

It was also emphasized occasionally that a Betawi governor would be able to provide Jakarta with a more authentic and unique identity. As one young man of Javanese descent on his mother's and of Sundanese descent on his father's side, who spoke of himself as Orang Jakarta, explained:

> Jakarta would somehow be more genuine if a Betawi was governor. You always get the impression that all kinds of ethnic groups live here but that there isn't really an indigenous culture. But Jakarta does have its own culture and a Betawi would be able to give that culture a public expression. After all Yogyakarta, for instance, isn't governed by a Sundanese but by a Javanese.

A young woman, herself Sundanese, said:

> Perhaps the people in Jakarta would identify more with Jakarta if a Betawi was governor. Then they would be represented by a native inhabitant of Jakarta [*Jakarta Asli*] and because a governor represents everyone in the city, they would identify with him and thereby feel more indigenous themselves. If the governor himself is not a native of the city, it is more difficult to identify oneself as a Jakartan [*Orang Jakarta*].

Indigeneity and local tradition are also deployed as arguments when it comes to the promotion of tourism in Jakarta. Since the Betawi, as natives of Jakarta, represent Jakartan tradition, it is assumed that they are particularly interesting for tourists and that a Betawi governor would therefore have a beneficial effect on tourism. A staff member of a tourist bureau who organizes city tours explained to me:

> If we want more tourists in Jakarta then this is best achieved by having something that is culturally specific to Jakarta. And that something is the Betawi. And that's why it would be good if the highest representative of Jakarta were himself a Betawi, because that person represents Jakarta not only within the city but also throughout Indonesia and the world.

In connection with the (public) positioning of the Betawi as representatives of indigeneity and local tradition in Jakarta, some Sundanese however also pointed to the fact that they are also indigenous inhabitants of Jakarta and would therefore also have the right to demand the election of a Sundanese governor. However, as the Sundanese regard their real roots and their ethnic territory as lying outside Jakarta, in West Java, most of them did not seem to dispute the Betawi's claim to indigenous status within Jakarta and therefore rarely rejected the claim for a Betawi governor. Furthermore, many of them feel closer to the Betawi than to Sundanese outside Jakarta and thus there is a common tendency among them to support the election of a Betawi. As one young man put it:

> I am a Betawi, a Betawi Sunda.... We are more Betawi than Sundanese in terms of our culture. We have always lived here in Jakarta. That's why I think it would be good for a Betawi to become governor. In any case, it shouldn't be a Javanese this time [2002].

When it comes to demanding greater political influence for the Betawi, indigeneity and local tradition are frequently mentioned as positive criteria. However, this view is also countered by the claim that the Betawi lack modernity, urbaneness and formal education. For long, many Betawi maintained a distance from political life because they felt themselves to be discriminated against and excluded by those in power and because they had reservations against the modernization efforts driven by the Indonesian state. Therefore they continue to be stigmatized as being averse to formal education, which is regarded as a disadvantage when it comes to a high political office such as governor of the national capital. As this Javanese man put it:

> The Betawi are not progressive enough to govern Jakarta, and they don't understand politics well enough. Jakarta is a modern city and must be run by a modern governor. If the person was a modern and politically experienced Betawi then okay, but otherwise I would be sceptical.

A young woman explained that there would be a danger of Jakarta's image as a modern city suffering 'if we were represented by a Betawi governor who regarded the mosque in his *kampung* as the centre of the world and discos, shopping centres and universities as foreign and dispensable.' This argument reflects the fact that – despite the promotion, valorization and 'Kota-ization' of the Betawi – many people still cling to old stereotypes associated with them.

Creole Identity in the Production of Commonalities

As already discussed, it is particularly the creoleness of Betawi culture and identity that makes it possible for the inhabitants of Jakarta to identify at least partially with the Betawi largely irrespective of their own ethnic identities. Creoleness also plays a major role in the public politicization of Betawi identity. On the one hand it has a particular integrative potential, which is highly significant in a city that is extremely heterogeneous in social and cultural terms. On the other hand, it also has the potential of being politically instrumentalized by outsiders.

It seems obvious that any campaign to gain political influence in Jakarta – a city with millions of inhabitants of many different ethnic origins – would be unwise to make ethnic interests central to its political program. Rather, it makes sense to represent and formulate political positions in such a way that they seem relevant and convincing to people irrespective of their ethnic identities. It is thus important that a governor possesses and communicates interethnic competence.

The discourses concerning the election of a Betawi governor accordingly saw emphasis being placed not merely on Betawi indigeneity but also on the Betawi's creoleness that was seen as having a high potential for transethnic identification. A middle-aged saleswoman argued as follows:

> It would be good if a Betawi became governor because the Betawi are the indigenous Jakartans and because their culture encompasses many other cultures found in Jakarta. It would be better than if a Javanese or a Sundanese became governor, because then the other ethnic groups wouldn't feel they were represented. With the Betawi it's somehow different because we know they are mixed on top of being natives of Jakarta.

As is the case here, the indigeneity of the Betawi and particular features associated with their creole background are often mentioned together when explaining one's preference for a Betawi governor. It is the combination of indigeneity and creoleness that makes the Betawi different from all other groups in Jakarta. Even if a Sundanese in Jakarta succeeded in publically staging Sundanese indigeneity, Sundanese identity, not having a creole background, would not offer the same kind of potential for transethnic identification – it has no pidgin potential, so to speak. This, of course, does not mean that a Sundanese candidate could not win an election in Jakarta – there are other criteria than ethnicity involved in (identity) politics and there are other ways of conveying one's transethnic competence than by being a member of a creole group. However, creoleness, on top of indigeneity, may significantly increase the potential for transethnic identification and seems to have a special appeal in the given context. In the words of a young Javanese woman:

> It would actually be great if a Betawi was governor, because people would be able to identify with him more because in Jakarta almost all of us are mixed in some way. It might also mean that ethnocentrism [*sukuisme*[6]] would decrease, because more people would be able to feel they were Orang Jakarta and less Batak, Sunda and so on. Because it is all in there, in the Betawi, I mean.

According to this view, the creole nature of the Betawi facilitates identification with Betawi-ness by virtue of it encompassing common roots. Indigeneity and creoleness thus mutually reinforce one another in terms of their integrative potential. If the Betawi had more political influence, their creoleness would – ideally – also allow others to share in this influence because a certain proximity to the Betawi due to the latter's original ethnic heterogeneity can easily be assumed irrespective of one's own ethnic background.

Inasmuch as the indigeneity of the Betawi is in itself a strong argument for the legitimacy of their political demands, it would unlikely provide a sufficient foundation for claims to representation at the gubernatorial level. The campaigns around the governorship have shown that it is above all the creole background of Betawi-ness that may unfold an integrative effect that enables people other than Betawi to join the Betawi camp. However, the fact that Betawi identity can easily be claimed and ascribed also implies the danger of the arbitrary ascription of something or someone as Betawi and may thereby facilitate (political) instrumentalization and manipulation.

Islam In and Out of Politics

In their deliberations concerning the election of a Betawi governor people sometimes link religious convictions to political ones. Some – like the Chinese quoted above – are afraid that more prominent Betawi representation in politics may radicalize Islam and increase violent oppression of what radical Muslims consider true Islam's enemies. Others hope that the increased participation of the Betawi in political life would give Islam greater influence in shaping public life. As one young man explained to me: 'It would be good if the Betawi were given more political posts in Jakarta because that would give Islam a more influential role in politics.'

People in favour of Islamist politics are generally less influenced by ethnic than by religious considerations when it comes to taking political decisions. They favoured a Betawi governor because they saw this as a way to strengthen the political role of Islam rather than as a way to strengthen the political influence of the Betawi. Their main concern is Islamization rather than Betawi-ization of social and political life. As an older man explained:

> It would be good for morality in Jakarta if a Betawi was governor. For instance, if a devout Muslim Betawi was governor, all these bars would finally be closed for the entire period of Ramadan. But he would have to be a genuine Muslim, that's the most important thing. That's more important than him being Betawi. But a Betawi who made sure that people in Jakarta respected Islam would be a good thing.

Not closing 'all these bars' during Ramadam was interpreted by many as indicative of subservience to foreign interests. One young woman expressed her indignation as follows:

> It is very bad that our governor permits bars to remain open during Ramadan. That is contrary to our faith. He is contradicting the religious will of his own people. He allows bars to remain open so that foreign men can continue to drink and hang around with Indonesian prostitutes. That is bad. It hurts our pride as Indonesians and as Muslims.

To many Indonesians particularly in Jakarta the behaviour of Westerners appears morally reprehensible and disrespectful in several ways. As one man put it, 'It is Christians who behave disrespectfully, who do not accept Ramadan, who associate with prostitutes, who hang around in "Tanamur".'[7] A young woman who worked serving drinks in a bar concluded 'that many foreigners forget they are guests here. They do not have any respect for Indonesians, behave badly, are impolite and injure our pride.' This attitude is amplified by the historical connection of colonialism, foreign domination and oppression with whites and Christianity, as is evident in a comment made by a taxi driver: 'The Dutch who colonized Indonesia and oppressed and humiliated Indonesians were of course also Christians; the Americans are helping the Jews to oppress the Palestinians and are waging war on Muslims.... Now why should we like Christians?' Islam has for long (also) been a symbol of resistance – resistance against the colonizers in colonial times and against the dominance of the West nowadays – a West that is in many ways perceived as humiliating and mocking Islam. Whereas Islam in Indonesia is generally considered to be particularly liberal, also because it is significantly shaped by Hindu-Buddhist influences, it is also part of this specific tradition of resistance to foreign rule and oppression.

A number of Betawi have taken leading positions in radical Islamic associations – particularly in the *Front Pembela Islam*[8] (FPI), the 'Islamic Defense Front' – a radical Islamic association founded in 1998 whose members and sympathizers see themselves as champions of Islam. The FPI's leader, Habib Rizieq, is himself a Betawi(-Arab).[9] Therefore, the FPI is considered an organization strongly influenced by the Betawi – whether this is really so or not. Although certain FPI demands have received widespread public support – like pressurizing the government to pass a strict anti-pornography law and to ban the Ahmadiyyah movement[10] – their paramilitary actions and commitment to violence have done more political harm than good both to the FPI and the Betawi.

It is my impression that most Jakartans disapprove of a closer connection of politics and Islam because they fear that Islamist politics would put the relatively new political freedom at risk. Many also fear that the Islamization of politics will lead to further discrimination and persecution of non-Muslims. Many Chinese, among them numerous who refer to themselves as Betawi and who have become involved in Betawi organizations to manifest their status as indigenous Jakartans, favoured the election of a Betawi governor in both the 2002 and 2007 elections. However, there are, at the same time, also concerns among them that political

Betawi-ization may lead to Islamization and, hence, to resentment and discrimination of non-Muslims. An older Chinese woman expressed her fears as follows:

> I have nothing against a Betawi as governor, but please, one who is tolerant and not a fanatical Muslim. Such people are also found among the Betawi, and they might become even more adverse to the Chinese, who are of course mostly Buddhists or Christians.

Jakarta between National and Local Representation

Jakarta is the seat of the national and the regional government. It is often pointed out in this context that the significance of the national should not be allowed to obscure the significance of the local. As Indonesia's largest and most important city and as the national capital, Jakarta has a level of influence that extends far beyond the city and the island of Java. For many people this is yet another reason for ensuring that the autonomy laws are also implemented in Jakarta – firstly because the same laws should apply to Jakarta as to other regions and secondly because what happens in Jakarta has a 'knock-on effect' throughout Indonesia. An indigenous governor in Jakarta as the national capital accordingly has not only local but also national significance. A young woman explained to me:

> The issue of who is governor in Jakarta is more important than who is in power in Surabaya. Jakarta is the capital of all Indonesians, and if a native of the city, a Betawi, becomes governor, then all of Indonesia will see this and it will give people the confidence to aspire to something similar.

Whereas beyond Jakarta the new autonomy laws have effected that regional forces are gaining more political representation and Javanese representation is declining this is complicated in the Jakartan context by the fact that Jakarta has political functions both as a city and region on the one hand and as the national capital on the other, with both levels requiring internal and external representation. Moreover, these different levels of representation are more closely and visibly interwoven in Jakarta with regard to state institutions and officials than is the case elsewhere in Indonesia.

In the view of many Javanese living in Jakarta, representation of the Javanese is also required at a regional, namely Jakartan, level. As they see it, Jakarta as the national capital should first and foremost represent the (ethnic) majority of all Indonesians, the Javanese, that is. In the words of two Javanese men:

> We Javanese are the majority in Indonesia, and therefore it is important that we are also represented as the strongest force in Jakarta. After all, this is not a Betawi city but the capital city of Indonesia.

Jakarta is not a city like other cities. Jakarta is the capital city for all Indonesians and not only the city of the Jakarta Asli and the Betawi. Jakarta has national significance. That's why national interests should take priority here, not local interests. And that's why it's wrong to claim a Betawi must be governor.

In this view the representation of the Javanese is of primarily national, the representation of the Betawi of primarily local significance in Jakarta and the significance of Jakarta's representation of the national precedes the significance of Jakarta's representation of the local. An older man of Sundanese-Javanese descent explained this as follows:

The Betawi are important for Jakarta and for everyone living here. They connect the people in Jakarta.... But Jakarta is also in Java and, what is even more important, Jakarta is the Indonesian capital. The majority of people in Java and in Indonesia are Javanese. Therefore it would be better to have a Javanese governor here.

However, this viewpoint is widely challenged. For many, the local and regional aspects of political representation should have priority also in Jakarta, as is evident in this (typical) statement by one Betawi resident: 'Jakarta belongs to the Betawi. We are the indigenous inhabitants who have always lived here. That is why we must have broad and top level representation in Jakarta. I think it is time for a Betawi governor.'

It was commonly asserted that ethnic criteria should not be the major forces guiding political decisions. 'It isn't about whether someone is Betawi or comes from Sulawesi', a young woman said to me. 'He or she should be competent and educated and should make a positive impression. It should be about good politics.' However, ethnic criteria do have an important impact on people's political preferences, and arguments against ethnic criteria at least in the 2002 run-up to the election were also motivated by Javanese fears of losing political influence, as is evident in the following statement made by an older Javanese, a longtime holder of high political office in Jakarta:

Sutiyoso is a good governor, and that is why he should remain governor. The fact that he is Javanese surely can't be a reason for voting him out. And in any case the Betawi don't have anyone competent enough to be governor. Furthermore, the Javanese make up the majority of the population in Java and in Indonesia.

There were people who claimed that granting a leadership role to the Javanese – as the national majority – was the only feasible way of ensuring Indonesia does not disintegrate as a nation. Precisely because of the enormous significance attached to Jakarta as the national capital[11] and its importance as a model for other regions, they feared that Javanese disempowerment in Jakarta could encourage similar developments elsewhere. They tended to neglect, however, that a considerable proportion of conflicts in Indonesia have been triggered by Javanese hegemony in the first place. Rather than having been a solution to ethnic and religious conflicts, the forced Javanization of the Indonesian archipelago, including the oppression of indigenous populations, has in fact been one of their causes.

Social Margins Going Ethno-politics

Since the fall of the Suharto regime, many new Betawi organizations have sprung up in Jakarta, the largest and most influential ones being situated at the social margins of Jakartan society. To demonstrate some of their effects concerning recent processes of exclusion and fragmentation among the Betawi themselves on the one hand and between the Betawi (margins) and non-Betawi on the other, it is sufficient to consider the most prominent one, i.e., the *Forum Betawi Rempug* (FBR) – the Betawi Brotherhood Forum that mainly recruits its members from the urban poor and whose membership has grown to around 100,000 since its foundation in 2001. The FBR understands itself as being the voice of the most marginalized Betawi and its official claim is to protect Betawi culture by defending its territories against outsiders (i.e., *pendatang*). The FBR often gets involved in violent fights against such newcomers and is making headlines for being involved in street brawls.

> According to the FBR, the Betawi have been oppressed in their own homeland, and have failed to benefit from either the economic development (*pembangunan*) of the New Order, or the process of democratization following its demise. In order to achieve their goal the FBR have undertaken a strategy of claiming their economic and political rights through the use of coercion, intimidation and force (Brown and Wilson 2007: 10).

The FBR tends to fight the newcomers to Jakarta who they feel are infringing upon the (poor) Betawi's (limited) native rights and resources (Noor 2012). Despite – or irrespective of – their creole background they engage in violent ethnocentrism directed against those who they consider non-natives, thereby also undermining the Betawi potential to function as a transethnic link in Jakarta and demonstrating that creole identity may be(come) just as ethnocentric and exclusive as any other ethnic identity.

Whereas the official goal is to fight for the rights of the indigenous Betawi, actual FBR activities have shown that such high aims 'coexist with the concern of individual gang members to use violence and intimidation in order to enrich themselves.' Whereas there are many supporters of the FBR, particularly among the poor, the majority of Jakartans – including the Betawi – have strong reservations against the organization due to their propensity to violence and their paramilitary appearance. There have also been widespread public demands to disband the FBR, and in response to growing resistance the latter has now and again dismissed some of its members for being involved in acts of public violence (Ruqoya 2010).

However, despite an abundance of thugs and thieves among them, the FBR is, together with more than a hundred Betawi organizations, affiliated with *Bamus* and officially acknowledged by *Bamus* as a Betawi organization. The relationship between *Bamus* and the FBR has nevertheless long been an ambiguous one. On the one hand, *Bamus* does not want to lose connection with an important Betawi organization at the (broad) margins of Betawi society. As well, it is an open secret, that social margins in particular may be – and have often been – manipulated to serve one's (political) needs (in election campaigns, most importantly). On the other hand, being associated with the often violent activities of the FBR is harmful to the kudos of the Betawi as a whole and damages their political reputation in particular (Guerin 2002). Reactions in view of the FBR's activities have so far been ambiguous, contradictory and undecided among members of *Bamus* and the wider Betawi community. Some would favour the expulsion of the FBR, others speak out for their continued integration in *Bamus,* also for fears of disintegration, should the Betawi margins go astray. After all, the majority of the Betawi are poor and abandoning the FBR may mobilize the Betawi margins against the more established Betawi and result in the disintegration of the Betawi as a whole. The FBR is rarely directly attacked by the more established Betawi. It seems that it is as yet too powerful and that people – high-ranking members of *Bamus,* the police and the government included – are afraid both of losing their potential support should the need arise and of the FBR's revenge should they be discredited or disbanded.

As has been pointed out previously, the creoleness of Betawi identity makes it relatively easy to adopt the Betawi label, and the latter's inflationary use among all sorts of groups in Jakarta has led many Betawi to demand caution with regard to what they perceive as a danger of being infiltrated and misused by people not actually Betawi. A leading member of *Bamus* explained to me:

> We will have to take greater care that we are not infiltrated by people who harm us. Today there are hundreds of associations who have 'Betawi' in their name without in fact being Betawi. We don't want to exclude anyone but we should ensure that these people do not bring the Betawi into disrepute. Therefore we have to be more careful about which groups we accept as Betawi. It is not about excluding people who perhaps have not

been Betawi for five generations. It is about protecting genuine Betawi from people who run riot in our name and thus bring the Betawi into disrepute.

The Betawi are facing a dilemma both with regard to their social and their institutional margins. They want to bring as many people as possible into the Betawi fold to increase the Betawi's influence and political clout as a group. At the same time experience has shown that groups such as the FBR may also discredit the Betawi as a whole. Thus, it is the social reputation of a (potentially) Betawi group that the more established Betawi are concerned about, and not so much their degree of Betawi authenticity.

Betawi as a Social Class and as Urban Identification

Besides being classified as an ethnic group and identity native to Jakarta, Betawi is also understood as a social class, namely the working class. There are, for instance, associations of *bejak* and *ojek* drivers that have the word Betawi in their name without thereby referring to the Betawi in ethnic terms. 'We belong to the class of the workers, the ordinary people in Jakarta,' one *bejak* driver said to me, and another one responded, 'You're asking if we are all Betawi? Well, somehow, yes. I don't mean to say we are Betawi Asli in that we are descendants of Betawi. We are Betawi because we live in Jakarta and we are all workers and all poor, like most of the Betawi.'

Young people in Jakarta also tend to describe themselves as Betawi on occasion and then regard this designation as linked not merely with the working class but with certain existential attitudes that are not limited to the Betawi in ethnic terms but are regarded as typical of them. The *bejak* driver quoted above also explained: 'I say I am Betawi because I was born in Jakarta and I am a typical Orang Jakarta. I am a small guy, I have to struggle to survive and to struggle for my rights. Whether my ancestors were Betawi or not doesn't matter.'

Even among the ethnic Betawi there are many who prefer to conceptualize Betawi as a social class. As one *bejak* driver put it, 'I am Betawi Asli, but someone can also be Betawi because of his lifestyle, because he has the courage to defy the powerful and doesn't conform. That's also Betawi.'

This connection between Betawi identity and, in the broadest sense, class consciousness, recalls the linking of the Betawi with the *jago* of the colonial period. Whereas the latter case frequently involves retrospective Betawi-ization of the so-called small anti-colonial heroes, the former involves de-ethnicization of a social feature originally classified as Betawi in ethnic terms. A specific combination of features – namely working-class membership, proletarian consciousness and a culture of resistance – is largely dissociated from ethnic references and defined as belonging to a social class instead. The Betawi, as it were, supply the ethnic background for specific features, which, once dissociated from their ethnic reference, may serve as features of class affiliation. An ethnonym is hence being translated into a socionym.

Despite the ambivalent attitudes concerning the Betawi's politicization – both among the Betawi and others –, transethnicization of Betawi identity seems to prevail. This process continues to encompass the incorporation of groups and individuals into Betawi society as well as the extension of the parameters governing who and what is to be conceptualized as Betawi. In the context of political mobilization, there is also a general tendency to speak of Orang Jakarta rather than of Betawi. The following extract from a conversation (2006) shows that this tendency may be related to identity politics rather than to identity as such.

IN: It really is time for a Jakarta Asli governor now [*Gubernur Orang Jakarta Asli*]
JK: You mean a Betawi?
IN: A Jakarta Asli.
JK: Not a Betawi?
IN: Yes, a Betawi.
JK: Why do you say Jakarta Asli and not Betawi?
IN: Why do you say Betawi and not Jakarta Asli?
JK: Isn't there a difference?
IN: Yes, there is. But it's better to say Jakarta Asli.
JK: Why?
IN: Because otherwise it seems like *sukuisme*.

The notion Jakarta Asli is thus preferred to avoid the impression of ethnocentrism. Because more people in Jakarta see themselves as Orang Jakarta than as Betawi the designation Jakarta (Asli) is preferred to Betawi when one aims to evoke a spirit of Jakartan communitas. Orang Jakarta (Asli) may encompass both the (ethnic) Betawi as well as all those who see themselves as Jakartans without being Betawi in ethnic terms. When it comes to asserting the political interests of all Jakartans (including the Betawi) it is thus strategically wiser to choose the (potentially) transethnic designation rather than the ethnic one, since the former does not run the risk of affronting either the ethnic Betawi or those who see themselves as Jakartans but not as Betawi.

However, this sort of terminological and strategical transethnicization does not imply that the boundary between the ethnic Betawi (Asli) and others who regard themselves as Orang Jakarta (Asli) is abrogated. In some ways, it is even more instrumental in political than in less politicized contexts. This is so because to function as a (master) symbol of transethnic connectivity that distinguishes the Betawi from other (merely ethnic) groups, the boundary between the Betawi and others has to be maintained. A boundary can only be transcended and crossed where it exists in the first place; only where a boundary is in place, it can be negotiated and made permeable and hence function as a symbol of the Betawi's capacities for transethnic connectivity and integration. Unity in diversity needs boundaries, across which diversified interaction and unification can occur.

Notes

1. *Betawi untuk Gubernur:* '(For) a Betawi as Governor' or 'Betawi for Governor'.
2. Bang Yos is an abbreviation of Sutiyoso.
3. Referring to Sutiyoso's announcement – which he soon retracted – that he would no longer campaign for the post of governor, the publisher of *LaksamaNet* commented on this Betawi 'leaning' of the governor as follows: 'While we wish Mas Yoso (we decline to use his self-adopted Betawi usage of Bang) a quiet retirement, we would also suggest that Jakarta's residents demand more of their next governor, especially if the potential nominees are to be veterans of his flawed reign over the city' ('Jakarta Arrogance on Display again', in *LaksamaNet,* 27 January 2002).
4. Fauzi Bowo was succeeded by Joko Widodo (a Javanese from Surakarta, Central Java) in 2013. Joko Widodo – nicknamed Jokowi – is very dedicated to the promotion and preservation of Betawi culture as Jakarta's native identity and heritage and is supported by most Betawi as well as other Jakartans.
5. *bejak:* roofed three-wheeler with a two-stroke motor.
6. *Sukuisme:* from *suku* = people, ethnic group. *Sukuisme* refers to ethnocentrism and discrimination based on specific ethnic affiliations and ethnic affiliations different from one's own.
7. Well-known bar in Jakarta heavily frequented by foreign men and Indonesian prostitutes.
8. On the background of the FPI and its activities see *Refugee Review Tribunal* (2009). See also the FPI's website at http://fpi.or.id/.
9. The name 'Habib' indicates direct descendancy from the Prophet Mohamed.
10. Many (orthodox) Muslims consider the Ahmadiyyah to be heretics because they do not believe that Mohammad was the last prophet.
11. Concerning fears of national disintegration in post-Suharto Indonesia, see e.g., Kingsbury and Aveling (2003).

Conclusion

Towards an Open End

The analysis of ethnic, local and national identifications in Jakarta has shown that the latter are constructed, transformed and socially enacted in close interaction with one another and according to situational and contextual demands. Identifications acquire social meanings and social relevance beyond the individual level in the context of ascriptions and demarcations that are shaped by specific belief systems, historical experiences and political exigencies. Social meanings of identity-related processes and social discourses reflecting them impact each other.

In Jakarta a specific creole culture and identity – namely Betawi culture and identity – plays a specific role for the interaction of ethnic, local and national identifications in – and due to – the given ethnically heterogeneous and postcolonial context.

The explicitly diverse origins of the Betawi allow for a partial (ethnic) identification with them and/or with their cultural representations largely irrespective of one's own ethnic identity. The categories Orang Jakarta and (Orang) Betawi both have ethnic and transethnic meanings, and people may ascribe themselves to one and/or the other category according to personal and situational preferences. Through the Betawi Jakarta is also invested with ethnic tradition and indigeneity without which a territory is not considered a real social place in Indonesia and which, due to its creole background, may be shared across ethnic boundaries. This being said, it is important to keep in mind that, despite their overlapping meanings, the categories of identification in question are by no means exchangeable and that demarcations between them are crucial to allow for their being crossed. Betawi-ness derives its integrative potential from being both an ethnic *and* a transethnic category of identification, thus allowing for ethnic *and* transethnic ascriptions.

Due to the fact that their ethnic identity is based on heterogeneous origins, the Betawi can function as a potent symbol of *Bhinneka Tunggal Ika* – unity in diversity – a motto that is highly significant for Indonesia as a whole and for Jakarta as Indonesia's capital and 'Indonesia en miniature'. The fact that the Betawi are located in Jakarta can be considered a stroke of luck in terms of their potential for serving as a symbol of *Bhinneka Tunggal Ika*. A creole group based in Surabaya, for example, would not have the same symbolic force with reference to both the local and national context.

The original diversity of the Betawi also functions as a historical model for the heterogeneous reality of present-day Jakarta and Indonesia. The Betawi provide an historical blueprint, so to speak, for a heterogeneous society in need of both diversity and diversity-transcending unity. It is important to note that the social significance of Betawi as a category of ethnic and transethnic identification in contemporary Jakartan and Indonesian society is not founded on *current* processes of creolization, but on creoleness as a product of *historical* creolization.

For the large majority among those who creolized and became Betawi, proximity to European culture was not an option to achieve upward social mobility in colonial society or political participation in the early postcolonial nation-state. The Betawi constructed indigeneity by incorporating local people and culture, on the one hand, and by keeping their distance from the colonizers, on the other. The Betawi resisted, rather than incorporated or appropriated, European norms. They maintained their Muslim faith or converted to Islam as part of their becoming Betawi. Not being associated with the Dutch but with resistance against them is an indispensable condition for Betawi identity being able to tap its potentials with regard to symbolizing and representing transethnic Jakartan and national identity in contemporary Indonesian society.

Today it is above all the pidgin factor of creoleness as a late consequence of historical creolization in colonial contexts, which is increasingly gaining social and political relevance and becoming more attractive as a form of identification in many postcolonial contexts of social and cultural diversity.[1] In historical processes of creole ethnogenesis local people and culture of different ethnic origins were incorporated and became integral constituents of creole identities. Therefore, local populations can find elements of their own ethnic culture reflected in contemporary creole culture and thus may feel both ethnically as well as transethnically connected with it while retaining their own respective ethnic identities. In addition to the more general knowledge of creole culture and identity having heterogeneous origins, it is thus also specific knowledge concerning its ethnic parts, which enables people of different ethnic belongings to identify with it, thereby creating an identitarian reference system, which makes use of and transcends ethnic identities and boundaries at the same time.

The transethnic relatedness of creole culture and identity can only be upheld if it is not experienced as exclusive, but as allowing for selective identification. However, in societies where ethnic identity is a matter of social relevance, creole groups are likely to feel a need to also retain their ethnic specificity and visibility at the same time. Since creole groups' origins are often conceptualized as particularly heterogeneous and as less indigenous than the origins of other groups, their being ethnic tends to be more contested. Hence, creole groups are likely to face social expectations that require them continuously to balance out between being 'different from' and 'the same as' other groups in different social, political and historical contexts and situations.

Integration and connectivity are likely to prevail where creole groups manage to mediate the ambivalence between difference and sameness by 'being different from' by means of 'being more the same as' others. The pidgin potential of creole identity tends to be high where diversity of origin is considered an ethnic marker of creole identity and where the heterogeneous roots of creole groups are conceptualized and represented as connections to different others within a given society and locality, thereby connecting ethnic specificity with transethnic connectivity.

The pidgin potential of creole identity tends to be low where a creole population seeks distance and exclusiveness, where its 'being different from' is seen as a result of its 'being better (off) than' others. In such cases, the heterogeneous roots of creole groups are conceptualized and represented as paths leading away from the different non-creole groups in a given society and locality, thereby disconnecting creole identity from the society within which it is situated.

The significance of creoleness, particularly in postcolonial, ethnically heterogeneous societies, stems from the very fact that creolization also involves ethnicization. The unique aspect of creolization is not that something old dissolves, but that something new evolves. The unique aspect of the result of historical creolization – contemporary creoleness – is that due to the combination of historical heterogeneity with indigenization and ethnicization, it allows for both ethnic *and* transethnic identification. Without indigenization and ethnicization having taken place in its historical formation, creoleness could not play such a prominent role in the processes of integration and differentiation, as it often does in societies, in which there is both a social requirement to acknowledge ethnic diversity *and* to substantiate transethnic – local, regional, national – ties. Particularly in such contexts creoleness may unfold its pidgin potential as an identitarian frame of reference, linking people across ethnic boundaries by enabling them to share (selected) ethnic *and* transethnic identifications.

At the same time, creole groups and identities tend to be ambivalent due to the fact that they emerged in colonial contexts and are therefore associated with the colonial heritage. The positioning of creole groups and identities in postcolonial contexts therefore also depends on their retrospective positioning in the colonial context and vice versa. The variations of creole identities and the social meanings and practices related to them can only be discovered and understood through more systematic and comparative research across different societies and historical periods of time.

Notes

1. See Knörr (1995, 2007a, 2010a). In Knörr (2010a) ethnographic data concerning creolization and creole identities in Sierra Leone and Indonesia are compared in terms of their historical, social and political impact. The analysis seeks to spell out some of the major criteria for the pidginization – the transethnicization – of creole identity. See also Knörr (2010b).

Bibliography

Aa, A.J. van der. 1846. *Nederlands Oost-Indië*, Vol. 2. Amsterdam: J.F. Schleijer.
Abdurachman, P.R. 1975. 'Portuguese Presence in Jakarta'. *Masyarakat Indonesia* 1(1): 89–103.
———. 1977. 'Kroncong Moresko, Tanjidor dan Ondel-Ondel', *Budaja djaja* 10(109): 338–47.
Abdussomad. 1997. 'Jatinegara Kaum: Kampung tertua di Jakarta penduduk Jakarta Asli yang bukan Betawi', in Y.Z. Shahab (ed.), *Betawi dalam Perspektif Kontemporer: Perkembangan, Potensi, dan Tantangannya*. Jakarta: LKB, pp. 35–70.
Abeyasekere, S. 1983. 'Slaves in Batavia. Insights from a Slave Register', in A. Reid (ed.), *Slavery, Bondage and Dependency in Southeast Asia*. New York: St. Martin's Press, pp. 286–314.
———. (ed.) 1985. *From Batavia to Jakarta: Indonesia's Capital 1930s to 1980s*. Clayton: Monash University.
———. 1989. *Jakarta. A History*, 2nd ed. Singapur and New York: Oxford University Press.
Adas, M. 1979. *Prophets of Rebellion. Millenarian Protest Movements against the European Colonial Order*. Chapel Hill: University of North Carolina.
Affandi, B. 1976. 'Shaykh Ahmad Al-Surkati; His role in the Al-Irshad Movement in Java in the Early Twentieth Century', M.A. thesis. Montreal: McGill University.
Ali, R. 1993. *Cerita Rakyat Betawi 1*. Jakarta: Gramedia Widiasarana Indonesia.
Allen, P. 2003. 'Contemporary Literature from the Chinese 'Diaspora' in Indonesia', *Asian Ethnicity* 4(3): 383–99.
Anderson, B.R. 1972. 'The Idea of Power in Javanese Culture', in C. Holt (ed.), *Culture and Politics in Indonesia*. Ithaca and London: Cornell University Press, pp. 1–69.
———. 1990. 'Old State, New Society: Indonesia's New Order in Comparative Historical Perspective', in B.R. Anderson (ed.), *Language and Power. Exploring Political Cultures in Indonesia*. Ithaca: Cornell University Press, pp. 94–120.
———. 1991. *Imagined Communities. Reflections on the Origin and Spread of Nationalism*. London and New York: Verso.
———. 1996. *Die Erfindung der Nation. Zur Karriere eines folgenreichen Konzepts*. New York and Frankfurt/Main: Campus.

———. 1998. *The Spectre of Comparison: Nationalism, Southeast Asia and the World*. London and New York: Verso.
Arrom, J.J. 1951. 'Criollo: Definición y matices de un concepto', *Hispania* 34: 172–76.
Aspinall, E. and G. Fealy (eds). 2003. *Local Power and Politics in Indonesia. Decentralisation & Democratisation*. Singapore, Institute of Southeast Asian Studies: Indonesia Update Series.
Assmann, J. 2002. *Das kulturelle Gedächtnis. Schrift, Erinnerung und politische Identität in frühen Hochkulturen*, 4th ed. München: C.H. Beck.
Aurora, L. 2004. 'Betawi Cuisine, Arts Make Comeback', *The Jakarta Post*, 10 September 2004.
Avé, J.B. 1989. '"Indonesia', 'Insulinde' and 'Nusantara': Dotting the I's and Crossing the T', *Bijdragen tot de Taal-, Land- en Volkenkunde* 145: 220–34.
Balutansky, K.M. and M.-A. Sourieau. 1998. 'Introduction', in K.M. Balutansky and M.-A. Sourieau (eds), *Caribbean Creolization. Reflections on the Cultural Dynamics of Language, Literature, and Identity*. Gainsville: University Press of Florida, pp. 1–11.
Barnard, A. and J. Spencer (eds). 1996. *Encyclopedia of Social and Cultural Anthropology*. London and New York: Routledge.
Barth, F. 1969. 'Introduction', in F. Barth (ed.), *Ethnic Groups and Boundaries. The Social Organization of Culture Difference*. Bergen and Oslo: Allen and Unwin, pp. 9–38.
Benda-Beckmann, F. and K. Benda-Beckmann. 2001. 'Recreating the *nagari*: Decentralization in West Sumatra', *Max Planck Institute for Social Anthropology Working Papers No. 31*. Halle/Saale: Max Planck Institute for Social Anthropology.
Berg, L.W.C. van den. 1886. *Le Hadramout et les colonies arabes dans l'archipel indien*. Batavia: Imprimerie du Gouvernement.
Berghe, P.L. van den (ed.). 1975. *Race and Ethnicity in Africa*. Nairobi: East African Publications.
Berlin, Ira 1998. *Many Thousands Gone. The First Two Centuries of Slavery in North America*. Cambridge, MA: Harvard University Press.
Bertrand, J. 2004. *Nationalism and Ethnic Conflict in Indonesia*. Cambridge: Cambridge University Press.
Blussé, L. 1986. *Strange Company. Chinese Settlers, Mestizo Women and the Dutch in VOC Batavia*. Dordrecht: Foris Publikations.
Boekhoudt. 1908. *Rapport reorganisatie van het politiewezen op Java en Madoera (uitgezonderd de Vorstenlanden, de particuliere landerijen en de hoofdplaatsen Batavia, Semarang en Soerabaja, 1906-07)*. Batavia: Landsdrukkerij.
Bommer, B. 1991. 'Zur Anlage der Urbanethnologie. Ansätze zur Konzeption des Forschungsgebietes im Rahmen der Zeitschrift *Urban Anthropology* und

einige grundsätzliche Fragen', in W. Kokot and B. Bommer (eds), *Ethnologische Stadtforschung*. Berlin: Reimer, pp. 15–28.

Brasseaux, C.A. 1990. *The Foreign French: Nineteenth-Century French Immigration into Louisiana*, 3 volumes. Lafayette: The Center for Louisiana Studies, University of Southwestern Louisiana.

Brathwaite, E.K. 1971. *The Development of Creole Society in Jamaica, 1770–1820*. Oxford: Clarendon.

―――. 1977. 'Caliban, Arien and Unprospero in the Conflict of Creolization: A Study of the Slave Revolt in Jamaica', in V. Rubin and A. Tuden (eds), *Comparative Perspectives on Slavery in New World Plantation Societies*. Annals of the New York Academy of Sciences 292. New York: New York Academy of Sciences, pp. 41–62.

Brockhaus Konversations-Lexikon, 16th ed. F.A. Brockhaus' Geographische Anstalt. Leipzig.

Brondgeest, B.T. 1927. 'Een Zonderlinge Appreciatie de Hadramieten bij een Deel de Bataviaasche Bevolking', *Djawa* 2: 117.

Brown, D. and I. Wilson 2007. 'Ethnicized Violence in Indonesia: The Betawi Brotherhood Forum in Jakarta', *Working Paper 145* (July 2007). Perth: Asia Research Centre, Murdoch University.

Brug, P.H. van der. 1994. *Malaria en malaise. De VOC in Batavia in de achttiende eeuw*. Amsterdam: De Bataafsche Leeuw.

Bruner, E. 1974. 'The Expression of Ethnicity in Indonesia', in A. Cohen (ed.), *Urban Ethnicity*. London: Tavistock Publications, pp. 251–80.

Budhinsantoso, S. 1976. 'Manfaat penelitian folklore Betawi', in H. Wijaya (ed.), *Seni-Budaya Betawi. Pralokakarya, Penggalian dan Pengembangannya*. Jakarta: Pustaka Jaya, pp. 47–53.

Budiati, T. 2000. 'The Preservation of Betawi Culture and Agriculture in the Condet Area', in K. Grijns and P.J.M. Nas (eds), *Jakarta-Batavia. Socio-Cultural Essays*. Leiden: KITLV Press, pp. 319–35.

Carey, P.B.R. 1980. 'Aspects of Javanese History in the Nineteenth Century', in H. Aveling (ed.), *The Development of Indonesian Society: From the Coming of Islam to the Present Day*. New York: St. Martin's Press, pp. 45–105.

Castles, L. 1967. 'The Ethnic Profile of Jakarta', *Indonesia* 1 (April): 153–204.

Chaudenson, R. 2001. *Creolization of Language and Culture*. Padstow, Cornwall: Routledge.

Chijs, J.A. van der (ed.). 1889. *Dagh-register gehouden int Casteel Batavia vant passeren-de daer ter plaetse als over geheel Nederlandts-India 1624-1682*. Batavia: Landsdrukkerij.

Coakley, J. 2003. 'Introduction: The Challenge', in J. Coakley (ed.), *The Territorial Management of Ethnic Conflict*, 2nd ed. London and Portland, Oregon: Frank Cass, pp. 1–22.

Cohen, A. 1974. *Urban Ethnicity.* London, New York: Tavistock Publications.
———. 1981. *The Politics of Elite Culture. Explorations in the Dramaturgy of Power in a Modern African Society.* Berkeley and Los Angeles: University of California Press.
Cohen, A.P. 2000. 'Boundaries of Consciousness, Consciousness of Boundaries', in H. Vermeulen and J.F. Boissevain (eds), *Ethnic Challenge. The Politics of Ethnicity in Europe.* Göttingen: Edition Herodot, pp. 59–79.
Cohen, R. and P. Toninato. 2009. 'Introduction. The Creolization Debate: Analysing Mixed Identities and Cultures', in R. Cohen and P. Toninato (eds), *Creolization. Studies in Mixed Identities and Cultures.* London: Routledge, pp. 1–21.
Collier, G. and U. Fleischmann (eds). 2003. *A Pepper-port of Cultures: Aspects of Creolization in the Caribbean (Matatu).* Amsterdam: Rodopi.
Coppel, C. and L. Suryadinata 1970. 'The Use of the Terms "Tjina" and "Tionghoa"', *Indonesia: An Historical Survey, Papers on Far Eastern History* 2 (September): 97–118.
Crawfurd, John 1971 [1856]. *A Descriptive Dictionary of the Indian Archipelago & Adjacent Countries.* Kuala Lumpur and New York: Oxford University Press.
Cribb, R. 1991. *Gangsters and Revolutionaries. The Jakarta People's Militia and the Indonesian Revolution 1945–1949.* Honolulu: University of Hawaii Press.
Da Franca, P.A. 1970. *Portuguese Influence in Indonesia.* Jakarta: Gunung Agung.
Dahm, B. 1971. *History of Indonesia in the Twentieth Century.* London: Pall Mall Press.
Damardini, P. 1993. 'Cerita Si Pitung sebagai sastra lisan; Analisis terhadap struktur cerita', M.A. thesis. Fakultas Sastra, Universitas Indonesia.
Danandjaja, J. 1976. 'Manfaat Penelitian Folklore Betawi', in H. Wijaya (ed.), *Seni-Budaya Betawi. Pralokarya Penggalian Dan Pengembangannya.* Jakarta: Pustaka Jaya, pp. 36–46.
Darmaputera, E. 1988. *Pancasila and the Search for Identity and Modernity in Indonesian Society: A Cultural and Ethical Analysis.* Leiden and New York: E.J. Brill.
Daus, R. 1989. *Portuguese Eurasian Communities in Southeast Asia.* Singapur: Institute of Southeast Asian Studies.
De Vos, G. and L. Romanucci-Ross (eds). 1982. *Ethnic Identity: Cultural Continuities and Change.* Chicago: University of Chicago Press.
Dhofier, Z. 1976. 'Social Interaction in Jakarta. A Study of the Relationships between Betaweenese and Newcomers', M.A. thesis. Australian National University.
Dorléans, B. 2002. 'Urban Land Speculation and City Planning Problems in Jakarta before the 1998 Crisis', in P.J.M. Nas (ed.), *The Indonesian Town Revisited.* Münster: LIT, pp. 41–56.

Drake, C. 1989. *National Integration in Indonesia. Patterns and Policies.* Honolulu: University of Hawaii Press.

Earl, G.W. 1850. 'On the Leading Characteristics of the Papuan, Australian, and Malayu-Polynesian Nations', *Journal of the Indian Archipelago and Eastern Asia* 4: 1–10; 66–74; 172–81.

Effendy, B. 2003. *Islam and the State in Indonesia.* Singapur: Institute of Southeast Asian Studies: Series on Islam.

Eisenstadt, S.N. 2005 [2000]. *Multiple Modernities.* New Brunswick and London: Transaction Publishers.

Elwert, G. and P. Waldmann (eds) 1989. *Ethnizität im Wandel.* Saarbrücken: Breitenbach.

Encyclopaedie van Nederlandsch-Indië 1919. Den Haag and Leiden, Vol. 1.

Eriksen, T.H. 1993. *Ethnicity and Nationalism. Anthropological Perspectives.* London: Pluto Press.

———. 1999. '*Tu dimunn pu vini kreol:* The Mauritian Creole and the Concept of Creolization', *Transnational Communities Programme, Working Paper No. 99*, 13.

———. 2002 [1993]. *Ethnicity and Nationalism. Anthropological Perspectives.* London and Ann Arbor: Pluto Press.

———. 2007. 'Creolization in Anthropological Theory and in Mauritius', in C. Stewart (ed.), *Creolization: History, Ethnography, Theory.* Walnut Creek, CA: Left Coast Press, pp. 153–77.

Errington, S. 1997. 'The Cosmic Theme Park of the Javanese', *Review of Indonesian and Malaysian Arts* 31(1): 7–36.

Evers, H.-D. 1982. *The Social Organization of the Subsistence Sector: Studies on Urbanization and on Social Development in Southeast Asia.* Bielefeld: UB, Forschungsschwerpunkt Entwicklungssoziologie.

Evers, H.-D. and R. Korff. 2000. *Southeast Asian Urbanism: The Meaning and Power of Social Space*, 2nd ed. Münster: LIT.

Faes, J. 1893. *Geschiedenis particulier landbezit op West-Java*, Vol. 1. Batavia: Ogilvie.

Foucault, M. 1991. *Die Ordnung des Diskurses.* Frankfurt/Main: Fischer Wissenschaft.

———. 2002. *Archäologie des Wissens.* Frankfurt/Main: Suhrkamp.

Fowler, R. 1991. *Language in the News: Discourse and Ideology in the Press.* London and New York: Routledge.

———. 1996. *Linguistic Criticism,* 2nd ed. Oxford: Oxford University Press.

Freedman, A. 2003. 'Political Institutions and Ethnic Chinese Identity in Indonesia', *Asian Ethnicity* 4(3): 439–52.

Friederici, G. 1947. *Amerikanistisches Wörterbuch.* Hamburg: Cram, De Gruyter and Co.

Furnivall, J.S. 1944. *Netherlands India: a Study of Plural Economy.* Cambridge: Cambridge University Press.

———. 1948. *Colonial Policy and Practice.* Cambridge: Cambridge University Press.

Fyle, C.M. 2000. 'Official and Unofficial Attitudes and Policy towards Krio as the Main Lingua Franca in Sierra Leone', in R. Fardon and G. Furniss (eds), *African Languages, Development and the State.* London: Routledge, pp. 44–54.

Gardels, N. 1991. 'Two Concepts of Nationalism: An Interview with Isaiah Berlin', *New York Review of Books* 21 (November).

Geertz, C. 1960. *The Religion of Java.* Glencoe, Illinois: Free Press.

———. 1999. *Dichte Beschreibung: Beiträge zum Verstehen kultureller Systeme,* 6th ed. Frankfurt/Main: Suhrkamp.

Gellner, E.1983. *Nations and Nationalism.* Oxford: Blackwell.

———. 1999. *Nationalismus: Kultur und Macht.* Berlin: Siedler.

Gerke, S. 1995. 'Symbolic Consumption and the Indonesian Middle Class', *Working Paper.* Bielefeld: UB, Forschungsschwerpunkt Entwicklungssoziologie.

Gilman, C. 1979. 'Cameroonian Pidgin English, a Neo-African Language', in I. Hancock (ed.), *Readings in Creole Studies.* Gent: E. Story-Scientia, pp. 269–80.

Glaser, B.G. and A.L. Strauss 1967. *The Discovery of Grounded Theory: Strategies for Qualitative Research.* New York: Aldine.

Glissant, E. 2000. 'Interview', *Label France* No.38.

Gobée, E. and C. Adriaanse (eds). 1959. *Ambtelijke adviezen van C. Snouck Hurgronje, 1889–1936,* Vol.2. 's-Gravenhage: Nijhoff.

Grijns, C.D. 1976. 'Lenong in the Environs of Jakarta: a Report', *Archipel* 12: 175–202.

———. 1979. 'A la recherche du "melayu betawi" ou parler malais de Batavia', *Archipel* 17: 135–56.

———. 1991. *Jakarta Malay: A Multidimensional Approach to Spatial Variation.* Leiden: KITLV Press.

Groenevelt, W.P. 1880. 'Notes on the Malay Archipelago and Malacca, compiled from the Chinese Sources', *Verhandelingen van Bataviasch Genootschap van Kunsten en Wetenschapen* 39(1): 41–50.

Guerin, B. 2002. 'Bully Boys Shame Indonesia', *Asia Times,* 3 April 2002.

Guinness, P. 1972. 'The Attitudes and Values of Betawi Fringe Dwellers in Djakarta', *Berita Antropologi* 8: 78–159.

Haan, F. de 1917. 'De laatste der Mardijkers', *Bijdragen tot de Taal-, Land- en Volkenkunde* 73: 219–54.

———. 1922. *Oud Batavia. Gedenkboek uitgegeven naar aanleiding van het driehonderjarig bestaan der stad in 1919.* Bataviaasch Genootschap van Kunsten en Wetenschappen. Batavia: Kolff.

———. 1935. *Oud Batavia*. Vol. I. Bandung: A.C. Nix & Co.

Haller, D. 2002. 'Das Lob der Mischung: Nationalismus und Ethnizität in Gibraltar', in A. Ackermann and K.E. Müller (eds), *Patchwork: Dimensionen multikultureller Gesellschaften: Geschichte, Problematik und Chancen*. Bielefeld: Transcript, pp. 211–56.

Hannerz, U. 1980. *Exploring the City: Inquiries toward an Urban Anthropology*. New York: Columbia University Press.

———. 1987. 'The World in Creolization', *Africa* 57: 546–59.

———. 1989. 'Notes on the Global Ecumene', *Public Culture* 1: 66–75.

———. 1998. *Transnational Connections. Culture, People, Places*, 2nd ed. London and New York: Routledge.

Headland, T.N., K.L. Pike and M. Harris 1990. *Emics and Etics: the Insider/Outsider Debate*. Newbury Park, Kalifornien: Sage Publications.

Heinrich, W. 1984. *Ethnische Identität und nationale Integration. Eine vergleichende Betrachtung traditioneller Gesellschaftssysteme und Handlungsorientierungen in Äthiopien*. Göttingen: Edition Herodot.

Henry, J.M. and C.L. Bankston III 1998. 'Propositions for a Structuralist Analysis of Creolism', *Current Anthropology* 39(4): 558–66.

Herskovits, M.J. 1958 [1941]. *The Myth of the Negro Past*. Boston: Beacon Press.

Heryanto, A. 2001. 'Ethnic Identities and Erasure. Chinese Indonesians in Public Culture, in J.S. Kahn (ed.), *Southeast Asian Identities. Culture and the Politics of Representation in Indonesia, Malaysia, Singapore, and Thailand*. London and New York: I.B. Tauris Publisher, pp. 95–14.

Heuken, A. 2000. *Historical Sites of Jakarta*. Jakarta: Cipta Loka Caraka.

Hobsbawm, E.J. and T. Ranger (eds) 1999. *The Invention of Tradition*. Cambridge: Cambridge University Press.

Hoffmann, L.-F. 2003. 'Creolization in Haiti and National Identity', in G. Collier and U. Fleischmann, *A Pepper-Pot of Cultures. Aspects of Creolization in the Caribbean*. Amsterdam and New York: Editions Rodopi, pp. 3–16.

Hollander, J.J. de 1895. *Handleiding bij de Beoefening der Land- en Volkenkunde van Nederlandsch Oost-Indië*, Vol. 1.

Houaiss – *Dicionário da Lingua Portuguesa*. 2001. Rio de Janeiro: Editora Objectiva.

Hubinger, V. 1992. 'The Creation of Indonesian National Identity', *Prague Occasional Papers in Ethnology* 1: 1–35.

Jäger, S. 2004. *Kritische Diskursanalyse. Eine Einführung*, 4th ed. Münster: Unrast.

Jayapal, M. 1993. *Old Jakarta*. Kuala Lumpur and Oxford: Oxford University Press.

Jonge, H. de 2000. 'A Divided Minority. The Arabs of Batavia', in K. Grijns and P.J.M. Nas (eds), *Jakarta-Batavia. Socio-Cultural Essays*. Leiden: KITLV Press, pp. 143–56.

Josselin de Jong, J.P.B. de 1977 [1935]. 'The Malay Archipelago as a Field of Ethnological Study', in P.E. de Josselin de Jong (ed.), *Structural Anthropology in the Netherlands: A Reader*. The Hague: Martinus Nijhoff, pp. 166–82.

Josselin de Jong, P.E. de (ed.). 1988. *Unity in Diversity: Indonesia as a Field of Anthropological Study*. Dordrecht: Foris Publications.

Jourdan, C. 2001. 'Creolization: Sociocultural Aspects', in N.J. Smelser and P.B. Baltes (eds), *International Encyclopedia of the Social and Behavioral Sciences*, pp. 2903–06.

Kahin, G. McTurnan. 1952. *Nationalism and Revolution in Indonesia*. Ithaca, NY: Cornell University Press.

Khan, A. 2007. 'Good to think? Creolization, Optimism, and Agency', *Current Anthropology* 48(5): 653–73.

Kingsbury, D. and H. Aveling (eds) 2003. *Autonomy and Disintegration in Indonesia*. London and New York: Routledge Curzon.

Knight, F. 1997. 'Pluralism, Creolization and Culture', in F. Knight (ed), *General History of the Caribbean, Vol. 3: The Slave Societies of the Caribbean*. London and Basingstoke: Unesco Publishing/Macmillan Education Ltd., pp. 271–286.

Knörr, J. 1990. *Zwischen goldenem Ghetto und Integration. Ethnologische Autobiographie und Untersuchung über das Aufwachsen deutscher und Schweizer Kinder und Jugendlicher in der Dritten Welt am Beispiel Ghanas und ihre anschließende Eingliederung in Europa*. Frankfurt and New York: Peter Lang.

———. 1991. 'Kreolisierung versus Pidginisierung auf kultureller Ebene', in M.S. Laubscher and B. Turner (eds), *Völkerkunde Tagung 1991*, Vol. 2. München: Akademie Verlag, pp. 15–25.

———. 1994a. 'Kreolisierung versus Pidginisierung auf kultureller Ebene', in M.S. Laubscher and B. Turner (eds), *Regionale Völkerkunde*, Vol. 2. München: Edition Anacon, pp. 15–25.

———. 1994b. 'Creolization and Pidginization as Categories of Cultural Differentiation: Varieties of Cultural Identity and Inter-ethnic Relations in Freetown', in J. Riesz and H. d'Almeida-Topor (eds), *Échanges Franco-Allemands sur l'Afrique*, Vol. 3. Bayreuth: Bayreuth African Studies, pp. 115–31.

———. 1995. *Kreolisierung versus Pidginisierung als Kategorien kultureller Differenzierung. Varianten neoafrikanischer Identität und Interethnik in Freetown, Sierra Leone*. Münster and Hamburg: LIT.

———. 2002a. 'Konstruktion und Transformation ethnischen und transethnischen Gemeinwesens in Jakarta', in U. Krasberg and B.E. Schmidt (eds), *Stadt in Stücken*. Marburg: Curupira, pp. 247–70.

———. 2002b. 'Im Spannungsfeld von Traditionalität und Modernität: Die Orang Betawi und Betawi-ness in Jakarta', *Zeitschrift für Ethnologie* 128(2): 203–21.

———. 2007a: *Kreolität und postkoloniale Gesellschaft. Integration und Differenzierung in Jakarta.* Frankfurt/Main and New York: Campus.

———. 2007b. 'Creole Identity and Postcolonial Nation-Building. Examples from Indonesia and Sierra Leone', *Série Antropologia* 416. Brasília: Universidade Brasília (DAN), Departamento Antropologia.

———. 2008a. 'Indigenisierung versus Re-Ethnisierung. Chinesische Identität in Jakarta'. *Anthropos* 1: 159–77.

———. 2008b. 'Towards Conceptualizing Creolization and Creoleness', *Max Planck Institute for Social Anthropology Working Papers No.100.* Halle/Saale: Max Planck Institute for Social Anthropology.

———. 2009a. 'Creolization and Nation-Building in Indonesia', in R. Cohen P. Tonninato (eds), *The Creolization Reader. Studies in Mixed Identities and Cultures.* London: Routledge, pp. 353–63.

———. 2009b. '"Free the Dragon" versus "Becoming Betawi". Chinese Identity in Contemporary Jakarta', *Asian Ethnicity* 10(1): 71–90.

———. 2009c. 'Postkoloniale Kreolität versus koloniale Kreolisierung', *Paideuma* 55: 93–115.

———. 2010a. 'Contemporary Creoleness, or: The World in Pidginization?', *Current Anthropology* 51(6): 731–59.

———. 2010b. 'Out of hiding? Strategies of Empowering the Past in the Reconstruction of Krio Identity', in J. Knörr and W. Trajano Filho (eds), *The Powerful Presence of the Past. Processes of Integration and Conflict along the Upper Guinea Coast.* Leiden: Brill, pp. 205–28.

———. 2011. 'Mardijker: Creoles in Batavia', in A.J. Andrea (ed.), *Encyclopedia of World History. Era 6: The First Global Age, 1450-1770.* Santa Barbara, CA: ABC-CLIO, pp. 184–85.

———. 2012. 'Creolization', in G. Ritzer (ed.) (2012), *Wiley-Blackwell Encyclopedia of Globalization.* New York: Wiley-Blackwell, pp. 335–42.

Koentjaraningrat, R.M. 1973. 'Village Life South of Jakarta. Brief Report of a Comparative Study on "Village Life Around Capital Cities of Southeast Asia"', *Discussion Paper No. 64.* Kyoto University: The Center for Southeast Asian Studies.

———. 1975. *Anthropology in Indonesia: A Bibliographical Review.* Den Haag: Martinus Nijhoff.

Koesasi, Basoeki 1992. 'Lenong and Si Pitung', *Working Paper No. 73.* Melbourne: Monash University, Centre of Southeast Asian Studies.

Kortendick, O. 1996. *Indische Nederlanders und Tante Lien: eine Strategie zur Konstruktion ethnischer Identität,* 2nd ed. Canterbury: CSAC Occasional Papers.

Krausse, G.H. 1975. 'The Kampungs of Jakarta, Indonesia: A Study of Spatial Patterns in Urban Poverty', Ph.D. dissertation. Pittsburgh: University of Pittsburgh.

Kurris, R. 1996. *Terpencil di Pinggiran Jakarta - Satu Abad Umat Katolik Betawi.* Jakarta: Obor.

Laffan, M.F. 2003. *Islamic Nationhood and Colonial Indonesia. The* umma *below the Winds.* London and New York: Routledge.

Latif, C. and E. Lay (eds) 2000. *Atlas Sejarah. Indonesia dan Dunia.* Jakarta: PT Pembina Peraga.

Lehmann, A. 1983. *Erzählstruktur und Lebenslauf: autobiographische Untersuchungen.* Frankfurt/Main and New York: Campus.

Lekkerkerker, C. 1918. 'De Baliers van Batavia', *De Indische Gids* 40(1): 409–31.

Leman, J. 1998. 'Indigeneous and Immigrant Ethnicities: Differences and Similarities', in J. Leman (ed.), *The Dynamics of Emerging Ethnicities: Immigrant and Indigenous Ethnogenesis in Confrontation.* Frankfurt/Main: Lang, pp. 149–60.

Lewis, O. 1969. 'The Culture of Poverty', *Scientific American* 215(4): 19–25.

Logan, J.R. 1850. 'The Ethnology of the Indian Archipelago: Embracing Enquiries into the Continental Relations of the Indo-Pacific Islanders', *Journal of the Indian Archipelago and Eastern Asia* 4: 252–347.

Lohanda, M. 1989. 'Lingkungan Budaya Betawi', *Jali-Jali* 3: 9–15.

———. 2001. *The Kapitan Cina of Batavia. 1837-1942,* 2nd ed. Jakarta: Djambatan.

Lombard, D. 1989. 'Une description de la ville de Semarang vers 1812 (d'après un manuscript l'India Office)', *Archipel* 37(2): 263–77.

———. 1990. *Le carrefour javanais: Essai d'histoire globale,* 3 vols. Paris: École des Hautes Études en Sciences Sociales.

Mandal, S.K. 2002. 'Forging a Modern Arab Identity in Java in the Early Twentieth Century', in H. De Jonge and N. Kaptein (eds), *Transcending Borders. Arabs, Politics, Trade and Islam in Southeast Asia.* Leiden: KITLV Press, pp. 163–84.

Marcus, G.E. 1995. 'Ethnography in/of the World System: The Emergence of Multi-sited Ethnography', *Annual Review of Anthropology* 24: 95–117.

Maryono, O'ong 1997. 'The "jago": friend or foe?', *Pencak Silat Seminar Nusantara.* Kuala Trengganu, Malaysia.

———. 2001. 'The Rise of the Jago in Colonial Times', *Rapid Journal* 6(1): 40–41.

Mastenbroek, W.E. van 1934. *De Historische Ontwikkeling van de Staatsrechtelijke Indeeling der Bevolking van Nederlandsch-Indiës.* Wageningen: H. Veenmann and Zonen.

Matsuda, T. (ed.). 2001. *The Age of Creolization in the Pacific: In Search of Emerging Cultures and Shared Values in the Japan-America Borderlands.* Hiroshima: Keisuisha.

Mertokusumo, R.D.G. 1977. 'Si Pitung dan persoalannya', *Berita Buana.*

Miles, W.F.S. 1999. 'The Creole malaise in Mauritius', *African Affairs* 98: 211–28.

Miller, I. 1994. 'Creolizing for Survival in the City', *Cultural Critique* (Spring): 153–88.

Milone, P. 1966. 'Queen City of the East: The Metamorphosis of a Colonial Capital', Ph.D. dissertation. Berkeley: University of California.

———. 1967. 'Indish Culture and its Relationship to Urban Life'. *Comparative Studies in Society and History* 9: 407–26.

Mintz, S.W. 1998. 'The Localization of Anthropological Practice. From Area Studies to Transnationalism', *Critique of Anthropology* 18(2): 117–33.

Mintz, S.W. and R. Price 1992 [1976]. *The Birth of African-American Culture: An Anthropological Perspective*. Boston: Beacon Press.

Moosmüller, A. 1989. *Die Pesantren auf Java: zur Geschichte der islamischen Zentren und ihrer gegenwärtigen gesellschaftlichen und kulturellen Bedeutung*. Frankfurt/Main: Lang.

———. 1999. 'Ethnische und nationale Identität: Die Konstruktion kultureller Gemeinsamkeit in Indonesien und Japan in vergleichender Perspektive', *Zeitschrift für Ethnologie* 124: 33–50.

Morgan, P.D. 1991. 'British Encounters with Africans and African-Americans, circa 1600–1780', in P.D. Morgan and B. Bailyn (eds), *Strangers within the Realm: Cultural Margins of the first British Empire*. Chapel Hill: University of North Carolina Press, pp. 157–219.

Mufwene, S.S. 2000. 'Creolization is a Social, not a Structural, Process', in I. Neumann-Holzschuh and E.W. Schneider (eds), *Degrees of Restructuring in Creole Languages*. Amsterdam and Philadelphia: Benjamins, pp. 65–84.

Muhadjir. 1986. *Peta Seni Budaya Betawi*. Jakarta: Dinas Kebudayaan DKI Jakarta.

Mulder, N. 1996: *Inside Indonesian Society. Cultural Change in Java*. Amsterdam and Kuala Lumpur: The Pepin Press.

Multatuli. 1992: *Max Havelaar of de koffiveilingen der Nederlandsche Handelmaatschappy*, 2 vols. Assen: Van Gorcum.

Nagata, J.A. 1974. 'What is a Malay? Situational Selection of Ethnic Identity in a Plural Society', *American Ethnologist* 1: 331–50.

Nas, P.J.M. and W. Boender. 2002. 'The Indonesian City in Urban Theory', in P.J.M. Nas (ed.), *The Indonesian Town Revisited*. Berlin: LIT, pp. 3–16.

Nas, P.J.M. and K. Grijns 2000. 'Jakarta – Batavia. A sample of Current Sociohistorical Research', in P.J.M. Nas and K. Grijns (eds), *Jakarta – Batavia: Socio-Cultural Essays*. Leiden: KITLV Press, pp. 1–23.

Nassehi, A. 1999. 'Fremde unter sich. Zur Urbanität der Moderne', in Senatsausschuß für Kunst und Kultur (ed.), *Individuum und Gesellschaft in der Stadt der 90er Jahre*. Münster and Hamburg: LIT, pp. 227–24.

Niel, R. van 1960. *The Emergence of the Modern Indonesian Elite*. Den Haag and Bandung: W. Van Hoewe Ltd.

———. 1992. *Java under the Cultivation System*. Leiden: KITLV Press.
Niemeijer, H.E. 2000. 'The Free Asian Christian Community and Poverty in Pre-modern Batavia', in K. Grijns and P.J.M. Nas (eds), *Jakarta-Batavia. Socio-Cultural Essays*. Leiden: KITLV Press, pp. 75–92.
Noor, F.A.2012. 'The "Forum Betawi Rempug" (FBR) of Jakarta: An Ethnic-Cultural Solidarity Movement in a Globalising Indonesia', *RSIS Working Paper No. 242*.
Onghokham. 1984. 'The Jago in Colonial Java: Ambivalent Champion of the People', in A. Turton and S. Tanabe (eds), *History and Peasant Consciousness in South East Asia*. Senri Ethnological Studies 13. Osaka, Japan: National Museum of Ethnology, pp. 327–43.
Palmié, S. 2007. 'The C-Word, Again: From Colonial to Postcolonial Semantics', in C. Stewart (ed.), *Creolization: History, Ethnography, Theory*. Walnut Cree, CA: Left Coast Press.
Parsons, T. 1975. 'Some Theoretical Considerations on the Nature and Trends of Change of Ethnicity', in N. Glazer and D.P. Moynihan (eds), *Ethnicity: Theory and Experience*. Cambridge: Harvard University Press, pp. 53–83.
Patterson, O. 1982. *Slavery and Social Death. A Comparative Study*. Cambridge: Cambridge University Press.
Pemberton, J. 1994. 'Recollections from "Beautiful Indonesia" (Somewhere beyond the postmodern)', *Public Culture* 6(2): 241–62.
Peoples, J. and G.A. Bailey 2001. *Essentials of Cultural Anthropology*. Belmont, CA: Wadsworth/Thompson Learning.
Pierce, B.E. 1998. 'The Historical Context of Nengre Kinship and Residence: Ethno-history of the Family Organization of Lower Status Creoles in Paramaribo (Suriname)', in A. Torres and N.E. Whitten (eds), *Blackness in Latin America and the Caribbean, Vol. 2: Eastern South America and the Caribbean: Social Dynamics and Cultural Transformation (Blacks in the Diaspora)*. Bloomington: Indiana University Press, pp. 215–35.
Ponder, H.W. 1988 [1934]. *Java Pageant*. Singapur: Oxford University Press.
Premdas, R.R. 2002. 'Identity in an Ethnically Bifurcated State: Trinidad and Tobago', in S. Fenton and S. May (eds), *Ethnonational Identities*. Basingstoke, Hampshire: Palgrave Macmillan, pp. 176–97.
Probonegoro, N. 1977. 'Satu malam dalam kehidupan teater topeng', *Berita Antropologi* 9(32/33): 99–116.
———. 1987. 'Teater topeng Betawi sebagai simbol transisi masyarakat Betawi', *Jali-Jali* 1: 12–21.
Purdey, J. 2003. 'Reopening the *Asimilasi* vs *Integrasi* debate: Ethnic Chinese Identity in Post-Suharto Indonesia', *Asian Ethnicity* 4(3): 421–37.
Raben, R. 2000. 'Round about Batavia. Ethnicity and Authority in the Ommelanden, 1650-1800', in K. Grijns and P.J.M. Nas (eds), *Jakarta-Batavia. Socio-Cultural Essays*. Leiden: KITLV Press, pp. 93–113.

Raffles, T.S. 1817. *The History of Java*. London: Murray.
———. 1988 [1817]. *The History of Java*. Singapore: Oxford University Press.
Ramelan, R. 1977. *Condet: cagar budaya Betawi*. Jakarta: Lembaga Kebudayaan Betawi.
Rath, R.C. 2000. 'Drums and Power. Ways of Creolizing Music in Coastal South Carolina and Georgia, 1730-90', in D. Buisseret and S.G. Reinhardt (eds), *Creolization in the Americas*. Arlington: University of Texas at Arlington, pp. 99–130.
Refugee Review Tribunal Australia 2009. RRT Research Response, Country: Indonesia. Research Response Number: IDN34570 (26 March 2009).
Ricklefs, M.C. 1984. *Chinese Muslims in Java in the 15th and 16th Centuries: the Malay Annals of Semarang and Cerbon*. Melbourne: Monash University.
———. 1993. *War, Culture and Economy in Java, 1677–1726. Asian and European Imperialism in the Early Kartasura Period*. Sydney: Allen and Unwin.
Roosens, E. 1989. *Creating Ethnicity: the Process of Ethnogenesis*. London: Sage.
———. 1995. 'Ethnicity as a Creation: Some Theoretical Reflections', in K. von Benda-Beckmann and M. Verkuyten (eds), *Nationalism, Ethnicity and Cultural Identity in Europe*. Utrecht: Ashgate, pp. 30–39.
Ruqoya, S. 2010. 'FBR siap pecat anggotanya'. Okezone.com. 2 August 2010. (http://news.okezone.com/read/2010/08/02/338/358613/fbr-siap-pecat-anggotanya).
Saidi, R. 1994. *Orang Betawi dan Modernisasi*. Jakarta: LSIP.
———. 1997. 'Sejarah Betawi', in Y.Z. Shahab (ed.), *Betawi dalam Perspektif Kontemporer: Perkembangan, Potensi, dan Tantangannya*. Jakarta: LKB, pp. 1–34.
Santoso, S. 1975. *Sutasoma, a Study in Old Javanese Wajrayana*. New Delhi: International Academy of Culture.
Schapper, H.P. 1970. *Aboriginal Advancement to Integration. Conditions and Plans for Western Australia*. Canberra: Australian National University Press.
Schlee, G. 2008. *How Enemies are Made. Towards a Theory of Ethnic and Religious Conflict*. Oxford and New York: Berghahn Books.
Schlee, G. and A. Horstmann (eds) 2001. *Integration durch Verschiedenheit: Lokale und globale Formen interkultureller Kommunikation*. Bielefeld: transcript Verlag.
Schlee, G. and K. Werner (eds) 1996. *Inklusion und Exklusion: die Dynamik von Grenzziehungen im Spannungsfeld von Markt, Staat und Ethnizität*. Köln: Köppe.
Schulte Nordholt, H. 1991. 'The Jago in the Shadow: Crome and "Order" in the Colonial State in Java', *Review of Indonesian and Malaysian Affairs* 25(1): 74–91.
Schulte Nordholt, N.G. 2002. 'Violence and the Anarchy of the Modern Indonesian State', in F. Hüsken and H. de Jonge (eds), *Violence and Vengeance. Discontent and Conflict in New Order Indonesia*. Nijmegen Studies in Devel-

opment and Cultural Change. Saarbrücken: Verlag für Entwicklungspolitik, pp. 52–70.
Seni-Budaya Betawi. Pralokarya Penggalian Dan Pengembangannya. 1976. H. Wijaya (ed.). Jakarta: Pustaka Jaya.
Sensus Penduduk Tahun 2010 Propinsi DKI Jakarta. Badan Pusat Statistik (BPS): Jakarta.
Shahab, Y.Z. 1994. 'The Creation of Ethnic Tradition. The Betawi of Jakarta', Ph.D. dissertation. London: SOAS London.
———. 2000. 'Aristocratic Betawi. A Challenge to Outsiders' Perception', in K. Grijns and P.J.M. Nas (eds), *Jakarta – Batavia. Socio-Cultural Essays.* Leiden: KITVL Press, pp. 199–209.
Sheller, M. 2003. 'Creolization in Discouorses of Global Culture', in S. Ahmed, *Uprootings/Regroundings. Questions of Home and Migration.* Oxford and New York: Berg, pp. 273–94.
Shepherd, V.A. and G.L. Richards (eds). 2002. *Questioning Creole. Creolisation Discourses in Caribbean Culture.* Kingston and Oxford: Ian Randle Publishers; James Currey.
Simbolon, P. 1991. *Tapping on the Wall: Ethnicity and Marketplace Trade in the Urban Context of Jakarta.* Amsterdam: VU University Press.
Sispardjo, S. 1978/1979. 'Aspek seni musik pada "topeng Betawi"', *Kawit* 20: 27–33.
Skinner, D. and B.E. Harrell-Bond. 1977. 'Misunderstandings Arising from the Use of the Term "Creole" in the Literature on Sierra Leone', *Africa* 47(3): 305–320.
Skinner, G.W. 1959. *Local, Ethnic, and National Loyalties in Village Indonesia: A Symposium.* Yale University: Cultural Report Series, South East Asia Studies 6.
———. 1963. 'The Chinese Minority', in R.T. McVey (ed.), *Indonesia.* New Haven, Southeast Asia Studies, Yale University: HRAF Press, pp. 97–117.
Slamet-Velsink, I. 1998 [1994]. 'Traditional Leadership in Rural Java', in H. Antlöv and S. Cederroth (eds), *Leadership on Java. Gentle Hints, Authoritarian Rule.* Richmond: Curzon Press, pp. 33–56.
Smith, A.D. 1994. 'The Origins of Nations', in J. Hutchinson and A.D. Smith (eds), *Nationalism.* Oxford and New York: Oxford University Press, pp. 147–54.
Somantri, G.R. 1995a. 'People Making the City: Pattern of Intra-City Migration in Jakarta', *Working Paper.* Bielefeld: UB, Forschungsschwerpunkt Entwicklungssoziologie.
———. 1995b. 'Looking at the Gigantic Kampung: Urban Hierarchy and General Trends of Intra-City Migration in Jakarta', *Working Paper.* Bielefeld: UB, Forschungsschwerpunkt Entwicklungssoziologie.
Somers Heidhues, M.F. 1974. *Southeast Asia's Chinese Minorities.* Hawthorne, Victoria: Longman.

Spitzer, L. 1974. *The Creoles of Sierra Leone. Responses to Colonialism 1870–1945.* Madison: University of Wisconsin Press.

Spitzer, N.R. 2003. 'Monde Créole: The Cultural World of French Louisiana Creoles and the Creolization of World Cultures', *Journal of American Folklore* 116(459): 57–72.

Steenbrink, K. 1993. *Dutch Colonialism and Indonesian Islam. Contacts and Conflicts 1596-1950.* Amsterdam: Editions Rodopi.

Stein, P. 1982. 'Quelques dates nouvelles de l'histoire de mot *créole*', *Ètudes Créoles* 5(1–2): 162.

Stephens, T.M. 1983. 'Creole, Créole, Criollo, Crioulo: The Shadings of a Term', *The SECOL Review* 7(3): 28–39.

———. 1999. *Dictionary of Latin American Racial and Ethnic Terminology.* Gainesville: University of Florida Press.

Stewart, C. (ed.) 2007. *Creolization: History, Ethnography, Theory.* Walnut Creek, CA: Left Coast Press.

Stockdale, J.J. 1995 [1811]. *Island of Java.* Singapur: Periplus Editions.

Strübing, J. 2004. *Grounded Theory: Zur sozialtheoretischen und epistemologischen Fundierung des Verfahrens der empirisch begründeten Theoriebildung.* Wiesbaden: VS Verlag für Sozialwissenschaften.

Surachimat, D. 1985. *Sejarah Kampung Marunda.* Jakarta: Pemerintah DKI Jakarta, Dinas Museum dan Sejarah.

Suryadinata, L. 1992. *Pribumi Indonesians, the Chinese Minority and China*, 3rd ed. Singapur: Heinemann Asia.

Suryadinata, L., E.N. Arifin, and A. Ananta 2003. *Indonesia's Population. Ethnicity and Religion in a Changing Political Landscape.* Institute of Southeast Asian Studies. Singapur: Indonesia Population Series 1.

Susetyo, G. 2011. 'Parading Betawi Pride', *KemangBuzz* 2(8). Retrieved February 2013 from http://www.kemangbuzz.com/content/previssue/view.php?edisi_id=14&art_id=150.

Sutherland, H. 1979. *The Making of a Bureaucratic Elite. The Colonial Transformation of the Javanese Priyayi.* Singapur: Heinemann.

———. 1994. 'Writing Indonesian History in the Netherlands. Rethinking the Past', *Bijdragen to de Taal-, Land- en Volkenkunde* 150: 786–804.

Sutter, J.O. 1959. 'Indonesianisasi: Politics in a Changing Economy, 1940–1955', *Ithaca* 1: 26.

Tambun, L.T. 2013. 'Civil Service Betawi Day Now on Fridays', *JakartaGlobe*, 9 February 2013 (http://www.thejakartaglobe.com/jakarta/civil-service-betawi-day-now-on-fridays/570515).

Tan, M.G. 1983. 'Ethnicity and Fertility in Indonesia', *Research Notes and Discussion Paper No. 53.* Singapore: South East Asian Studies.

———. 1991. 'The Social and Cultural Dimension of the Role of Ethnic Chinese in Indonesian Society', in A. Kahin (ed.), *Indonesia: The Role of the*

Indonesian Chinese in Shaping Modern Indonesian Life. Ithaca, NY: Cornell Southeast Asia Program, pp. 113–25.

———. 2008. *Etnis Tionghoa di Indonesia: Kumpulan Tulisan [Ethnic Chinese in Indonesia: Collected Writings].* Jakarta: Yayasan Obor Indonesia (in English and Indonesian).

Taylor, J.G. 1983. *The Social World of Batavia. European and Eurasian in Dutch Asia.* Madison, Wisc.: University of Wisconsin Press.

Till, M. van 1995. 'In Search of Si Pitung. The History of an Indonesian Legend', *Bijdragen tot de taal-, land- en volkenkunde* 152(3): 461–82.

Tregle, J.G. Jr. 1992. 'Creoles and Americans', in A.R. Hirsch and J. Logsdon (eds), *Creole New Orleans: Race and Americanization.* Baton Rouge: LSU Press, pp. 131–88.

Turner, S. 2003. 'Setting the Scene. Speaking Out. Chinese Indonesians after Suharto', *Asian Ethnicity* 4(3): 337–52.

Unidjaja, F. and A. Gunawan 2004. 'Chinese-Indonesians Rising to Political Stage', *The Jakarta Post,* 15 March 2004.

Vermeulen, H. and J.F. Boissevain (eds) 1984. *Ethnic Challenge. The Politics of Ethnicity in Europe.* Göttingen: Edition Herodot.

Vermeulen, H. and C. Govers 2000. *The Anthropology of Ethnicity. Beyond 'Ethnic Groups and Boundaries'.* Amsterdam: Het Spinhuis.

Veur, P.W. van der 1968. 'The Eurasians of Indonesia: A Problem and Challenge in Colonial History', *Journal of Southeast Asia History* 9(2): 191–207.

———. 1969a. 'Race and Color in Colonial Society: Biographical Sketches by an Eurasian Woman Concerning pre-World War II in Indonesia', *Indonesia* 8: 69–80.

———. 1969b. *Education and Social Change in Colonial Indonesia.* Athens, Ohio: Papers in International Studies, Southeast Asia Series No. 12, Ohio University.

Vlekke, B.H.M. 1959. *Nusantara: A History of Indonesia.* Den Haag: van Hoeve.

Volkstelling. 1930. Batavia: Landsdrukkerij. 1933–1936.

Wahid, A. 1974. 'Pesantren Sebagai Sub-Kultur', in D. Rahardjo (ed.), *Pesantren dan Pembangunan.* Jakarta: LPES, pp. 39–60.

Wallerstein, I. 1974. *The Modern World-System.* New York: Academic Press.

Wandelt, I. 1988. *Der Weg zum Pancasila-Menschen: die Pancasila-Lehre unter dem P4-Beschluss des Jahres 1978.* Frankfurt/Main: Lang.

Warnaen, S. 1978. 'Stereotipe Etnik Didalam Suatu Bangsa Multi-Etnik. Suatu Studi Psikologi Sosial di Indonesia', Ph.D. dissertation. Jakarta: Universitas Indonesia.

Waters, M.C. 1990. *Ethnic Options: Choosing Identities in America.* Berkeley: University of California Press.

Widiadan, R.A. 2000. 'Chinese Puppets Perform Once More', *The Jakarta Post*, 5 February 2000.

Wijaya, H. (ed.) 1976. *Seni Budaya Betawi. Pralokarya Penggalian Dan Pengembangannya*. Jakarta: PT Dunia Pustaka Jaya.

Willis, J. 2000. *Mombasa, the Swahili, and the Making of the Mijikenda*. Oxford: Clarendon Press.

Wodak, R. 1994. 'Formen rassistischen Diskurses über Fremde', in G. Brünner and G. Gräfen (eds), *Texte und Diskurse: Methoden und Forschungsergebnisse der funktionalen Pragmatik*. Opladen: Westdeutscher Verlag, pp. 265–84.

Wyse, A.J.G. 1979. 'On Misunderstandings Arising from the Use of the Term "Creole" in the Literature on Sierra Leone: A Rejoinder', *Africa* 49(4): 408–417.

———. 1989. *The Krio of Sierra Leone. An Interpretive History*. Washington, D.C: Howard University Press.

Young, C. 1993. 'The Dialectics of Cultural Pluralism: Concept and Reality', in C. Young (ed.), *The Rising Tide of Cultural Pluralism: the Nation-State at Bay?* Madison: University of Wisconsin Press, pp. 3–35.

Index

A
abolition of discrimination, 144
abolition of segregated administration, 110–11, 113
adat, 125, 133n50
administrative structure of Jakarta, 42
Ahmadiyyah movement, 190, 197n10. *See also* Muslims
amalgamation (of cultures), 20, 27, 55, 165
anti-Islamic policy, 159, 181n3. *See also* Suharto regime
Arabs, 48, 58–59, 62, 110–13, 166. *See also* wulaiti
Asli/asli, 11, 82
    Betawi, 10, 11, 74, 77, 78–86, 91, 102, 195, 196
    Depok, 59, 72n36, 116, 122–23
    Jakarta, 74, 76–77, 81, 82, 83, 84, 86, 87–88, 91, 100, 102, 118, 125, 126–27, 152–53, 186, 192, 196
    Kristen, 114
    orang, 78–79, 81, 153
    penduduk, 167
authenticity, 11, 37, 68, 81–82, 84–85, 90, 130, 150, 185–87
    lack of, 107

B
Badan Pusat Statistik (BPS), 41, 70n1
Bali, 49, 50, 115. *See also* slaves
    Balinese, 49, 52–56, 88, 97n16, 137, 165
Bamus, 101, 104, 130n4, 185, 194
bangsawan Betawi, 124–28. *See also* Betawi: aristocracy
banyan tree, 160, 163
Batak, 130

Bekasi (city), 11, 41, 104, 105, 121, 165
Belanda Depok, 72n36, 122, 123
Belles Creoles, 23–24, 39n15
Betawi
    activists, 78, 130, 153–54, 164, 171
    ancestors of the, 60–61, 68, 79–80, 83, 87–88, 104–5, 118, 126, 129, 148–49, 152, 171, 195
    Arab, 60
    aristocracy, 124–29 (*see also* bangsawan Betawi; Iwarda)
    associations, 87–88, 101, 109, 131n5, 147, 194–95 (*see also* Bamus)
    becoming, 136, 150, 199
    Baru, 84, 86, 93, 96n11
    Cerita Rakyat, 171–72, 173, 178
    and Chinese culture, 138, 146, 153
    Chinese/Cina, 60, 136, 148, 149, 154, 156n28
    Muslim, 116, 118, 119, 122, 149, 189
    Ora, 105, 108, 131n10
    Tengah, 101, 130n1
    wedding, 100–101, 169
Betawi-ization, 81, 106, 128, 129, 130, 154, 169–70, 180, 181, 189, 191, 195
Betawi-ness/Betawiness, 77, 83, 86, 90, 96, 98–101, 109–14, 118, 120–21, 130, 136, 149–50, 153, 155, 165, 166–67, 169, 188–89, 198
    genuine, 84–85
    revival of, 127, 151

Betawi untuk Gubernur Campaign, 183–85
Bhinneka Tunggal Ika, 9, 108, 152, 158–66, 180, 198. *See also* unity in diversity
black Portuguese, 114–15, 132n28. *See also* Tugu
boundaries
    ethnic and identity boundaries, 2–4, 22, 23, 27, 29, 56, 74, 80, 88, 113, 136, 198–200
    nation-state, 7, 26, 197
    open boundaries, 30, 37, 82
Bowo, Fauzi, 183–84, 197n4
Buddhism, 45, 56, 106, 163

C

categories, 28
    ethnic categories, 23, 45, 48, 69, 74, 77, 92–93, 152, 184, 198
    of identification, 4, 10–13, 16, 17n3, 22, 56, 163, 180–81, 198
    subcategories, 48, 77, 109
Catholicism, 10, 150. *See also* Christianity
central Jakarta, 16, 65, 105, 146
Ceylon, 49, 114, 140
China, 46, 135, 136, 137, 138, 141, 149, 152
Chinese revival, 147, 151, 153
Chinese-ness, 153–54
Christianity, 51, 53, 56, 62, 97n16, 115, 118, 122, 138, 150, 179, 190
Ciliwung River, 46, 58, 124, 137
Cina Benteng, 137, 151
city of Jakarta, 11, 90, 101, 117, 164
collective identities, 1–2, 25, 163
    construction of, 1, 8, 10–11, 26–27, 31, 34, 72n38, 158, 164
colonialism, 1, 7, 56, 87, 120, 126, 127, 128, 190
    colonial period, 11, 59, 61, 171, 179–80, 195

    colonial regime, 50, 138, 140, 170, 178
    colonial rule, 61–62, 70n12, 87, 126, 129, 137–39, 158, 170, 171
    colonial system, 62–64, 175, 179–80
    Dutch colonial rulers, 126, 138, 139
colonization, 55, 73n49, 97n16
communism, 106, 131n12, 159, 162
construction and transformation of identity, 1, 7, 8, 10–12, 13, 23, 109, 116, 158, 163, 164
contemporary Jakarta, 91, 95, 129
conversion
    ethnic, 30, 44, 64, 85, 129–30
    religious, 20, 56, 114, 122, 135, 138, 150–51
creole continuum, 29
creole terminology, 19–21, 26–27
creoleness, 1, 19, 23–25, 27, 33, 36, 37, 38, 39n17, 180, 187–89, 194, 199, 200
créolité (Caribbean context), 21–23
    model of/model for, 22
creolization
    historical, historical context of, 19–20, 22, 23, 25, 29, 36, 37, 84–85, 93, 97n16, 105, 110, 129, 199–200
    linguistic, 28, 31, 39n20, 40nn29,33
    process(es), 11, 12, 21, 25–29, 33, 34, 36, 38n5, 51, 55–57, 60, 112, 135, 138, 163, 174
    versus pidginization (CvP), 30–32, 34
cultural diversity, 6, 9, 22, 25, 31, 37, 94, 155, 164, 199. *See also* creolization
culture
    as process of interaction, 9
    common, 3, 25, 31

cultural features, 2, 21, 28, 33, 37, 59, 82, 105, 169
European, 10, 39n21, 119, 199
indigenous, 69, 76, 118, 146, 173, 186
local, 10, 33, 38, 155
of poverty, 65–66
shared, 27, 53, 55
traditional, 69, 70, 76, 87, 165, 173
urban, 7, 8, 28, 169

D

de-strangement, 10
defender(s). *See* jago
democratization, 113, 144, 169, 193
dependency theory, 28
descent, 3, 20, 82, 83, 84, 123, 125, 126
  Arabic, 111, 113
  Chinese, 71n28, 135, 136, 144, 147, 148, 150, 152, 153–54
  European, 23
  indigenous, 21, 29, 33, 37, 50, 66, 70n13, 74, 76, 78, 80, 83, 90, 94, 122, 135, 137, 141, 144, 163, 167, 171, 174, 181, 185, 186, 188, 191–93
  Javanese, 43–44, 48–49, 52, 78, 80, 91, 154, 165–66, 170, 185–88, 191–92
  Sundanese, 43–44, 46, 48, 64, 78–80, 83, 88, 113, 126, 165, 177, 186–88, 192
diaspora, 20, 21, 34–35
diasporization, 34
Dinas Kebudayaan DKI Jakarta, 78, 96n6
discrimination, 36–37, 64, 65, 110–11, 122, 127, 141, 143, 144, 151, 190–91, 197n6
Dutch, 46–51, 54, 56, 58, 59, 61, 62, 68, 71n21, 78, 81, 83, 87, 96n12, 110, 111, 114, 115, 119, 122, 124–26, 128, 129, 137–41, 158, 166, 170, 172, 176, 178, 179, 190, 199

E

East India Company, 70n8, 138. *See also* Vereenigte Oostindische Compagnie
education (formal), 61, 62, 65, 66, 67, 102, 103, 107, 119, 187
  Western education, 63, 65
election, 94–95, 183–84, 186, 187, 188, 189, 190, 192
emic/etic model, 17n13
endogenous, 38n6
Ethical Policy, 59–60, 61, 63, 72n40
ethnic affiliations, 6, 8, 11, 69–70, 90, 94
ethnic ascriptions, 4, 25, 29, 35, 36, 45, 56, 84, 85, 92, 198
ethnic criteria, 54, 192
ethnic diversity, 9, 12, 27, 34, 59, 163, 180, 200
ethnic groups, 2–6, 8, 11, 29, 33, 36, 38, 44, 49–50, 54, 64, 69, 70n3, 78, 80, 84, 105, 112, 141, 142, 144, 155, 163–66, 169, 174, 186, 188
ethnic identity, 2–6, 14, 27, 29, 30, 32, 35, 38, 40n34, 44–45, 55, 56, 64, 76, 79, 83–86, 91–93, 99, 102, 118, 129–30, 135–36, 150, 152, 154, 165–66, 188, 193, 198–99. *See also* collective identities
ethnic reference, 4, 5–6, 12, 30–31, 33, 37, 77, 82–87, 91, 92, 94, 195–96
ethnic traditions, 7, 85, 92, 96, 100, 166, 198
ethnicization, 22, 30, 31, 32, 39n22, 59, 85–86, 135, 166, 200
  process of, 4, 25, 27, 93
ethnocentrism, 188, 193, 196, 197n6. *See also* sukuisme
ethnogenesis, 25–27, 55, 84, 180, 199

ethnonyms, 19, 60
etymology (of the term creole), 19, 25, 26
Eurasians, 51, 53, 97n16, 115, 116
Europe, 20, 21, 34, 48, 107, 137
    Europeans, 21, 51–52, 53, 58–61, 78, 110, 115, 137, 140
    European model(s), 35–36
exclusion, 36, 56, 85, 143, 144, 151, 171, 193
    inclusion and exclusion, 12, 13, 18n22, 85, 36, 147
exogeneity, 20, 36, 135

F

Fatawi, 125–26, 128–29, 133n47
foreigners, 45, 56, 154, 167, 190
Forum Betawi Rempug (FBR), 168, 193–95
free citizens (*vrijburghers*), 48, 49, 50, 60, 115, 138
Front Pembela Islam (FPI), 114, 131n24, 190

G

globalization, 21, 36
Glodok, 139, 140, 141, 151, 176
Golkar (party), 125, 133n46
government, 41, 50, 58, 59, 63, 65, 67, 68–69, 113, 116, 122
    Indonesian, 41, 78, 116, 136, 141, 159–60, 165, 190
    Jakartan, 41, 65, 67, 68, 69, 127
Gunawan Semaun, 125

H

Hadhramaut, Hadhrami, 110–12
heritage (cultural), 31, 94, 117, 166
heroism, 170–80
heroization, 174, 178. *See also* Si Pitung
heterogeneity, 1, 6, 8, 9, 28, 33–36, 38, 77, 84–85, 89, 90, 121, 148, 153, 163–65, 173, 189, 200
hierarchies (social), 23, 59, 60, 101, 109, 127

Hinduism, 45, 55, 56, 97n16, 163
Hitachi, 136, 148, 149, 151–52, 156n28. *See also* Cina Betawi
Holland, 46, 48–50, 58, 59, 119
Hollandization, 51–52
homeland, 20–21, 34–35, 51, 93, 112, 113, 136, 193

I

identification(s), 1–2, 198–200
    and delimitations, 15–16
    ethnic and transethnic, 4, 23, 32, 33, 62, 88–90, 105, 107, 129, 135–36, 163, 167, 168, 169, 179, 180–81, 188
    national, 2, 5, 10, 35, 69, 75, 92–93, 152
    processes of, 7, 12–14, 19
    territory, 4, 5, 158, 166, 188, 198
    urban, 90–93, 169, 174, 195–97
immigrants, 32, 40n36, 52, 54, 58, 81, 110, 122, 137
immigration, 46, 49, 81, 111, 140
independence, 34–35, 56, 60, 63–65, 91, 111, 117, 120, 122, 140, 158–59, 170, 178, 180, 181, 185
India, Indians, 32, 45, 46, 48, 110, 114, 166
indigeneity, 20, 34, 36, 77, 79, 102, 116, 120, 135, 136, 152, 161, 163, 165, 166–68, 180, 183, 185–87, 188, 189, 198, 199
indigenization, 22, 24, 25–27, 30, 34, 36, 39n22, 50, 59, 93, 113, 135, 180, 200
indigenous population of Jakarta, 78, 80, 163, 167, 185
indirect rule, 50, 71n20
Indonesian archipelago, 15, 53, 115, 138, 169, 193
Indonesian-ness, 165
Indonesian Robin Hood. *See* Si Pitung
Indonesian society, 90, 94, 113, 136
Indos, 50, 51, 58, 59

inner circle of the Betawi, 98–99, 103, 121
International Monetary Fund (IMF), 180
Islam, 46, 49, 51, 55–57, 62–63, 67, 68, 104, 106, 110–13, 115, 124, 127, 135, 137, 150–51, 179, 189–91, 199
Islamization, 106, 189, 190–91. *See also* Betawi-ization; Iwarda (Mangkudat)
Iwarda (Mangkudat), 125. *See also* Betawi: aristocracy; bangsawan Betawi

J

jago, 171, 174–80, 195
Jakarta (capital), 153, 163–68, 171, 174, 180
Jakartan, 4–5, 11, 69, 77, 81, 85–86, 91, 92–94, 120, 171. *See also* Orang Jakarta
  genuine Jakartans (*see* Asli: Betawi, Jakarta)
Jam'iyyat Khair, 112–13
Japan, 47, 115
Jatinegara Kaum, 124–29
Java, Javanese, 6, 41, 43–44, 46, 48, 49, 52, 56, 58, 60, 61, 64, 70n3, 78, 80, 88, 91, 94, 116, 119, 124, 128, 137, 141, 146, 148, 152, 154, 156n4, 158, 159, 161, 163–66, 169–70, 175, 185–86, 188, 191–93
  East Java, 167, 171, 180
  (Hindu-)Javanese kingdom, 45–46, 161
  West Java, 78–79, 83, 124
Java War, 58

K

kampung, 15, 17, 18n26, 43, 49, 54, 56, 57, 60, 62, 79, 100, 178
  inner-city, 64, 81, 88
Kampung Buda, 106

kapitan, 49, 54, 71n19, 139–40, 143
Keroncong, 116, 117–18, 122, 132n33, 133n42
Kiyai (religious leaders), 103–4, 131n8. *See also* syech
Koran, 62
Kota, 58
Krio (Sierra Leone), 25, 39n21

L

language, 11, 21, 51–52, 69, 107, 112, 121, 123, 138, 142, 144, 158
  Bahasa Indonesia, 159
  Betawi, 88, 95
  creole, 24, 28, 29, 31, 40n33, 114–15, 116
  Dutch, 51–52
  ethnic, 31, 40n34, 85
  pidgin, 28, 30–31
liberalization, 113, 144, 145, 151
linguistic concept of creolization, 29
Louisiana, 21, 23

M

madrasah, 62, 72n45
Majapahit (kingdom), 161, 163
Makassar, 49
Mardijkers, 48, 50, 52, 53, 58
marriages, 20, 48, 50, 54, 59, 85, 97n16, 111–12, 122, 169
  interethnic, 88, 96n15, 110, 137
Marunda, 174, 176–77
Mataram (kingdom), 46, 49, 124
Mauritius, 21, 29, 39n23
Mestizos, 52, 53
migration, 34, 44, 59, 109
  immigration, 46, 49, 81, 111, 140
Minangkabau, 43, 90
minority (group), 65, 85, 88, 111, 119, 121, 128, 142
mixing of groups, 24, 27, 34, 44, 51, 53, 59, 85, 105, 120, 121, 138, 155
  processes of, 134n61, 135

modernity, 7, 86, 89–90
    perceived lack of, 66, 75, 100, 151, 170, 187
    tradition and modernity, 7, 17n10, 36, 38, 94–96
modernization, 7, 38, 103, 113, 159, 187
Moors, 48, 54, 110, 131nn15,17
mulawad, 113
Muslims, 56, 65, 68, 104, 106, 111, 113, 117, 119, 121, 132n40, 148, 151, 152, 189, 190

N

NASAKOM, 159, 161, 162
nation(-state), 5, 6, 7, 9, 35, 37, 141, 142, 158–59
    imagined, 5
    Indonesian, 12, 141, 142, 161, 162, 163, 164
    postcolonial, 6, 7, 36, 199
national identity, 5–6, 9, 10, 12, 34–35, 69, 94, 113, 136, 142, 150, 154, 158–64, 167, 169–71, 180–81, 199
national ideology, 9, 142, 163. *See also* Pancasila vision, Pancasila ideology
nationalism, 5, 6, 17n7, 159, 161, 162, 181
natives, 33, 36, 46, 48, 49, 50, 53, 56, 59, 61, 70n13, 78–79, 81, 89, 95, 100, 107, 115, 118, 121, 128–29, 155n1, 158, 164, 167, 172, 186, 188. *See also* pribumi
nativization, 34, 40n38
Netherlands, 51, 58, 59, 115
New World, 20, 21, 34
newcomers, 20, 81, 112, 193
non-creoles, 33, 34, 38

O

Ommelanden, 46, 48, 49–50, 52, 53, 55–58, 78, 79, 96n4, 104, 115, 138, 139, 140, 175
Ottoman Empire, 111
Oud Batavia, 47

Orang Jakarta, 5, 10, 11–12, 17, 18n19, 45, 69, 74–96, 102, 152, 169, 184, 186, 188, 195, 196, 198. *See also* Jakartan

P

Pancasila vision, Pancasila ideology, 142, 161, 165. *See also* national ideology
Papangers, 48, 54, 71n15
Partai Nasional Indonesia (PNI), 159
Pejambon, 115, 116
Pekojan, 110, 131n14
pencak silat (martial art), 174, 176, 179, 180, 182n20
Peranakan, 54, 59, 60, 71n28, 109, 112, 113, 135–55, 178–79
Persatoean Arab Indonesia, 113
pesantren, 62, 72n45, 103, 131n7, 179. *See also* madrasah
pidginization. *See* creolization: versus pidginization
politicization of identity, 125, 187, 196
Portuguese, 45–46, 48, 70n6, 114–15, 117, 119, 120, 166. *See also* Tugu
preservation (tradition and culture), 7, 69, 118, 124, 172, 179, 181
pribumi, 70n13, 155n2
    Indonesian leaders, 142
    non-Pribumi, 135, 141, 143
Prince Jayawikarta, 124
priyayi, 63, 72n48

R

radical Islamic associations. *See* Front Pembela Islam (FPI)
Ramadan, 141, 189, 190
rampok, 176
religion, 61–63, 66, 82–83, 98, 112, 117, 119, 138, 144, 148–49, 151, 159, 161–62, 181n6. *See also* Christianity; Islam
    Confucianism, 144, 148, 149, 150

Index

repression, 127–28, 141–43, 144, 146, 149, 170–71
revitalization
　of Betawi culture, 100, 105
　of Chinese culture, 144–45
　of identities, 59
rituals, 103, 114, 138, 150
　religious, 106
Robin Hood Betawi, 177. *See also* Si Pitung
roots, 6, 13, 22–23, 33, 35, 77, 82, 85–86, 88, 90, 118, 119, 185, 186, 188–89, 200
　'tree with roots', 17n8

S
Sadikin, Ali, 69, 117
sayid, 110–13
Si Pitung, 172, 176–79
Sierra Leone, 25, 31
slavery, 53, 55, 64, 68, 87, 128
　abolition of, 138
slaves, 20–21, 48, 50, 52–53, 55, 56, 57, 60, 68, 78, 87, 111, 114, 115, 119, 126, 137
　freed, 21, 40n36, 49, 54, 60, 114
social
　advancement, 40n37, 63, 64, 112
　classes, 48, 99, 102, 111–12, 137, 156n28
　meanings, 1, 9–10, 12, 13, 22, 198, 200
　status of the Betawi, 60, 62, 65, 66, 67, 102, 104–5, 169
struggle for independence, 56, 111, 158, 170
Suharto regime, 135, 141–44, 146, 147, 159, 160–62, 181n3, 185, 193
Sukarno, 141, 159, 161
sukuisme, 188, 196, 197n6
Sulawesi, 49, 53, 79, 88, 91, 92, 166, 192
Sultan Agung, 124
Sultanate of Bantam, 137
Sultanate of Banten, 46, 49, 124–25
Sumatra, 49, 68, 77, 79, 82, 83, 91, 93, 95, 169
Sunda, 70n5
　Banten, 125
　Kelapa, 45–46
Sundanese, 43, 44, 46, 48, 64, 78, 79–80, 82, 88, 106, 113, 126, 146, 169, 170, 176, 177, 186–87, 188
Surabaya, 191, 198
Surkati, 113
Sutiyoso (Governor), 183–84, 185, 192
syech (Islamic scholars), 110, 111
symbol (national), 6, 15, 37, 108, 159–60, 163, 165, 180–81, 198. *See also* unity in diversity

T
Taman Mini Indonesia Indah (TMII), 15, 18n27, 75
Totok, 59, 72n39, 135, 136, 141
tourism, 69, 76, 94–95, 186
trade, 45–46, 58, 70n8, 110, 124, 138, 140. *See also* East India Company; Vereenigte Oostindische Compagnie (VOC)
tradition
　indigenous, 103, 181
　local, 38, 186, 187
　modernity and tradition, 17n10, 36, 38, 94–96
　national, 35
　precolonial, 161
traditional culture of Jakarta, Jakartan traditions. *See* Betawi; culture
transethnic
　category, 11, 33, 198
　identity, 2–5, 8, 9
　links, 90, 119, 120, 193
　reference, 5–6, 33, 37, 38, 77, 120
transethnicization, 196, 200n1
transnationalization, 26
true Islam, 103–4, 106, 112, 189

Tugu, 114–21, 122, 123

U
unity in diversity, 9, 35, 37, 108, 121, 152, 163–66, 171, 174, 180, 181, 197, 198
'ur-creoles', 24
urban anthropology, 7, 17n9

V
Vereenigte Oostindische Compagnie (VOC), 46, 48–52, 53, 54, 58, 61, 70nn8,12, 115, 138. *See also* East India Company; trade
Vreemde Oosterlingen, 48, 60, 70n12, 111

W
Wahid, Abdurrahman, 144, 167
Warga Negara Indonesia Keturunan Tionghoa (WNI), 135, 155n1
Westernization, 7, 9
white creole, 20, 23, 34
wulaiti, 112, 113